ACTION GUIDE

for

EFFECTIVE DISCIPLINE
IN THE HOME AND SCHOOL

by

Margaret K. Cater

*This **Action Guide** is for individual or group study of the book **Effective Discipline in the Home and School** by Genevieve Painter and Ray Corsini.*

ACCELERATED DEVELOPMENT INC
PUBLISHERS
3400 KILGORE AVENUE
MUNCIE, INDIANA 47304

ACTION GUIDE FOR EFFECTIVE DISCIPLINE IN THE HOME AND SCHOOL

Technical Development: Tanya Benn
Cynthia Long
Marguerite Mader
Sheila Sheward

LCN: 91-77889

ISBN: 1-55959-027-0

Order additional copies from:

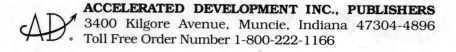

ACCELERATED DEVELOPMENT INC., PUBLISHERS
3400 Kilgore Avenue, Muncie, Indiana 47304-4896
Toll Free Order Number 1-800-222-1166

ACKNOWLEDGEMENTS

This author expresses appreciation to Doctors Raymond Corsini and Genevieve Painter for their confidence that she could produce this manual and their assistance, both with editing and helpful comments.

And to my husband, Walter Cater, for his patience and encouragement while I labored along with this effort, while he often did without my company; also, for his vitally concrete help in word-processing and re-processing of pages. I couldn't have done without it.

CONTENTS

PART I
ACTION GUIDE FOR PARENTS

Organizational Meeting

Week 1

Week 2

Week 3

Week 4

Week 5

Week 6

Week 7

PART II
ACTION GUIDE FOR TEACHERS

Organizational Meeting

Week 1

Week 2

Week 3

Week 4

Week 5

PART I
Action Guide for Parents Related to Effective Discipline in the Home

SECTION P-1
INTRODUCTION

The *Action Guide* for group *or* individual study of *Effective Discipline in the Home and School* by Painter and Corsini is designed to assist the reader in understanding and using the theories and techniques offered. This *Action Guide* will take those who like to study thoughtfully on their own through the material, suggesting where and when to start, putting the ideas and methods into use, clarifying important points, and giving step-by-step ways to put into effect each of the essential skills. All of us have habits of thought and action that do not give way easily and, if you are seeking new ways of influencing children as one of their teachers (parents or their teachers in school), the children of our increasingly democratic society need new approaches. Organized group study with a leader/facilitator or counselor as a leader is also an excellent way to study and may be your preferred way to study and, perhaps, help yourself change. This method does have the added influence of group support and group insight into where you are with your children as a parent or a teacher in school. This *Action Guide* is designed to work for both the needs of the individual and the group. You will note two *Outlines of Study*, one for the individual and one for the group with ten Study Plans for each. The Chapter Questions and other materials are to be used for both ways of studying, as and when indicated in the Study Plans.

Studying Alone

If you are an individual wanting to study this book on your own, the *Action Guide* has been established for you, with this section containing an overview of this project and the initial steps for you to take. Then you get down to considering these parenting ideas and skills at a measured pace so you can absorb these viewpoints and begin to really understand them and use them if you wish. There are ten different blocks of study, with chapter questions including answers to read and ponder, along with connected study materials to explore, evaluate and think about using. If you are going to study alone, then skip over the rest of this introduction and move to the page entitled *Individual Study Overview, Section P-4,* and begin.

Studying As A Group

All of you who are interested in forming a group and those of you who are leader/facilitators looking for material that parents and teachers can use to study together in a group will find the *Action Guide* helpful in assisting you to organize such an effort, using the book, *Effective Discipline in the Home and School,* along with this *Action Guide.* A group may consist of as few as three to as many as twenty people and may meet in private homes, church buildings, schools, community halls, or social agencies. The leader/facilitator may be a parent, teacher, social worker, psychologist, counselor, etc.

These groups ordinarily meet for a definite period of time, such as every Wednesday morning from 9:00 to 10:30 or every Thursday evening from 7:00 to 9:00 p.m. for ten or more weeks. Usually, a small fee is charged that covers the cost (1) of the two books; (2) of paying for a babysitter for any children brought to the meeting, if needed; (3) for refreshments, such as coffee and doughnuts that may be served during the meeting; and (4) for the meeting room or a donation to the institution permitting use of the room. Usually, the fee for individuals is only a few dollars for the whole program. Generally, the leader is not paid.

While all persons benefit from participating in such groups, the leader/facilitator often benefits most. These groups, especially if held during the day, are composed mostly of women but some fathers' groups have been started. In the evenings the groups often contain both fathers and mothers. The leader/facilitator usually starts the group through placing notices in public places and schools with the cooperation of the school principal, and by notices in local newspapers. The leader/facilitator then reads the whole book through, and reviews the *Action Guide.* In other words, he/she, the typical leader/facilitator gets to understand and be familiar with the whole system before the first meeting.

Leader/Facilitator

IMPORTANT! You are to be the facilitator of the group more than the leader! You must resist all impulses to become the expert. The purpose of these groups is to encourage and facilitate open discussion, and your job is to lead discussion, not settle arguments, not give opinions. **The authority is the text book.** Any disputed issue is to be checked by examining the index of that book. If the answer is not found there, one of the resource books may have the answer. Dreikurs and Soltz's CHILDREN: The Challenge is the most likely supplement.

The books, not you, are to be the authorities. If a particular problem cannot be answered, say "I don't know. Who will want to check what is the Adlerian position on the question?" This permits people to think about the problem, check on authorities, and permits fuller participation and discussion.

Any attempt on your part to give answers (even if they are in the book) must be resisted strongly. Let us suppose you *know* what is in the book and let us suppose this common type problem arises:

> **Parent:** My problem is how to stop bed wetting. Do you know what to do?
>
> **Leader/Facilitator** (who has read Chapter 29 in the text and knows what is said in the book and who has already successfully used this method recommended in the book): This subject is covered in Chapter 29. We will get to it eventually. But if you wish, and if there are no objections, we can all read this chapter, which is only 4 pages long, right now, or we can read it during the week and discuss it next week, or hold off until the regular time.
>
> **Parent:** Well, it really bothers me, and I don't like to wait.
>
> **Another Parent:** Why don't you read that chapter and then, if it makes sense, try doing what the authors say?

First Parent: I'd so much like to know right now. (To the leader/facilitator) Do you know what to do?

Leader/Facilitator: I have read the chapter, but I would prefer to simply help you individually and as a group discuss it. I am no expert myself, I am just a parent like the rest of you.

Starting the Group

Any person can start a group as a leader/facilitator. A good way is to inform a school principal of your intention. Another way is to pass copies of *Effective Discipline in the Home and School* around to friends, asking them if they would like to form a parents' study group, and, if so, to ask other friends to join. Still another way is to place a notice in a public place. Thousands of such groups of parents have been started by ordinary parents as well as counselors. See also Chapter 35 in *Effective Discipline in the Home and School* for additional suggestions.

The First Meeting

The books and the *Action Guides* should be distributed and all financial arrangements made and settled. Then the first meeting may begin by everyone introducing themselves and your co-leader, if you have one. The leader/facilitator can state that we have gathered for the purpose of studying the book, *Effective Discipline in the Home and School* and to make sure that everyone is where he/she belongs and wants to be. Someone could have wandered in, looking for the Neighborhood Improvement Council! Following this, one by one, group members introduce themselves and state how they happened to become interested in studying this book. Parents could also tell how many children they have and their ages and sex. Teachers in a Teachers' Study Group could state their background and the age group of the students they are now teaching. Do this "round robin" fashion. This helps everyone to relax and become really interested in the whole proceeding.

Next, hold an open discussion on the ground rules of your group. What time will you meet? Will you start on time? Will you serve refreshments? How long will the meetings be? What babysitter arrangements are there, if any? You must be firm about no one bringing children into the meeting itself. The distraction will not be tolerable—it will wipe you out. All these matters must be made clear and be agreed on at the outset, along with any other points your group might find important. Holding your meetings down to two hours, with possibly, a ten minute break midway, is suggested. Or you can elect to have coffee already made and nearby, so that individual members can get some coffee quietly, as they wish. A final meeting that ends with some special cookies or cake is very pleasant for all.

When all of you have introduced yourselves and determined that everyone has his or her own book and an *Action Guide* and is settled down, someone can volunteer to read the first paragraph of the *Preface* of the book out loud. Next direct your attention to the outline of the book, noting that you will spend the first sessions going over the fundamentals of this system of parenting or classroom teaching, discussing and gaining understanding of them. Notice that in the last one-half of the ten Parenting Sessions, you will be actively considering techniques and methods of handling specific problems in line with the principles and concepts of child rearing already studied. During the questions for each chapter on techniques and methods, an effort should be made by everyone to continually refer back to the principles which are being applied. The Chapter Questions will help you with this. Together, go through the rest of the outline of the chapters, noting the kind of problems that are going to be taken up. In the *Group Outline of Study*, Section P-3 of the *Action Guide*, take note of the chapters to be read by each study session. As soon as everyone is satisfied and comfortable with the textbook and what they are going to be studying, turn to the *Family Relationship Index*, Section P-6 of the *Action Guide*, and go through it together, following the directions. This will be a good ice breaker and help everyone to begin to locate his/her chief areas of difficulty in the family. You will sometimes be surprised to learn that what you see as a difficulty with your children is different from what your spouse sees. This is why each parent does his/her own Questions Sheet and why they are asked not to check with each other until each is finished with the task. (The leader/facilitator should have extra *Family Relationship Index* sheets to hand out, if needed). Time allowing, together, go over the *Basic Adlerian Concepts*, Section P-11 in the *Action Guide*, noting the new viewpoints that are going to form the basis for this study. If time does not permit, then close by agreeing to have each person read it at home, along with the other pages to be covered by the next meeting, and bring any questions or doubts he/she may have about the material covered to next week's session. A step-by-step outline to follow for the *Organizational Meeting* is Section P-5 in this book. It should help your group move along with confidence through your first meeting together. For each subsequent meeting, a *Group Meeting Format/Study Plan* is available for your convenience and assistance when meeting together to study.

Preparation for Leading the Discussion

True, you can lead a study group without preparing ahead of time, but you probably will not do it as well, and you and your parents probably will not learn as much. We will be urging our group members to take time for training and time for fun—we might urge ourselves *to take time* to lead them in this study course. Using five sessions (at least four) to cover the theory and principles of Adlerian parenting and teaching which are dealt with in the first chapters of *Effective Discipline in the Home and School* (hereafter entitled *Effective Discipline*), is recommended. In the *Action Guide*, the *Group Outline of Study*, Section P-3, is suggested because it, along with *The Individual Outline of Study*, Section P-2, has been used and found workable. Each parent (or at least each couple) needs to have, as an additional aid, his/her own *Action Guide*. It has been designed to help you, the leader/facilitator, develop, in more depth, particular areas of this study and is to be used along with the text as stated in each meeting format. The *Action Guide* is designed for use with your parents or teachers when you are going over particular topics with them, as directed in your group meeting formats. You will be best prepared if you read over the indicated pages ahead of time, perhaps highlighting some points you particularly want to call to their attention, using a bright ink or colored liner, maybe writing in little explanatory notes you might want to add.

The *Group Outline of Study, Section P-3,* as you can see, has the chapters of the book divided in blocks of ten. The chapters listed are to be assigned for reading and study at home at the end of each meeting as shown in the outline and in your meeting format. Leader/facilitators leading the discussion might find it helpful to purchase a bright, *light* green or *light* blue writing pen (avoid using red or lavender ink, as these colors tend to run and smear over time) and mark the margin of the pages in their books in the manner below, also bracketing the beginning sentence which answers the particular question being taken up in the study questions, marking too, where the answer ends, as: example—see page 25 in the text—the next to last and last paragraphs of the page:

> Adlerians see problems—and this is an example of a problem—as opportunities. Ralph and Carol can use this situation to actually strengthen relationships—if they are wise enough to deal with it sensibly.
>
> *Example*
>
> [When an act occurs which we consider negative it helps to look for the child's *good purpose* (good intention) so that we can overcome our own anger.] If we continue to be angry, the relationship worsens. [In this case Chris was trying to be helpful (his *good purpose*); he carried out his parents' wishes but made a mistake.]

Rewards and Punishments: A Mistake, p. 25

The "10" stands for the question number of Section P-27, *Study Questions for Chapter 4, Rewards and Punishment: A Mistake,* found in this book. Through this method you can quickly locate *the author's answer* and point out to the group members the page and the line number so all may read along as you or one of your group members read it out loud. Discussion can then follow. When quiet ensues, move along to the next question. If you do not think you are going to have time to use all the questions, the suggestion is that you look them over and choose some key ones you want to use, underline circling them with your bright ink, as in *Section P-10, Study Questions for Chapter 1,* in this book:

(1.) Have you seen any children lately with the characteristics described on page 5, line 9? (Read. This should bring a laugh.)

(2.) Do you think such children as are described on page 5, lines 14-15, are possible? (Read lines— if you know of such transformations, give examples.)

(3.) Why do you think many children become "rebellious, uncooperative, hostile, or vengeful?" (Let the group members give their ideas.) What do the authors think causes this in children? (Page 9, line 8, ff. and page 8, line 10 to "train them")

NOTE: ff. is used to indicate "and the following as it pertains to the subject."

Also on Section P-10, the *Study Questions for Chapter 1*, underlining the page number following the question is helpful, and it also can be useful to place a ruler directly under the question you are presently using to help you keep your place on the Study Questions page, moving it down as you go. In your own book, you may want to underline in your bright ink any phrase or sentence you want to highlight by additional discussion or concrete examples. One of your main aims is to get the parents/teachers talking about what they are studying, asking questions, raising objections, etc. This helps everyone to feel a part of it and keeps them from getting bored. It also promotes learning and understanding. For additional advice and help on group leadership and discussion techniques, refer to *Systematic Training for Effective Parenting—Leader's Manual* (Dinkmeyer, Don, Ph.D., and McKay, Gary, D., M.A. *S.T.E.P. Leader's Manual*, Circle Pines, Minn.: American Guidance Service, Inc., 1976).

The last five sessions dealing with the methods and techniques of handling specific problems will take special managing. You probably will not be able to discuss all of the problems the authors take up in each block of chapters. The suggestion is that you ask the group members at the beginning of these sessions what particular difficulties covered in their reading would they like to take first and list them as they are named. You can then take them up for discussion in that order. Or you can ask for volunteers the week before, to go over the different particular chapters using the chapter questions and to report to the group at the next meeting what they learned. This last method often assists in maintaining everyone's enthusiasm and interest. At each subsequent meeting, you can go on with the next block of chapters—any specific problems that were not discussed, the group members can study at home for themselves, as the approach will be similar to those that were used for discussion. To really cover the material in the book adequately, you are urged to follow the opening meeting with ten additional meetings, as shown in the *Group Outline of Study*, Section P-3, in the *Action Guide*.

Other Helpful Hints for the Group Leader/Facilitator

1. Often a good procedure is to look up a key word in the dictionary (like "respect") and have the definition ready to read to the group. This sometimes sheds more light on the word's application to parenting because, often, only a wavy idea of what is meant by a word is drifting about in the group members' heads and more clarification is sometimes needed to get a handle on how to use many of these techniques and to really accept some of these principles and concepts.

2. At some points in the sessions you could have members of the group form "buzz groups" of approximately six or so each, to discuss together a specific aspect of one topic, e.g., What was it like to have an authoritarian parent? How did it make you feel? What did you do about it? A permissive parent? A democratic parent? etc. All the members would then cluster in the group that matched their own childhood condition in the family. After about six minutes of discussion in these "buzz groups" everyone returns to the main group and shares the findings of the separate groups with the rest. This encourages the shyer members to speak and gives everyone an opportunity to take a larger part. Each "buzz group" needs to appoint a recorder to take down the findings of their discussion for later sharing with the main group. For many other helpful participant exercises to aid your parents' understanding of what they are studying, refer to Maple Ridge

Family Guidance Center's *Parent Study Group Leaders' Manual* (Maple Ridge Family Guidance Center, 21489 Cherry Avenue, Maple Ridge, British Columbia, V2X 4L5).

3. Many times, members in your group are experiencing distressing times at home. Feeling bankrupt, they probably are desiring immediate changes, or at least, being able to see hope directly ahead. The discussion launches into theory in the beginning; they could become discouraged and not stay with the group long enough to get help. To prevent such premature disenchantment, it helps to pass around 3" x 5" cards so that anyone who wishes may write down a pressing problem on which he/she would like some discussion. Usually two or three will do so and you can spend the last few minutes of each meeting going into a specific problem, enlisting the help of the group, along with what you know from your own Adlerian experience and pointing out what pages in the book are applicable (a quick look at the Table of Contents and the index of *Effective Discipline in the Home and School* could assist with this). Midway in the series of meetings, you can pass the cards around again, encouraging members to get some of their own worst difficulties talked about without pointedly calling attention to themselves. If, on the other hand, you find some members are constantly bringing up personal concerns and getting the group off the main point of discussion, you can pass over a card to that person, saying "Would you jot that problem down on this card and we can take it up in more detail in the last part of the meeting?" or, "Could you and I talk about this after class?" You are going to have to be tough about this or your group will dissolve, if one member is allowed to hog all the attention.

4. Relating concrete examples of applying the training techniques and the experienced results is often very helpful in holding the attention of the group and in convincing them that these new ideas can really be helpful and work for them— parents and teachers alike. Describing other positive authoritarian or permissive methods that you might have used in the past and their results also can be helpful. Even experiences that you have observed others having, that highlight the principles or the method being considered, can be described. Such examples, drawn from life, help enliven the discussion

and encourage other members to share their thoughts and experiences.

Soooo—on to your study group—and GOOD LUCK!

Margaret K. Cater

Margaret K. Cater

SECTION P-2
INDIVIDUAL OUTLINE OF STUDY

Week 1

Reading Assignment

Textbook: Chapters 1 and 2, pp. 5-14

Study in *Action Guide*

1. Basic Adlerian Concepts, Sec. P-11
2. Family Constellation, Sec. P-13

Topics to Be Covered

1. The ideal child
2. Child development

Home Practice Activity

1. Fill out *Observe Yourself as a Parent*, Sec. P-7

Week 2

Reading Assignment

Textbook: Chapter 3, pp. 15-20, and Chapter 36, pp. 262-267

Study in *Action Guide*

1. Mutual Respect, Sec. P-19
2. Disrespectful Acts, Sec. P-23
3. Ways to Spoil a Child, Sec. P-22
4. Bill of Rights for Healthy Parents and Healthy Children, Sec. P-24

Topics to be Covered

Democracy (equality) versus authoritarianism

Home Practice Activity

1. The Family Constellation, Sec. P-13.
2. Using point No. 7 of the Family Constellation, *Action Guide*, consider each child.

Week 3

Reading Assignment

Textbook: Chapters 4 and 5, pp. 21-33

Study in *Action Guide*

1. Punishment and Reward Versus Consequences, Sec. P-30
2. Times When A Parent Says " No," Sec. P-29
3. Characteristics of a Logical Consequence, Sec. P-31
4. Discouraged Child's Mistaken Goals, Sec. P-32

Topics to be Covered

1. Rewards and punishment
2. Natural and logical consequences

Home Practice Activity

Consulting Sec. P-23, Disrespectful Acts of Parents, notice whether you do any of them and observe the effect they have on your children.

Week 4

Reading Assignment

Textbook: Chapter 6, pp. 34-39

Study in *Action Guide*

1. Encouragement and Recognition, Sec. P-38
2. These Foster Competition, Sec. P-36
3. Dreikurisms, Sec. P-39

Topics to be Covered
   1. Encouragement
   2. Praise
   3. Competition
   4. Failure

Home Practice Activity

Pick out a "Misbehavior" and try a "Consequence". (Use The Discouraged Child's Mistaken Goals, Sec. P-32.)

Week 5

Reading Assignment

Textbook: Chapter 7, pp. 40-44

Study in *Action Guide*

   1. Redirecting Your Child, Sec. P-44
   2. Large Mistakes, Sec. P-42
   3. How to Ruin Your Child, Sec. P-33

Topics to be Covered

General rules for child training and re-training.

Home Practice Activity

Stop all critical remarks.

Week 6

Reading Assignment

Textbook: Chapters 8-13, pp. 46-90.

Study in *Action Guide*

   1. Order and Limits, Sec. P-47
   2. Training Steps, Sec. P-55
   3. Four Ways to Learn, Sec. P-54

Topics to be Covered

Problems of routine living

Home Practice Activity

Watch for a chance to make a positive commitment to each child.

Week 7

Reading Assignment

Textbook: Chapters 14-18, pp. 92-147

Study in *Action Guide*

1. Encouragement for Mom and Dad, Sec. P-58
2. When an Order Must Be Obeyed, Sec. P-60
3. Children Respond To . . ., Sec. P-61
4. Characteristics of a Parent Date, Sec. P-66

Topics to be Covered

Problems of order and cooperation

Home Practice Activity

Notice how many times you get angry. Did it help?

Week 8

Reading Assignment

Textbook: Chapters 19-24, pp. 150-184

Study in *Action Guide*

1. Magic Words, Sec. P-69
2. Ways to Have a Good Relationship, Sec. P-77
3. Benefits of a Good Relationship, Sec. P-78
4. Extra Points for Fighting in the Car, Sec. P-72

Topics to be Covered

Interaction problems

Home Practice Activity (Try either activity.)

1. Plan a regular playtime.
2. Try a parent date. (See Characteristics of a Parent Date, Sec. P-65.)

Week 9

Reading Assignment

Textbook: Chapters 25-31, pp. 185-231

Study in *Action Guide*

1. Parental Obligations, Sec. P-81
2. Mistaken Ideas of Parents, Sec. P-89

Topics to be Covered

Special problems

Home Practice Activity (Try either activity.)

1. Try the "Fighting Advice."
2. Practice not scolding—Find another way to say it, or shut your mouth and act.

Week 10

Reading Assignment

Textbook: Chapters 32-34, pp. 235-253

Study in *Action Guide*

1. Communication, Sec. P-94
2. Criticism, Sec. P-95
3. Principles of Problem Solving, Sec. P-98

4. Benefits of a Family Meeting, Sec. P-99
5. Playing Board Games, Sec. P-101

Topics to be Covered

Building a cooperative family

Home Practice Activity

1. Check on how much needless talking you are still doing.
2. Plan some family fun.

SECTION P-3
GROUP OUTLINE OF STUDY

Week 1

Reading Assignment

Textbook: Chapters 1 and 2, pp. 5-14

Study in *Action Guide*

1. Basic Concepts, Sec. P-11
2. Family Constellation, Sec. P-13

Topics to be Covered

1. The ideal child
2. Child development

Home Practice Activity

Fill out Observe Yourself as a Parent, Sec. P-7.

Week 2

Reading Assignment

Textbook: Chapter 3, pp. 15-20 and Chapter 36, pp. 262-267

Study in *Action Guide*

1. Mutual Respect, Sec. P-19
2. Disrespectful Acts, Sec. P-23
3. Ways to Spoil a Child, Sec. P-22
4. Bill of Rights, Sec. P-24

Topics to be Covered

Democracy (equality) versus authoritarianism

Home Practice Activity

1. Look for The Family Constellation, Sec. P-13.
2. Using point No. 7 of The Family Constellation, *Action Guide,* consider each child.

Week 3

Reading Assignment

Textbook: Chapters 4 and 5, pp. 21-33

Study in *Action Guide*

1. Punishment and Reward Versus Consequences, Sec. P-30
2. Times When a Parent Says "No", Sec. P-29
3. Characteristics of a Logical Consequence, Sec. P-31
4. Discouraged Child's Mistaken Goals, Sec. P-32

Topics to be Covered

1. Rewards and punishment

2. Natural and logical consequences

Home Practice Activity

Consulting Sec. P-23, Disrespectful Acts of Parents, notice whether you do any of them and observe the effect they have on your children.

Week 4

Reading Assignment

Textbook: Chapter 6, pp. 34-39

Study in *Action Guide*

1. Encouragement and Recognition, Sec. P-38
2. These Foster Competition, Sec. P-36
3. Dreikurisms, Sec. P-39

Topics to be Covered

1. Encouragement
2. Praise
3. Competition
4. Failure

Home Practice Activity

Pick out a "Misbehavior" and try a "Consequence" (Use The Discouraged Child's Mistaken Goals, Sec. P-32.)

Week 5

Reading Assignment

Textbook: Chapter 7, pp. 40-44

Study in *Action Guide*

1. Redirecting Your Child, Sec. P-44

2. Large Mistakes, Sec. P-42

3. How to Ruin Your Child, Sec. P-33

Topics to be Covered

General rules for child training and re-training

Home Practice Activity

Stop all critical remarks.

Week 6

Reading Assignment

Textbook: Chapters 8-13, pp. 46-90.

Study in *Action Guide*

1. Order and Limits, Sec. P-47
2. Training Steps, Sec. P-55
3. Four Ways to Learn, Sec. P-54

Topics to be Covered

Problems of routine living

Home Practice Activity

Watch for a chance to make a positive commitment to each child.

Week 7

Reading Assignment

Textbook: Chapters 14-18, pp. 92-147

Study in *Action Guide*

1. Encouragement for Mom and Dad, Sec. P-58
2. When an Order Must Be Obeyed, Sec. P-60
3. Children Respond To . . ., Sec. P-61
4. Characteristics of a Parent Date, Sec. P-66

Topics to be Covered

Problems of order and cooperation

Home Practice Activity

Notice how many times you get angry. Did it help?

Week 8

Reading Assignment

Textbook: Chapters 19-24, pp. 150-184

Study in *Action Guide*

1. Magic Words, Sec. P-69
2. Ways to Have a Good Relationship, Sec. P-77
3. Benefits of a Good Relationship, Sec. P-78
4. Extra Points for Fighting in the Car, Sec. P-72

Topics to be Covered

Interaction problems

Home Practice Activity (Try either activity.)

1. Plan a regular playtime.
2. Try a parent date. (See Characteristics of a Parent Date, Sec. P-65.)

Week 9

Reading Assignment

Textbook: Chapters 25-31, pp. 185-231

Study in *Action Guide*

1. Parental Obligations, Sec. P-81
2. Mistaken Ideas of Parents, Sec. P-89

Topics to be Covered

Special problems

Home Practice Activity (Try either activity.)

1. Try the "Fighting Advice."
2. Practice not scolding—Find another way to say it, or shut your mouth and act.

Week 10

Reading Assignment

Textbook: Chapters 32-34, pp. 235-253

Study in *Action Guide*

1. Communication, Sec. P-94
2. Criticism, Sec. P-95
3. Principles of Problem Solving, Sec. P-98
4. Benefits of a Family Meeting, Sec. P-99
5. Playing Board Games, Sec. P-101

Topics to be Covered

Building a cooperative family

Home Practice Activity

1. Check on how much needless talking you are still doing.

2. Plan some family fun.

SECTION P-4
OVERVIEW FOR
INDIVIDUAL STUDY

1. Play tape No. 1 of *Parenting Tapes* by Dr. Corsini and Dr. Painter, if you have it. This is an introductory discussion to the parents and teachers which will help you get started. However, these tapes are not mandatory.

2. Do the *Family Relationship Index*, Section P-6. This task will help you spot any major areas of trouble. You may be surprised.

3. At the front of this book, look over Section P-2, *Individual Outline of Study.* You will note the chapters are divided into separate blocks of study with accompanying *Action Guide* material for deeper study.

4. An activity to be done at home with your children is included in every study section which will help you start to put this information to practical use in your life as a parent.

5. Areas are provided for your own individual notes or insights as you pursue this study under the heading of "Notes."

6. Do *Observe Yourself as a Parent.* This will help you spot patterns of action in your parenting. Some of these you might want to consider eliminating.

7. On to the *Individual Study Plan No. 1,* Section P-8 in this *Action Guide.*

SECTION P-5
ORGANIZATIONAL MEETING
FOR GROUP STUDY

1. As the parents come in, everyone buys books—*Effective Discipline* and *Action Guide.* If both mother and father are attending, each could buy an *Action Guide,* if they wish.

2. When sitting down, everyone introduces himself or herself, starting with the leader/facilitator, and also says how he/she got interested, and so forth. (As in the Introduction of this book under heading "The First Meeting.")

3. On 3 x 5 cards, each parent should write his/her name, address, phone number, business phone, spouse's name, children's names, their ages and sex. "Star" the name of the child that motivated him/her to come to the study group. On the back of the card, state how you learned about the class and what you hope to gain by attending these sessions. If a chalkboard is available, the format may be shown, along with questions for information, and the cards could then be made out as participants arrive and are waiting for the session to begin.

4. Establish together the ground rules (discussed in the Introduction of this book):

   a. Day or night and time of the meeting and the number of meetings. Usually ten study meetings are held after the organizational meeting.

   b. Will you start on time?

   c. Will you have coffee during a mid-break, or available when wanted individually?

   d. Will it be a closed group after the second study meeting? (This is strongly urged.)

   e. Will baby-sitting be available? Where? Costs? Sitters?

f.   Anything else important to your group?

5. If you have it, play the first ten minutes of tape No. 1 of *Parenting Tapes* by Drs. Corsini and Painter which is an introductory discussion, and which will help all of you to get started in taking part in the discussion. The leader/facilitator may listen to this tape ahead of time, if desired. Should you want to order these tapes, you are urged to do so. Drs. Corsini and Painter's tapes are interesting and helpful. However, *Effective Discipline in the Home and School* and the *Action Guide* are all you need to study and make use of these ideas.

6. Everyone turn to Section P-6, *Family Relationship Index (FRI)* in the *Action Guide,* and with the help of your leader/facilitator, do it together, following the instructions.

7. Give attention to Section P-3, *Group Outline of Study,* in the *Action Guide.* Become aware of the Reading Assignment, the Study Assignment, the Topics to be Covered, and the Home Practice Activity. Discuss the value of each and the differences.

8. Every group member will gain from taking part in the discussions of the material being considered. Ask questions, raise objections, and put these ideas into your own words. Doing so will help you absorb these theories and principles and begin to adopt them as your own valuable assets to parenting. The more you take part, the more likely you will continue to attend the meetings all the way through the ten sessions, and the more you will gain.

9. Talk together about the usefulness and the purpose of pages supplied for taking notes or recording insights gained, etc.

10. If any time remains, look together and discuss Section P-11, *Basic Adlerian Concepts,* in the *Action Guide.*

11. Look together at Section P-3, *Group Outline of Study* in the *Action Guide,* and note the work to do before next week's meeting.

SECTION P-6
FAMILY RELATIONSHIP INDEX

INSTRUCTIONS FOR ADMINISTERING
OR TAKING INDIVIDUALLY

Materials Required

> Instruction Sheet
> Double-sided rating form
> Pencils

Procedures:

The following procedures are applicable to individuals studying alone or in groups.

1. Before filling in this form, parents should wait and go over the instructions together. "Please wait for instructions." Ask if anyone needs a pencil.

2. When all have the right page, the leader/facilitator can point out: "This form will help show problem areas in your family. Each person is to fill in his/her name and the date and check mother or father." The individual studying on his/her own can fill out this form, also following the instructions above.

3. "Fill in the name, sex, and age of the children living at home, beginning with the oldest child, going down by age."

4. "Note that the word *rating* refers to the degree of difficulty you are having with that child overall.

> An 0 means **no problem.**
> 1 means **minor problem.**
> 2 means **moderate problem.**
> 3 means **serious problem.**
> X means you **cannot rate** the child. An example of inability to rate is as follows: A one-year old would

not be in school and therefore would have an 'X' rating for the 'home-school.' "

5. "Only you can judge the degree of difficulty. Please fill out the forms independently. Each parent should fill out his/her own form without discussing it with the other."

6. The leader/facilitator can read each item on the next page with a brief explanation, and the participants are to put in the boxes on the *Family Relationship Index* the degree of problem they are having with each child by writing in the box, '0,' '1,' '2,' '3,' or 'X.' Use the *Family Relationship Index* marked with the number 1. When the parents are ready, the leader/facilitator can read verbatim each item, allowing some time for decision making on the part of the parents.

7. After the 24 items have been read, look together at the lines provided for any problem the parents may have that is not listed. Put such problems in the spaces labeled "Other Problems" and rate accordingly.

8. Lastly, find a numerical total for each child and place in the rating box after each child's name. this will point out which of your offsprings is causing you the most difficulty.

General Information

An individual administration will last about ten minutes. A group administration will last about fifteen minutes. The *Family Relationship Index* marked with the number 2 is for use at the end of your study to evaluate what progress has been made.

PROBLEM AREAS AND SPECIFIC QUESTIONS
Explanation of Items
on the *Family Relations Index*

1. **Getting Up** (Any difficulty in getting children out of bed in the morning?)

2. **Dressing** (Any problems about getting dressed: selection of clothing, color combinations?)

3. **Eating** (Does child decline to eat properly, refuse certain foods, show bad manners?)

4. **Cleanliness** (Does child resist washing, bathing, tooth-brushing?)

5. **Home-School** (Are there problems about school that spill over at home, notes from teachers?)

6. **Bedtime** (Do you have difficulty persuading child it's bedtime; does child keep getting up?)

7. **Conformance** (Does child comply with family rules without resistance—and parent pressure?)

8. **Chores** (Does child do assigned work without hassles, remember what to do and do it properly?)

9. **Own Room** (Does child keep own room clean and neat, make bed, put things away?)

10. **Clutter** (Does child leave toys, papers, books cluttering up house and/or yard?)

11. **Possessions** (Does child take adequate care of own toys, books, games?)

12. **Fighting** (Does child quarrel and fight with brothers, sisters, or other children?)

13. **Car Behavior** (Any problems with fighting, fidgeting, making noises, teasing other children?)

14. **Public Misbehavior** (Are there problems in stores, restaurants, visiting in friends' homes?)

15. **Aggression** (Does child show aggressive or brutal behavior with persons outside family?)

16. **Social** (Is child shy, fearful, critical of or uncooperative with others?)

17. **Attention Seeking** (Does child demand undue and/or constant attention—show off, whine, talk back?)

18. **Dawdling** (Is child slow to do what is requested or required—draggy about getting started?)

19. **Temper Displays** (Does child get upset too easily, cry without real cause, throw tantrums?)

20. **Fears and Terrors** (Is child afraid of dark, strangers, animals, being alone?)

21. **Harmful Habits** (Does child bite nails, suck thumb, pull hair, eat dirt, put objects in nose?)

22. **Bedwetting** (Not much explanation needed here . . .)

23. **Incontinence** (Is child unable to retain urine or feces during day?)

24. **Character** (Does child lie, cheat, steal?)

1   FAMILY RELATIONSHIP INDEX

(   ) Mother

Family Name _____   (   ) Father   Date _____

Please fill in below, using the following ratings:

RATINGS: 0—No problem   2—Moderate problem   X—Cannot rate
            1—Minor problem   3—Serious problem

Names of children at home—oldest first.

Child	Age	Sex	Total Rating		Child	Age	Sex	Total Rating
I _____	( )	( )	( )		IV _____	( )	( )	( )
II _____	( )	( )	( )		V _____	( )	( )	( )
III _____	( )	( )	( )		VI _____	( )	( )	( )

CHILD	I	II	III	IV	V	VI		**CHILD**	I	II	III	IV	V	VI
1. Getting up								13. Car						
2. Dressing								14. Public						
3. Eating								15. Aggression						
4. Keeping clean								16. Social						
5. Home-School								17. Attention						
6. Bedtime								18. Dawdling						
7. Conformance								19. Temper						
8. Chores								20. Fears						
9. Own room								21. Habits						
10. Clutter								22. Bedwetting						
11. Possessions								23. Incontinence						
12. Fighting								24. Character						

Other problems:

(1) _____ Rating (   )

(2) _____ Rating (   )

Comments: _____

_____

2   FAMILY RELATIONSHIP INDEX

Family Name _____

(   ) Mother
(   ) Father   Date _____

Please fill in below, using the following ratings:

RATINGS: 0—No problem   2—Moderate problem   X—Cannot rate
           1—Minor problem   3—Serious problem

Names of children at home—oldest first.

Child	Age	Sex	Total Rating		Child	Age	Sex	Total Rating
I _____	( )	( )	( )		IV _____	( )	( )	( )
II _____	( )	( )	( )		V _____	( )	( )	( )
III _____	( )	( )	( )		VI _____	( )	( )	( )

CHILD

	I	II	III	IV	V	VI
1. Getting up						
2. Dressing						
3. Eating						
4. Keeping clean						
5. Home-School						
6. Bedtime						
7. Conformance						
8. Chores						
9. Own room						
10. Clutter						
11. Possessions						
12. Fighting						

CHILD

	I	II	III	IV	V	VI
13. Car						
14. Public						
15. Aggression						
16. Social						
17. Attention						
18. Dawdling						
19. Temper						
20. Fears						
21. Habits						
22. Bedwetting						
23. Incontinence						
24. Character						

Other problems:

(1) _____ Rating (   )

(2) _____ Rating (   )

Comments: _____

_____

SECTION P-7
OBSERVE YOURSELF AS A PARENT

Now, for one week observe **yourself** in the act of parenting. Look at your own behavior relative to the following and check your answer to each.

Yes   No

___ ___ 1. How do I act toward my child(ren)? Is my attitude friendly, courteous, and encouraging?

___ ___ Or is it critical, nagging, impatient?

___ ___ 2. Do I use bribes (promises of rewards) as incentives?

___ ___ 3. Do I continually issue orders, directives, and commands?

___ ___ 4. Do I accompany instructions and demands by threats of punishments?

___ ___ 5. Do I use physical punishment (slaps, spankings, etc.) to control?

___ ___ 6. Do I berate or put the child down when I disapprove of his/her actions?

___ ___ 7. Is my attitude that of trying in a friendly and kindly manner to educate my child?

___ ___ 8. Is (are) my child(ren) "disciplined" (punished, that is) as I think other adults expect me to, rather than treated in ways that actually benefit him/her?

___ ___ 9. Do I humiliate my child by publicly scolding him/her when he/she "lets me down" by failing to say "please," "thank you," or failing to shake hands?

Yes   No

___ ___   10. Do I insist on adult standards and manners from my child (such as forcing a two-year-old to share, or sit still too long with nothing interesting to do, or to exhibit perfect table manners)?

___ ___   11. Do I jump on my child for faults that I accept or ignore in myself?

___ ___   12. Do I talk so much (lecture, moralize, correct, nag, "bitch," scold, complain, criticize) that the child becomes "deaf" to my words?

___ ___   13. As a parent, do I regard respect, consideration, and friendly cooperation as something to be earned rather than demanded?

___ ___   14. Do I show more approval than disapproval of my child(ren)?

___ ___   15. Do I find things to like about my child/children?

___ ___   16. Do I build my child(ren) up, encourage, and boost his/her (their) confidence?

___ ___   17. Am I more interested in helping the child be right than proving to him/her how wrong he/she is?

___ ___   18. Do I show partiality or favoritism and negatively compare my child(ren) with other children—either in or out of the family?

NOTES
Related to the Organizational Meeting

SECTION P-8
INDIVIDUAL STUDY PLAN NO. 1

Chapters 1 and 2, Pages 5-14

1. Read Chapters 1 and 2 in *Effective Discipline in the Home and School.*

2. Play tape No. 1 of *Parenting Tapes* by Drs. Corsini and Painter again. It will tell you a lot about this study. If you would like to order these tapes, you are urged to do so. Drs. Corsini and Painter's tapes are interesting and helpful. However, *Effective Discipline in the Home and School* and the *Action Guide* are all you need to study and make use of these ideas.

3. Having completed the preceding sheets, Section P-7, *Observe Yourself as a Parent,* make a note of anything you want to change in yourself as a parent on the page for notes.

4. Go to Section P-10, *Study Questions for Chapter 1.* The answers can be read in your text following the directions given in the Introduction, Section P-1 in this book, under the topic "Preparation for Leading the Discussion" <u>page No. and line No.</u> locating as material is found in your text. Just count the lines up or down on the page designated.

5. Study in the *Action Guide,* Section P-11, *Basic Adlerian Concepts.* The connection between discouragement and misbehavior in a child is a foundation idea in this viewpoint. The worse the behavior, the more discouraged the child is—about himself/herself, about the world he/she lives in, and his/her part in it.

6. Do Section P-12, *Study Questions for Chapter 2,* which is in this book. After the first four questions, proceed to Section P-13, *The Family Constellation.* Using these ideas, consider how birth order positions affected you and your brothers and sisters. Also, your own children. Using points Nos. 6 and 7, what can a parent do to remedy

any misinterpretations your children may have? How could this help you? Use the notes page for any conclusions.

7. Finish Section P-12, *Study Questions for Chapter 2.*

8. Follow the *Individual Outline of Study,* Section P-2, provided on prior pages in this book. It will pace your study and use of these ideas and methods. Think about these ideas during the week—reflect on them.

9. Do the home practice activity for each week. Doing so is a very important part of your success with this system of parenting. Therefore, be sure to give it a try. For the coming week, follow directions given for Study Week No. 2 in the *Individual Outline of Study,* Section P-2, at the front of this book.

SECTION P-9
GROUP MEETING NO. 1 FORMAT

Chapters 1 and 2, Pages 5-14

1. Sell books and *Action Guides* to any new members of the group.

2. If you have it, play the first part of tape No. 1 of the *Parenting Tapes* by Drs. Corsini and Painter. Start with the discussion of the "4 R's." Play for ten minutes and shut off. The leader/facilitator can then announce that the tape for each meeting will begin exactly at the starting time so that those who are there promptly will be putting their time to good use, while those who may have been delayed can slip in and seat themselves quietly. This policy should reward those who have gotten there on time and encourage late comers to make it on time, for these tapes are interesting and helpful. These tapes *are* an asset but it is not necessary to have them.

3. Any new members can introduce themselves, etc.

4. Everyone shares about the home study practice, *Observe Yourself as a Parent*, Section P-7. Did they fill it out? Did they learn anything about themselves that they might want to change, etc.? Those who wish, share with the group.

5. If sufficient time is available and/or not much discussion has occurred, go to Section P-10, *Study Questions for Chapter 1*. (The leader/facilitator needs a watch or clock to help keep aware of the passing time and gauge the group's pace.) Do the most important questions which you have circled. (See in Section P-1 the topic entitled "Preparation for Leading the Discussion.")

6. Review Section P-11, *Basic Adlerian Concepts* which hopefully has been studied the week before.

7. Move next to Section P-12, *Study Questions for Chapter 2.* Do the first four questions.

8. Then give attention to Section P-13, *The Family Constellation,* in the *Action Guide.*

   Do "buzz groups" (See Section P-1, Introduction, Item 2, under the topic "Helpful Hints"). Those who were firstborn, middle children, and the baby in the family or an only child, form in separate groups and share for six minutes maximum, what they felt in this birth position and what they did about it. Each group is to appoint a recorder and spokesman, who will share their findings with the whole group—what it was like to be firstborn child, etc. Can refer also to the description of the child's birth order position of their group in Section P-13, *The Family Constellation* work up page. Everyone consider how their position in the family has affected the kind of person they have become as adults—leader, follower, shy, etc. Sharing these experiences will help all of you to better understand the birth-order process and its effects.

9. Look at further use of Section 13, *The Family Constellation* work up as

   a. answers,

   b. understanding children and themselves, and

   c. "What else can we do?" (Refer to Item 7 in Section P-13, *The Family Constellation.*)

10. Do remaining questions for Chapter 2 if sufficient time.

11. Look in Section P-3, *Group Outline of Study,* for the reading assignment in the text, the study assignment to be done by next meeting, and the home practice activity for the coming week. (All are to be found under "Week 2.")

SECTION P-10
STUDY QUESTIONS FOR CHAPTER 1

The Ideal Family—The Ideal Child, Pages 5-9

1. Have you seen any children lately with the characteristics described on page 5 of the textbook? (Line 9. Read. This should bring a laugh.)

2. Do you think such children as are described on page 5, line 3 from bottom, are possible? (Read lines—if you know of such transformation—ask members to share examples.) Individuals recall and consider. Ask group members to share their ideas.

3. Why do you think many children become "rebellious, uncooperative, hostile, or vengeful"? Individuals use notes page— group members give their ideas. What do the authors think causes this in children? (Page 9, line 6 from bottom, and page 8, line 10.)

4. What hope and solution do the authors offer? ("Parents do learn to change their ways, children do learn to accommodate to new parental strategies," page 6, line 1 from bottom to page 7, top.)

5. The parents described in Chapter 1 are trying something different. What new strategies have they used? (Family Council, page 6, line 18 through line 21, and Logical Consequences, page 6, line 3 from bottom.)

6. Consider this statement about a family meeting: "It's how their family operates . . . a weekly family meeting where they discuss things, make decisions, settle problems." (Page 6, line 19.) Does this idea appeal to you? If so, what do you like about it? What do you not like? Individuals consider and make notes—group members share their ideas.

7. Here is a key statement: "The essence of the Adlerian system of family relationships is respect." (Page 7, line

11.) Who in the family is to receive respect? (Page 7, lines 12 and 13.)

8. In what ways do many parents behave with their children which the authors call disrespectful? (Page 7, line 17 from bottom through list.)

9. Do these acts seem disrespectful to you? (Page 7, line 17 from bottom through list.) Would you accept such actions from your husband or wife towards you? What might be disrespectful about each act? (Individuals reflect, using notes page. Group members discuss together.)

10. What are the four R's of the ideal child? (Pages 8 and 9.)

11. According to the authors, how does a child become respectful, responsible, resourceful, and responsive ("the four R's.")? (The heavy type on pages 8 and 9 and page 9, line 5.)

12. What other qualities do you like to see in a child? Individuals use notes page. Group members volunteer their thoughts.

NOTE: Group members can always use notes pages to record any good ideas and insights during discussions.

SECTION P-11
BASIC ADLERIAN CONCEPTS

Related to Rearing Children

1. All people strive towards goals.

2. The most important goal is to belong—to be part of a group, to have a place in this group, to be valued by this group.

3. The normally behaving child finds his/her place in the family group through participation, contribution, and usefulness.

4. The misbehaving child seeks his/her place in the group through one of the four mistaken goals: undue attention, power, revenge, assumed disability.

5. The misbehaving child is discouraged.

    a. He/she is discouraged about his/her place in the family group, in his/her play group, in his/her school group.

    b. His/her discouragement leads him/her from natural tendency to be cooperative and useful, into the four mistaken goals of misbehavior:

c. Adlerian ways of thinking and training aim to guide the misbehaving child back to the goals of useful contribution and cooperation.

6. Children need encouragement like plants need water.

   a. Encouragement increases self-confidence and self-respect.

   b. Our world, our culture, can be discouraging to a child.

   c. The child can be encouraged so as to counteract the discouragement he/she will receive outside the home.

   d. Children often are discouraged by us without our realizing it.

7. A child has a need to feel equal, e.g.,

   a. has needs important to him/her,

   b. wants the right to make self-decisions (where appropriate),

   c. wants to take part in decisions made about him/her, and

   d. wants to be recognized as important and of value.

8. In a democratic society (a society of equals) institutions such as the family also should be democratic.

9. Dominating parents produce shy, sly, withdrawn, resentful, rebellious, and hostile children.

10. Respect is needed by children, e.g.,

    a. the child needs to be respected, and

    b. the child needs to respect others.

       (1) Parents' deeds and actions earn respect.

       (2) Respect for the child earns respect.

11. A child needs to be accepted for what he/she is now, no matter how few in number his/her good points may be.

12. Respect implies freedom of choice.

    Agreement can be sought about limits in choices of actions as much as possible except where parents have exclusive responsibility—then they alone must decide.

13. Kindness implies a genuine respect for another individual.

14. Love is wonderful but it is not enough—love with respect is the optimum.

15. Rearing your child the Adlerian way will give you a child who is responsible, respectful, resourceful, responsive, and cooperative.

SECTION P-12
STUDY QUESTIONS FOR CHAPTER 2

Fundamentals of Child Development, Pages 10-14

1. Each of us as a child tries to gain recognition in some way (Page 11, line 14 to end of paragaph). Why do we do this? (To show to ourselves and to our family and later, the world, our secure place or position in the scheme of things. Page 11, line 4 from bottom to end of paragraph.)

2. How does each child find place or position in his/her own way? (Page 11, line 8 to "give up.") Name some examples of children finding recognition or their place. (Scholar, athlete, good girl, clown, etc., page 11, line 14 ff.)

3. What choice of "place" in the family would amount to a basic mistake in the child's future life-style or personality? (Page 11, line 21 to end of quote.) Why are these seen as basic mistakes? ("Because they spring from mistaken attitudes." Page 11, line 13 from bottom.)

4. How does a child happen onto these basic mistakes? (By his/her unique interpretations and reactions within his/her family. Page 10, line 7, and line 6 to "own way" page 11, and finally, line 1, ff. page 10.)

5. What inherent motivation do we all share? (To move toward competence. Page 11, line 8, from bottom ff.)

6. Name a second basic urge. (Desire to belong. Page 11, line 3 from bottom.)

7. What does a wise parent understand about the child? (Page 12, line 11 from bottom ff.) Why is this important to keep in mind? (The one can undermine the other, page 12, line 1 to "group.") Can anyone give an example of this in his/her own life? (Individuals record on notes page. Group members share and make notes.)

8. Describe a child with social interest. (Page 12, line 13 to "for others.") See Section P-20 in the *Action Guide* on what having social interest means.

9. What is the importance of social interest? (The child will become an adult who will be a joy to know—not some sort of nuisance or worse. Page 12, line 18 to end of paragraph.)

10. How can a parent successfully guide the child's development and behavior? (Page 12, line 6 from bottom.)

11. How does each child choose which actions of behavior will be adopted in the family? (Whichever ones help him/her along towards his/her chosen goal. Page 10, line 4.)

12. What is the goal of an encouraged child? (Page 12, line 5 from bottom.)

13. What are the four possible useless goals of a discouraged child? (Page 13, points 1 through 4.) How does the discouraged child feel? (They feel unfairly treated. Page 12, line 3 from bottom to "useless ones.")

14. What is the connection between misbehavior and the four useless goals of children? (Page 13, line 13 to end of paragraph.)

15. How can you determine which useless goal your child's misbehavior is pursuing? (Page 13, line 12 from bottom.) And why is it helpful to know the goal of your child's misbehavior? (Page 12, line 6 from bottom.)

16. According to the authors, what instills the inner motivation for successful living? (Page 14, line 2 from bottom.) What are some ways to develop the will? (Page 14, line 6 ff.) What is the definition of "the will"? (Page 14, line 4, starting " . . . will—. . ." to end of sentence.)

SECTION P-13
THE FAMILY CONSTELLATION

Its Effect and What We Can Do About It

1. The family constellation refers to the particular grouping of the family members which grows out of children's birth order.

2. What develops in the family constellation depends upon the interpretation each child gives to the family structure and upon the strategies which the child makes for coping with brothers, sisters, and parents.

3. The Adlerian view sees the attitude brothers and sisters take towards each other as having more effect than that of even the parents on children's personalities.

4. How the child sees and uses his/her position in the family constellation sets the pattern of movement and characteristic traits of that child as an adult.

5. Recognizing how a child sees and uses his/her position in the family birth order can assist the parent in finding ways to stimulate and guide the child in a more desirable direction (responsible, respectful, resourceful, responsive, and cooperative).

6. Children in the different positions of the family birth order often show the following characteristics:

First child tends

   a. to feel dethroned by the second child;

   b. to be conservative—negative about change;

   c. to take responsibility; and

   d. to want to be the very best most likely, and/or give up and be the very worst (if can't be the best).

Solutions for Parents

a. When a new baby comes, arrange parent dates with your older child.

b. Make the first child feel part of the family group— baby is ours.

c. Offer the older child opportunities to help with baby.

d. Point out advantages of being an older child:

    (1) has more freedom;

    (2) is capable of more things;

    (3) can take more responsibility—do this when younger child is not around; and

    (4) has had a chance to acquire more things, toys, etc.

Second child tends

a. to feel outdistanced;

b. to welcome any change;

c. to become the personality opposite of the older child; and

d. to form alliance with older child, and/or have an easier time of life because parents are more relaxed, more experienced.

Solutions for parents

a. Help child find an area of interest that does not compete with brother or sister.

b.   Separate children—put oldest in nursery school.

c.   Send them to different schools if possible.

Second child who becomes middle child tends

a.   to be a pace maker and is dethroned;

b.   to become good diplomat and negotiator;

c.   to become bitter and revengeful—feeling that he/she has been crowded out of the affection of the parents; and/or

d.   to feel squeezed out of the rights and privileges of others—will either give up and think life is unfair or will succeed in overcoming both competitors.

Solutions for parents

a.   Encourage any constructive traits that appear, without comparing children to other children.

b.   Arrange parent dates to reassure.

Youngest child tends

a.   to have an easier role, is never displaced;

b.   to expand extra efforts to find a place—many that would interest him/her are already taken;

c.   to be the "super baby";

d.   to have a lot of chances to be loved—by other children in family as well; and/or

e. to establish a special place for himself/herself, frequently through characteristics that are passive and non-productive. He/she may become the cutest, the most charming, or the most helpless or become discouraged about being the smallest, weakest, etc.

Solutions for parents

a. Avoid giving extra service.

b. Encourage self-sufficiency.

c. Show respect for all his/her efforts.

d. Make a point of noticing him/her.

Only child tends

a. to be a child in an adult world;

b. to be dominant, perfectionistic, and verbal;

c. to have a strained and uncertain relationship with other children.

d. to become adept at pleasing and manipulating adults; and/or

e. to be lonely and introspective.

Solutions for parents

a. Send him/her early to nursery school or arrange other group experiences with children.

b. Be aware of helping him/her learn to share (attention as well as toys).

7. Once we see that the child's place in the family constellation affects him/her, what else can we do?

   a. Detach ourselves, step back and take a good look at our children:

      (1) How has the child dealt with his/her

         (a) inner environment?

         (b) hereditary environment?

         (c) development rate?

         (d) assets?

         (e) liabilities?

      (2) What compensations or overcompensation has he/she developed? What has he/she given up?

      (3) How does he/she compare himself/herself with other children?

      (4) What does his/her place in the family constellation mean to him/her? (Children make good observers but poor interpreters.)

   b. Try to become aware of mistaken concepts so you can then guide your child into more correct evaluations. (When we perceive a situation, we are much better able to cope with it.)

   c. Try to determine how the child has perceived the situation and is using his/her place in the family birth order. Other things also can affect him/her, such as the sex of the different children and the number of years between the children.

   d. Try to become familiar with the child's beliefs and assumptions about life and about self.

   e. Help the child to correct any mistaken evaluations.

NOTES
Related to Week 1

SECTION P-14
INDIVIDUAL STUDY PLAN No. 2

Chapter 3, Pages 15-20

1. Review how place in the birth order has affected your children and what you can do about it. Write your response, using space for notes.

2. Having done your reading for the week, play tape No. 3 by Drs. Corsini and Painter, if you have it.

3. Look at Section P-16, *Seven Causes of Disobedience*, according to Dr. Dreikurs. These seven causes give us something to think about. Also, look at Section P-17, *Kinds of Misbehavior* that we would like to see disappear or at least, diminish.

4. Having read Chapter 3, *Democracy—Not Authoritarianism*, do the first *four* questions in Section P-18, *Study Questions for Chapter 3*, in the *Action Guide*.

5. Next, turn in the *Action Guide* to Section P-19, *Mutual Respect Between Parents and Children*, and note especially points No. 4, 5, 6, and 7. This Adlerian view of parenting is very serious about the importance of respect and equality between family members.

6. Do next, Section P-21, *Study Questions for Chapter 36*, and then pages 262 and 267 in the textbook. Probably, all of us need help with our own self-esteem. This chapter hopes to do that. The better we feel about ourselves, the more easily we can give our children the respect they need. They need this respect, especially from their parents.

7. Then review pages 18 and 19 in your textbook covering the statements in heavy black type. Unless these four statements are followed, large mistakes in parenting will result.

8. Take a detailed look in the *Action Guide* at what it means to spoil or pamper a child, Section P-22. The material is to help us consider more closely what is involved (spoiling). Dr. Dreikurs considered rejecting and pampering a child the two most harmful things that parents can do.

9. Next, go over Section P-23, *Disrespectful Acts of Parents to Children*. Section P-23 will help you to be aware of how respectful you are being to your children and how respectful they are being to you.

10. Now, return to Section P-18, *Study Questions for Chapter 3*, in the *Action Guide*, beginning with Item No. 5. Finish them.

11. Consult Section P-2, *Individual Outline of Study*, and find for Week 3, the reading assignment in your book and Sections P-27 and 28, *Study Questions for Chapters 4 and 5*. You are now going to look at a new way to discipline children. Use the entire week for study. This is important. To understand and use this parenting view and these parenting skills takes slow and steady study and consideration. *And* it is worth it. Do the home practice activity. This will help you be aware of the amount of respect that exists between you and your children.

SECTION P-15
GROUP MEETING NO. 2 FORMAT

Chapter 3, Pages 15-20

1. If you have the audio tapes by Drs. Corsini and Painter, play No. 3. Begin at the place where Dr. Corsini starts talking about "love," and play the tape for ten minutes. Start exactly at the time the meeting is to commence.

2. Ask any new members to introduce themselves, etc. Leader/ facilitator reminds everyone that from now on, it will be a closed study group. Any additional members may be placed on a waiting list for the next study group sessions.

3. Have each person share his/her experience with the home practice for this week, Section P-13, *The Family Constellation*, and, using point No. 7 in *The Family Constellation Work-Up*, consider each child. Did you find any differences? Do some areas need help?

4. Look at Section P-16, *Seven Causes of Disobedience* as listed by Dr. Dreikurs. This could start some discussion. Are we surprised by any of them? Are we doing any of them? Also, review Section 17, *Kinds of Misbehavior.* Would you add to any of these?

5. Start Section P-18, *Study Questions for Chapter 3.* Go through to Question 4.

6. Have members turn to Section P-19, *Mutual Respect Between Parents and Children,* and discuss together, emphasizing Nos. 4, 5, 6, and 7. Understanding as clearly as possible the meaning of respect and equality between and among family members is of great importance.

7. Do Section P-21, *Study Questions for Chapter 36,* in order to help strengthen "self-respect" in ourselves. Our children need us to do this so we can really give them our respect.

8. Review the statements in heavy black type on pages 18-19 in the textbook, *Effective Discipline in the Home and School*. Unless these four statements are followed, large mistakes in parenting will result.

9. Have group members discuss the eight points of pampering or spoiling a child, Section P-22. Discuss these together. They are not what we usually think of as "spoiled," are they?

10. Look at Section P-23, *Disrespectful Acts of Parents*. Everyone may be surprised to find that such behavior on their part could be up for question today. If we are no longer the top ones on the totem pole with the children way down below, then new ways of doing and thinking are needed. As a child, how would the group members have responded and felt themselves? Discuss.

11. Go back to Section P-18, *Study Questions for Chapter 3*, and finish, if time is sufficient.

12. Close by looking together at Section P-3, *Group Outline of Study* for Week 3, the reading assignment in the textbook, *Effective Discipline in the Home and School*; the study assignment in the *Action Guide*: Sections P-29, P-30, and P-31 which are to be done by the next meeting; and the home practice activity for the coming week. A faithful performing of the home practice activity will help everyone become more familiar with these ideas and better able to evaluate and use them.

SECTION P-16
SEVEN CAUSES
OF DISOBEDIENCE

1. Inconsistency in giving orders.

2. Indecisiveness of tone of voice.

3. Violent approach or expression.

4. Humiliating approach (Sarcasm).

5. Impatience that does not wait for compliance.

6. Repetition of an order.

7. Parents arguing about an order.

Dreikurs

NOTE: It does not say that the punishment is not severe enough.

SECTION P-17
KINDS OF MISBEHAVIOR

We Would Like to Disappear

1. Defiant behavior

2. Destructive behavior

3. Provocative behavior

4. Hurtful behavior

5. Annoying behavior

6. Testing behavior

7. Deceitful behavior

8. Disrespectful behavior

9. Irresponsible behavior

10. Angry behavior

11. Defeated behavior

12. Manipulative behavior

13. Whining behavior

14. Withdrawing behavior

SECTION P-18
STUDY QUESTIONS FOR CHAPTER 3

Democracy—Not Authoritarianism, Pages 15-20

1. Besides the primary bond of love between the parent and child, what else must parents emphasize? ("Respect," page 15 in textbook, line 3 from the bottom.) How will it help? (Page 15, line 3 from bottom to "respectful.") *Definition of "respect":* to esteem, to value highly, to treat with consideration, courteous regard.

2. How can love sometimes hurt the child? (Page 16, line 2 from top.) Is there a time when respect can hurt? All think about this—is there? Individuals use notes page.

3. How do many children react to arbitrary orders from parents today? (Page 15, line 4 to "punishment.")

4. What do you think the authors mean by mutual respect between parent and child? (Page 15, line 9 to end of paragraph.) How can we show respect? (Page 15, line 10 to end of paragraph.)

5. Do you ever speak to your children in the manner quoted in the "Democratic" column on page 17? Or are you more apt to use the sentences stated in the "Authoritarian" column? How do the democratic ones sound to you? How would you have felt if they had been said to you as a child? (Individuals think about it and use notes page, group members share their responses.)

6. What political ideal is thought by the authors and many others to be suitable for families today? ("Democratic." A democracy is a group of equals. Page 16, line 6.)

7. Does this mean we vote? (Page 16, line 11 to end of paragraph.)

8. In what ways are we equal?

a. Everyone has free will (babies, too). Can you think of an example?

b. Everyone is capable of making good common sense decisions about themselves and others if encouraged to develop this capacity.

c. Everyone is capable of developing the four R's.

d. Everyone is capable of developing the qualities that make up social interest.

e. Everyone is capable of becoming a mature human adult, the highest form of creation on this planet.

f. Everyone's needs are equally important.

g. Everyone's obligations need to be taken equally seriously.

h. Everyone is capable of making valuable, though differing contributions to the group.

9. Does a parent ever say "no" to the child? When? (Page 16, line 16 to end of paragraph.)

10. Do you disagree with any of the features of the democratic system of child raising advocated by the authors? (Beginning page 16, line 7 from bottom to page 18 through point 12.) If you disagree, why? (Individuals use notes page. Group members talk together.)

11. Does any of the advice in heavy black type on pages 18 and 19 apply to you? If so, what might be hurtful in what you have been doing with your child? Have you observed any other parents caught up in any of these well-meaning parental mistakes? What did you see it doing to the child involved? (Individuals use notes page. Group members discuss together.)

12. Do you disagree with any of the statements, 1 through 9 on pages 19-20)? If you do disagree, in what way would you be different and why? (Individuals use notes page. Group members share.)

13. Even though you might possess all the attitudes outlined on pages 19 and 20, according to the authors, what are you probably still in need of? (Some guidelines for training your child, page 20, line 3 from bottom.)

14. In what ways might our children educate us? (Page 20, line 6, ff.)

SECTION P-19
MUTUAL RESPECT BETWEEN PARENTS AND CHILDREN

1. If we respect our children, they will respect us.

2. Respect, like love, cannot be forced. (Children can be frightened into pretending respect. Often, actually they are thinking and feeling the opposite.)

3. Respect usually finds expression in courteous and considerate behavior.

4. Why should we respect our children?

   a. They are human beings, the highest form of creation on this planet; therefore, they have the capacity:

      (1) to think and comprehend;

      (2) to feel and to care;

      (3) to invent and to imagine;

      (4) to enjoy and to bring joy;

      (5) to grow and develop;

      (6) to remember;

      (7) to learn to talk, to write, and to read; and

      (8) to make tools, using a tool-making hand with its opposable thumb, accompanied by advanced intelligence.

   b. They have an ineffable uniqueness.

   c. They have a potential goldmine of talents.

5. Children are our equals because they

    a.   have free will.

    b.   are capable of making good common sense decisions or choices if encouraged to develop this capacity.

    c.   are capable of developing the four "R's":

        (1) Responsibleness,

        (2) Respectfulness,

        (3) Resourcefulness, and

        (4) Responsiveness.

    d.   are capable of developing the qualities that make up social interest. (This Section in the *Action Guide* and page 12, line 12, in *Effective Discipline in the Home and School.*)

    e.   are capable of becoming mature human adults, the highest form of creation on this planet.

    f.   have equally important rights and needs.

    g.   have obligations which can and should be taken seriously, as

        (1) no clutter,

        (2) their chores, and

        (3) being responsible for themselves (when appropriate), etc. (See Section P-47.)

    h.   are capable of making valuable, though differing, contributions to the family group.

6. What are children's rights and needs in regard to us?

a. To have their particular physical and emotional needs for their age and development, noted and filled.

b. To receive training in group-living procedures and routines.

c. To learn desired skills from training and by having a chance to practice them when ready.

d. To be permitted to choose between alternatives appropriate to their age:

    (1) Even *the wrong choice* should be allowed, providing it is not a matter of life endangerment, severe injury, breaking the law, seriously damaging their health, or interfering with the comfort of the whole family.

    (2) Allowing a *wrong decision* to stand and the results to happen allows them to learn from experience.

e. To have some fun times with us.

7. What can we expect our children to respect in us?

a. Our humanness and humaneness. (See point No. 4, a., (1)-(8).)

b. Our uniqueness and our potential qualities.

c. Our particular set of talents and contributions.

d. Our rights and needs (that they be equally noted and filled).

    (1) Not to say the least—our right to make choices when indicated by the situation. As, we choose to say what *we will do* or *will not do* if they misbehave.

    (2) Also our right to be wrong (in our parenting) and learn from the results.

(3) Our right to have the opportunities to grow and develop.

Not to the child's neglect.

8. Family members who respect each other (or who value each other highly and have an appreciation of each other's worth) will enjoy each other more.

9. Respect for each other results in a desire to cooperate with each other.

NOTE: Important extra point: We need to be aware of and value our own specialness and uniqueness as human beings and have respect for ourselves as a creation—only then can we give respect to our children.

SECTION P-20
WHAT HAVING
SOCIAL INTEREST MEANS

1. Respecting the rights of others.

2. Being tolerant of others.

3. Being interested in others.

4. Cooperating with others.

5. Encouraging others.

6. Being courageous.

7. Having a true sense of your own worth.

8. Having a feeling of belonging.

9. Having socially acceptable goals.

10. Putting forth genuine effort.

11. Being honest.

12. Assuming responsibility.

13. Being willing to share rather than "How much can I get?"

14. Thinking of "we" rather than just "I."

NOTE: All of us can equally develop these qualities if we want to make the effort. One could say, "This is our fundamental equality."

SECTION P-21
STUDY QUESTIONS FOR CHAPTER 36

Unconditional Love, Pages 262-267

1. What kind of attitude can prevent parents from creating a harmonious home? (Page 262, line 3 to "results.")

2. What is unconditional love? (Page 263, line 1 to "other person.") What are its benefits? (Page 263, line 15 from bottom.)

3. What would happen if we did manage to always love the behavior of our children, good or bad? (Page 263, line 5 to end of paragraph.)

4. How do you keep from feeling anger when your child or children are misbehaving? (Page 263, line 11 to "get angry.")

5. How can we train ourselves to become more positive in our lives? (Page 264, "Positivity Drill" ff.)

6. What is a "good purpose?" (Page 264, line 10 from bottom.) How does finding the "good purpose" in upsetting actions of others help us? (Page 265, line 6 ff., and line 2.)

7. What often causes us to criticize a trait of another person? (Page 265, line 10.) How could a person change his/her attitude of criticism to one of acceptance? (Page 265, line 11 ff.)

8. What else is suggested as a solution? ("Criticism Drill," pages 265 and 266.)

9. What surprising statement is made in regard to our emotions? (Page 266, line 12 from bottom to end of paragraph.)

10. What is suggested to help ourselves with negative emotions we might have, other than bottling them up or pretending

they aren't there? (Page 266, line 6 from bottom, to end of paragraph on page 267.)

11. Why would feeling less angry and critical, but more accepting of our children and people in general, help strengthen "self respect" in ourselves? (We would more successfully influence and train our children and they would show us more love. Our spouses, friends, and associates also would feel more drawn to us and positive about us. Anger begets anger and no one likes being criticized.) Read again "Important Extra Point" at the end of Section P-19, *Mutual Respect Between Parents and Children.*

SECTION P-22
WAYS TO SPOIL A CHILD

A child is getting you to spoil (pamper) him/her if you allow him/her to

1. demand undue or constant attention,

2. put others in his/her service,

3. avoid responsibility, or

4. disturb the order of the household.

Or if you

5. protect him/her from all hurt and hardship,

6. rescue him/her from all difficulties and never let the child practice solving problems,

7. treat him/her as someone who is special or superior to others, or

8. forget he/she is only special as everyone is special but not in a superior sense or above the restraints and obligations of ordinary humans.

NOTE: Even though our talents are outstanding, does this change our obligations to the family?

SECTION P-23
DISRESPECTFUL ACTS OF PARENTS

1. Using "baby talk" with children.

2. Using a special, really belittling, and patronizing tone of voice with children.

3. Reprimanding or correcting them in front of others.

4. Speaking sarcastically to them alone or in front of others.

5. Doing for them what they can or should be doing for themselves.

6. Making decisions for them that they could now make for themselves.

7. Not bothering to listen when they are speaking to you.

8. Not bothering to be courteous to them.

9. Making a servant out of them.

10. Not seeking their views about matters that affect them.

11. Constantly giving them orders, sometimes disguised as requests.

12. Not viewing their needs, desires, and contributions of equal importance to yours.

NOTE: Would you act in these ways with a friend?

SECTION P-24
BILL OF RIGHTS
FOR HEALTHY PARENTS
AND HEALTHY CHILDREN

(Original Source Unknown)

1. *YOUR RIGHTS ARE AS IMPORTANT AS YOUR CHILD'S, IF NOT MORE SO!!*

Because you are an adult, your responsibility is far greater than that of a child. You are responsible to the child and to the outside world. You must have authority commensurate with the responsibility you have to carry. The child should not have more authority in those things that pertain to you than you have—if as much. The Bible says, "Do not muzzle the ox that treads out the grain,"— if you need the sanction of Holy Writ to take your rights!

2. *TAKE YOUR FULL SHARE EVERY TIME!!*

The best way to teach children to know you have rights is to use your rights. They see you use them. Rights that are not used are like a vacant lot that is not protected; children move into it and dump refuse on it. The child will respect your value when he/she sees you assert your worth, and he/she thereby, learns to respect the value and worth of those with whom the child comes in contact.

3. *HAVE A PRIVATE LIFE OF YOUR OWN AND HAVE SOME FUN EVERYDAY!!*

Recreation means re-creation or the renewal of the spirit. You cannot be a good fellow man to anyone, least of all to your children, if your morale is broken. Life loses all meaning when joy goes out of it, and when that happens, we become as blind as moles.

4. **_KEEP YOUR PERSONAL AMBITION SEPARATE FROM YOUR CHILDREN'S AMBITIONS!!_**

Do not try to fulfil your life's ambition through your children. Find fulfillment in terms of your own accomplishments, not theirs. Then you will not need to hate your children for "defrauding" you. And they will not need to hate you for smothering their inner gleam!

5. **_LEARN TO MIND YOUR OWN BUSINESS AND MAKE IT PROFITABLE FOR YOUR CHILDREN TO DO LIKEWISE!_**

Remember that children are not your possessions. They are only transients or visitors who pass through your home on their way to the outside world, where they will be expected to be a help and not a burden. As husband and wife, you have your whole lives to spend together after your children have ended their visit in your home. Your relationship to each other should be paramount. Your children should never be allowed to steal the interest of one of you from the other. Do not your children's keepers be, and do not allow yourself to be kept by them!

NOTES
Related to Week 2

SECTION P-25
INDIVIDUAL STUDY PLAN NO. 3
Chapters 4 and 5, Pages 21-33

1. Review the home practice. Did you find yourself being disrespectful to your children sometimes? If so, seeing them in a different way can help you change your ways with them. We urge you to keep checking yourself on this point.

2. Play tape No. 2 by Drs. Corsini and Painter on logical consequences.

3. Read and reflect about the new meanings of reward and punishment for this study, as given by the authors in the text, page 22, line 14 and page 21, line 9, and in the *Action Guide,* Section P-27, *Study Questions for Chapter 4* at the top of the page. This view of rewards and punishments *leads* to new ideas and methods for influencing today's child.

4. Go next to Section P-27, *Study Questions for Chapter 4.*

5. Move on to Section P-28, *Study Questions for Chapter 5.*

6. Understand again that this Adlerian viewpoint *includes* "Times When a Parent Says 'No'" as listed in the *Action Guide,* following chapter questions on natural and logical consequences—also on page 29, line 11, ff. in your book. Allowing a child to learn from the consequences of his/her actions at such times is not possible. Instead, he/she will learn that some limits (rules) must be observed without exception or negotiation.

7. In your *Action Guide,* when studying Section P-30, *Punishment and Reward versus Natural and Logical Consequences,* look closely at the points about logical consequences. They are designed to be used as a quick

reference when you need it. **Logical Consequences** can be tricky and seen by the child to be punishment. **Natural Consequences** can be used for all misbehaving goals, if one *fits* the offending behavior. A Natural Consequence flows just naturally out of the natural order of things.

8. Look over Section P-32, *The Discouraged Child's Mistaken Goals*, which is provided to help you eliminate a misbehavior by the use of consequences.

9. Go next to Section P-2, *Individual Outline of Study* for Week 4 and view what you are to do. Your home practice activity for this week is to try using a consequence for a misbehavior. Start with an easy one and consult Section P-32, *The Discouraged Child's Mistaken Goals*, for extra assistance.

SECTION P-26
GROUP MEETING NO. 3 FORMAT

Chapters 4 and 5, Pages 21-33

1. Play tape No. 2 by Drs. Corsini and Painter for 10 minutes starting with the part about logical consequences.

2. Discuss together the home practice for Week 3. Did any of you catch yourselves in any of the disrespectful acts listed? How were the children affected? Talk together again about the importance of mutual respect between family members and how this respect from their parents helps our children.

3. Review the meanings of reward and punishment for this study as given at the top of the page of Section P-27, *Reward and Punishment: A Mistake*, and in the textbook on page 22, line 14 and page 21, line 2 from bottom ff. to end of paragraph.

4. Go next to Section P-27, *Study Questions for Chapter 4.* The leader/facilitator will help with this.

5. Move to Section P-28, *Study Questions for Chapter 5.* Make sure to have sufficient time to look over Section 30, *Punishment and Reward vs. Natural and Logical Consequences.* Turn your attention especially to point 11d.

6. Take time to discuss together and to gain an understanding of Section P-29, *Times When a Parent Says "No."* Also review together page 16, line 16, ff. *Effective Discipline in the Home and School.* Consult on why these times would be the exception to learning from the consequences of the actions.

7. Review Section P-31, *Characteristics of a Logical Consequence.* Gaining a clear understanding of a Logical Consequence is crucial to this method of discipline. This

list also can be used as a quick reference when planning and applying a logical consequence.

8. End the study session by looking together at Section P-3, *Group Outline of Study*, Week 4 at the reading assignment in *Effective Discipline in the Home and School*, the study assignment in the *Action Guide*, and the home practice activity for the coming week. Notice Section P-32, *The Discouraged Child's Mistaken Goals*. It offers extra assistance when applying a consequence to a misbehavior.

9. To the leader/facilitator: If time is not sufficient to preview with your group members their next week's home practice activity, you can always suggest that they refer to the discussion at the end of the corresponding *Individual Study plan*, Section P-2, for further clarification.

NOTE: Natural Consequences can be used for all misbehaving goals if one fits the offending behavior.

SECTION P-27
STUDY QUESTIONS FOR CHAPTER 4

Reward and Punishment: A Mistake

For this study, by **reward** we will mean a bribe or largesse. By **punishment** we will mean hitting, spanking, scolding, humiliating, depriving, isolating, grounding, threatening, and anything done in anger.

1. What aspects of reward and punishment (as described above) when used on children, can be called a "flaw?" (Page 21, line 9, ff.)

2. Even though reward and punishment often work, what are some undesirable side effects resulting from their use? (Page 21, line 6.)

3. Consider this statement: "In each case we have a superior bossing an inferior." (Page 22, line 10). What other kind of relationship is possible between parent and child? (A democratic, friendly relationship between equals. See point 5 a-h, in Section P-19, *Mutual Respect.*)

4. Name some of the examples of punishment that are best avoided by parents. (Page 22, line 14, ff.)

5. Do you argue with any of the authors' "additional points" about reward and punishment? (In heavy black type, pages 22-24.) (Individuals consider and use notes page. Group members discuss together.)

6. What capacity in the child do reward and punishment not help to develop? (Inner controls for good behavior. Page 23, line 9 from bottom.)

7. According to the authors, what should be the parents' primary, overriding goal? (Help the child become cooperative.) (Page 23, line 7 from bottom.)

8. What negative qualities in your child are you trying not to arouse? (Humiliation, alienation, or hostility. Page 25, line 16, from bottom, ff.)

9. How do Adlerian parents see problems? (As opportunities they can use to strengthen relationships. Page 25, line 11 from bottom.)

10. What else can we look for in negative behavior that can help our parenting? (Page 25, line 7, ff. from bottom. Example: line 4 from bottom.)

11. What effect does our continual anger have? (Page 25, line 5 from bottom.)

12. What is a win/win statement? (Page 26, line 2.) How did this one help? (Page 26, line 4 to end of paragraph.)

13. What do the authors see as the best way to correct misbehavior and yet maintain good relations with your child? (The method called "logical and natural consequences." Page 26, line 4, from bottom.)

SECTION P-28
STUDY QUESTIONS FOR CHAPTER 5
Natural and Logical Consequences, Pages 27-33

1. If we give up punishment and reward, what are some ways to obtain voluntary cooperation? (Page 27, line 1 to "home." List three ways.) What are some "democratic procedures"? (See page 16, line 12 ff. to "rights," and list 1 through 12 on page 16 to page 18.)

2. If voluntary cooperation is not possible, name the additional method to obtain cooperation. (Natural and logical consequences. Page 27, line 4 ff. to "behavior.")

3. What is the essence of natural consequences? (Page 27, line 2 from bottom.)

4. Where do we draw the line on the use of natural consequences? (Page 29, line 11 to end of paragraph.)

5. What do the authors see as one obligation parents have when using natural consequences? (Page 29, line 15.) How many times do they warn the child? (Page 29, line 18.) What is wrong with repeated warnings? (Page 29, line 16.)

6. Besides natural consequences, what other deterrent can parents make use of? (Page 29, line 2 from bottom to "draw backs" on page 30.)

7. In logical consequences, what two facts have to be expressed or implied by the parent to the child? (Page 30, line 2 to "misbehave.")

8. What two features do logical consequences contain to keep them from being punishment? (Page 30, line 15 from bottom to end of sentence.) Why does the child not feel resentment with this method? (Page 31, line 1 ff.)

9. Name two logical consequences that are often used. (Page 31, line 5, ignoring or withdrawing.) Why is such withdrawal not defeat? (Page 31, line 13 from bottom to "you.") What must we be careful about when withdrawing? (Page 31, line 1 to end of paragraph.)

10. What makes the "withdrawal technique" so effective with many misbehaviors? (Page 32, line 1 to end of paragraph.)

11. What is the "bathroom technique?" (Page 32, line 11 to "bathroom.") Would anyone like to describe it? When should the mother leave the bathroom? (Page 32, line 2 from bottom to end of paragraph.) (Individuals put into own words and then compare with book. Group members volunteer answers.)

12. What do the authors mean when they ask parents to start "thinking logically rather than punitively?" (Page 33, line 3 from bottom.) *Punitively:* meaning in a "payback sense"—"You'll suffer for this," or "You can't get away with that. I'll show you who is boss." *Logically:* You ask yourself what relates to this conduct that is discomforting— unpleasant for the child?

13. When we withdraw from a child, what should we be careful not to project? (Rejection—page 33, line 4 ff. to end of paragraph.)

14. What is the key to not rejecting a child? (Page 33, line 12 from bottom.)

SECTION P-29
TIMES WHEN A PARENT SAYS "NO."

(These areas are not negotiable.)

1. Life endangerment or severe injury.

2. Seriously damaging to their health.

3. Breaking the law.

4. Interfering with the comfort of the whole family or the group.

5. Idiosyncratic family values, such as diet, religion, etc.

See for review, page 167, line 16 ff. in *Effective Discipline in the Home and School.*

SECTION P-30
PUNISHMENT AND REWARD VERSUS NATURAL AND LOGICAL CONSEQUENCES

When Training Children

1. Punishment and reward are based on the superior, personal power of the parent.

   Also on the belief and conviction of the parent that they have a responsibility and a right to apply punishment and reward as learning and training techniques.

2. Use of *punishment* has drawbacks.

   a. **Punishment** teaches the child to respect stronger power.

   b. Often the child tries to become an even stronger power.

      And the power struggle begins.

   c. Being hit insults a child's sense of dignity.

   d. Being hit frightens a small child.

      His/her beloved parent, his/her source of love and joy and support hits him/her—it does not make sense.

   e. Yields only temporary success—it has to be repeated and then repeated again.

   f. Sometimes the child only half complies—the chore is sloppily done, the hands are barely washed, etc.

      It can also encourage deceit.

   g. Cooperation can become something that is forced or bribed— which is not quite cooperation.

h. A show of power often incites rebellion and its difficulties.

3. Use of a *reward* also has drawbacks.

   a. **Rewards** emphasize a superior vs. inferior relationship.

     (1) We reward our inferiors for favors or for good deeds.

     (2) The child can come to resent our superior vantage point, thereby hurting our relationship with him/her.

   b. A system of rewards can cause children to assume that they need not do anything unless there is something in it for them.

     We may run out of satisfying rewards.

   c. When we bribe a child for good behavior with a reward, we are, in effect, showing him/her that we do not trust him/her to do it, which is a form of discouragement.

   d. Since rewards are usually only given for success, the child can only feel worthwhile when he/she succeeds. This can be discouraging.

   e. Reward for a success puts some children under the pressure of continued success.

     (1) Effort and improvement not being honored with reward.

     (2) Fear of falling short can threaten his/her future abilities.

4. While we suggest discontinuing the use of personal power through punishment and reward, we stress the importance of establishing respect for order and limits through the use of natural and logical consequences.

5. **Consequences** differ from punishments and rewards by expressing the power of the natural order and the social order, rather than compliance with the demands of an individual authority—you and your power.

   a. **Natural consequences** occur as a result of a violation of the natural order of things.

   b. **Logical consequences** occur as a result of a violation of the social order of things.

6. The parent allows the child to experience the discomforts of lack of respect for order and reality through the use of natural and logical consequences.

7. Order and reality itself bring about the unpleasant consequences—not the arbitrary power of the adult.

   The parent is standing by as a concerned friend and your relationship is safeguarded.

8. Consequences, natural and logical, must be impersonal, involve no moral judgements (the child is learning), and be applied in a friendly manner—there is no need to be angry; your child is learning.

   a. Consequences deal with what is happening now—not with past transgressions.

   b. They must offer the child a choice of alternative actions—the correct act, or the misbehaving act.

   c. He/she must have a chance to try again—there is hope.

9. When the consequences take effect, the child gets angry at himself/herself—not at you.

10. He/she has been warned (once!) and he/she has chosen the act.

a.   This protects your relationship with him/her.

b.   This allows learning to take place.

He/she does not digress into anger and conflict with you.

11. An important factor in the use of consequences is that the child is relieved of feeling that he/she is subject to the whim of an authority over which he/she has no control.

With consequences, he/she decides for himself/herself whether or not he/she wants to repeat a given act, while you remain mostly neutral. (Being sure only that the promised results, the consequences, occur.)

12. A logical consequence in contrast to a natural consequence is arranged by the parent or another adult rather than being solely the result of the child's own act.

a.   It is logically connected to the act of misbehavior.

b.   It is directly related to the social order of man.

c.   It is not applicable in all situations but is most successful in dealing with attention-getting misbehavior.

d.   However, in a **power contest,** one can rarely succeed with a logical consequence.

(1) The parent is not objective enough.

(2) No anger, retaliation, or secret glee can be used (now I've got you).

(3) Instead, interest is shown in the situation, the outcome, and feelings of sympathy and understanding.

(4) The parent needs to have an awareness that the child is involved in a learning process, not a judicial proceeding.

(5) Withdrawal from the power contest and *improvement of your relationship* with positive attention could precede the eventual use of logical consequences. This is very important.

13. By using consequences instead of punishment and reward, the parent permits the child to discover for himself/herself the advantages of respect for the natural and social orders.

   a. Instead of external deterrents and incentives, internal deterrents and incentives are used.

   b. Experiencing the consequences, the child develops a sense of self-discipline and internal motivation for reasons of his/her own.

   c. He/she respects order (natural or social) not because he/she will be punished otherwise, but because he/she has learned it is necessary for effective functioning.

   No side benefits will come from the parent to encourage the continuance of the negative acts.

14. The most important means of avoiding conflicts and implementing consequences in a family is by use of the family council or family meeting.

SECTION P-31
CHARACTERISTICS OF A
LOGICAL CONSEQUENCE

1. An information session takes place first, so there is a spoken or implied agreement to the consequence from your child and he/she understands it.

2. The consequence is always logically connected to the misbehavior.

3. A choice of actions is available—the misbehaving action or the behaving action.

4. No anger is felt or expressed.

   Your child is learning; you are the teacher.

5. No second warnings of any kind are given, just immediate action in a friendly, teaching manner.

6. A chance to try again will be available so that hope is ever present.

7. Once the misbehavior and the resulting consequence are finished, it is over. You smile, and you talk of something else, etc.

NOTE: Unless your logical consequence has these characteristics, it is just the same old punishing thing and will have the same disappointing results.

SECTION P-32
THE DISCOURAGED CHILD'S MISTAKEN GOALS

As a parent, remove yourself and do not reinforce mistaken behavior. You can do retraining by coming back at neutral and positive times to "teach" and reinforce acceptable behavior.

The following four mistaken goals are the ones that discouraged children have. The more discouraged they are, the farther down the list they go in their mistaken goals.

For each mistaken goal are listed in outline form five important considerations.

1. *UNDUE ATTENTION*

    a. What the child is feeling (self image)

        (1) I only count when I am noticed, have your constant attention, keep you busy with me.
        (2) I am not important or happy on my own.

    b. How the parent feels

        (1) Frustrated
        (2) Annoyed
        (3) Bugged
        (4) Irritated
        (5) Always being bothered

    c. How parent reinforces

        (1) Gives constant attention
        (2) Serves
        (3) Reminds
        (4) Coaxes
        (5) Nags
        (6) Delighted with and praises "good" child
        (7) Does not give attention when child is not asking for it

d.　How child responds to parent reinforcement

(1) Temporarily stops, then uses misbehavior again.

e.　How parent can redirect

(1) Avoid the first impulse
(2) Don't get sucked in
(3) Ignore misbehavior
(4) Disappear
(5) Do the unexpected
(6) Encourage independence
(7) Give attention to deed not doer
(8) Give attention when child is not asking for it

2. **POWER**

a.　What child is feeling (self image)

(1) I am only significant when: I am the boss; I defeat you; I get my way; I involve you in a struggle.
(2) I am only important when I win.

b.　How parent feels

(1) Provoked
(2) Angry
(3) Enraged
(4) Ready to fight
(5) Determined to control
(6) Determined to be the boss

c.　How parent reinforces

(1) Fights back
(2) Blows up
(3) Punishes
(4) Tries to win

d.　How child responds to parent reinforcement

(1) Continues and intensifies conflict
(2) Is determined to win, to be boss

(3) Is less and less cooperative

    e.   How parent can redirect

        (1) Refuse to fight, stop your end of the power
        (2) Don't argue, get away
        (3) Take action not words
        (4) Do the unexpected
        (5) Admit inability to control
        (6) Provide and encourage cooperative activities

3. **REVENGE**

    a.   What child is feeling (self-image)

        (1) I am not accepted
        (2) I am not liked
        (3) I am going to: get even, hurt you back, show you how bad I am
        (4) I am at war

    b.   How parent feels

        (1) Hurt
        (2) Mad
        (3) "How could you do this to me?"
        (4) "I can't let you get away with this"

    c.   How parent reinforces

        (1) Strikes back
        (2) Punishes
        (3) Labels child "bad"
        (4) Treats the child like the enemy

    d.   How child responds to parent reinforcement

        (1) Intensification of war
        (2) Wants to get even, to retaliate
        (3) Wants to make them feel sorry for their success

    e.   How parent can redirect

(1) Remove yourself from the situation
(2) Avoid retaliation
(3) Don't be so easily hurt
(4) Refuse to accept child's "badness"
(5) Accept child
(6) Encourage child to find other ways to relate

4. **HELPLESSNESS—WITHDRAWAL**

  a. What child is feeling (self-image)

   (1) Leave me alone
   (2) I can't: do anything right, do anything for myself, ever win
   (3) I'm no good, a lost cause, a failure
   (4) Why try—I can at least survive by giving up

  b. How parent feels

   (1) Hopeless
   (2) Full of despair
   (3) Extremely discouraged
   (4) "I give up"

  c. How parent reinforces

   (1) Labels and treats child as helpless
   (2) Does for the child what he/she can do for self
   (3) Pressures and has too high expectations
   (4) Expects the child to fail

  d. How child responds to parent reinforcement

   (1) Continues to be helpless
   (2) Retreats further
   (3) Is passive

  e. How parent can redirect

   (1) Accept the child as is
   (2) Remove standards of performance
   (3) Stop feeling helpless yourself

(4) Show faith that child can do it
(5) Encourage all efforts to try
(6) Trust the child with small responsibilities so he/she can experience success
(7) Have patience

SECTION P-33
HOW TO RUIN YOUR CHILD

(Original source unknown)

1. Begin with infancy to give the child everything he/she wants. In this way the child will grow to believe the world owes him/her a living.

2. When the child picks up bad words, laugh at him/her. This will make the child think the behavior is cute. It will encourage him/her to pick up "cuter" phrases that will blow off the top of your head later.

3. Never give the child any spiritual training. Wait until he/she is 21 and then let him/her decide for himself/herself.

4. Avoid use of the word "wrong." It may develop a guilt complex. This will condition him/her to believe later, when he/she is arrested for stealing a car, that society is against him/her and he/she is being persecuted.

5. Pick up everything he/she leaves lying around—books, shoes, clothes. Do everything for him/her so that he/she will be experienced in throwing all responsibility on others.

6. Let the child read any printed matter he/she can get his/her hands on. Be careful that the silverware and drinking glasses are sterilized, but let his/her mind feast on garbage.

7. Quarrel frequently in the presence of your children. In this way, they will not be too shocked when the home is broken up later.

8. Give a child all the spending money he/she wants. Never let him/her earn on his/her own. Why should the child have things as tough as you had them?

9. Take the child's part against neighbors, teachers, policemen. They are all prejudiced against your child.

10. When the child gets into real trouble, apologize for yourself by saying, "I never could do anything with him/her."

11. Prepare for a life of grief. You will be likely to have it.

NOTES
Related to Week 3

SECTION P-34
INDIVIDUAL STUDY PLAN NO. 4

Chapter 6, Pages 34-39

1. If your home practice last week, applying a consequence to a misbehavior, is having results already—fine! Keep it up! If your child's behavior is worse—continue on— do not move to another misbehavior yet. Your child is asking, "Do you really mean it?"

2. Having read Chapter 6, play tape No. 8 by Drs. Corsini and Painter if you have it. The last part is on encouragement.

3. Notice the parental actions that foster competition, Section P-36, *These Foster Competition.* Competition between and among family members kills cooperation. Who wants to cooperate with their rival? These parental actions also increase discouragement in children.

    See page 12, top, *Conflict of Directions* in **Effective Discipline in the Home and School** and page 236, No. 3.

4. Go to Section P-37, *Study Questions for Chapter 6.* Do all the questions through question No. 8.

5. Turn to Section P-38, *Encouragement and Recognition.* First, look at points 9, 10, and 11 on *"Praise."* Then go over points 1 through 8.

6. Back to Section P-37, *Study Questions for Chapter 6,* and do Nos. 9 and 10.

7. Then return to Section P-38, *Encouragement and Recognition,* and look over the ways to discourage and encourage children—points 12 and 13.

8. Lastly, go over points 14 through 17 in Section P-38, covering training a child in how to handle and use *failure.*

Mastering this will greatly strengthen your child's assurance for now and always.

9. Our increased understanding about what does and does not encourage a child can loom alarmingly large to a parent. Keep heart. Try first to cut out all critical remarks. This is your home practice activity for Week 5. In your reading assignment, you will be reviewing theories, ideas, and principles of the Adlerian approach to child rearing. Look at Section P-2, *Individual Outline of Study*, for your next reading assignment and study assignment for Week 5.

SECTION P-35
GROUP MEETING NO. 4 FORMAT

Chapter 6, Pages 34-39

1. Play tape No. 8 by Drs. Corsini and Painter—the last part on encouragement for about 10 minutes.

2. What about the home practice for Week 4? How did the use of consequences go? What misbehavior did you work on? Is it working? An important point is not to move to another misbehavior until this one goes. Talk about this together.

3. Also look at the list of parental actions, Section 36, *These Foster Competition*, that foster competition between and among your children. A very important point is to eliminate competition in the family. Whatever its value in the outside world, competition is a killer of cooperation in the family. Who wants to cooperate with his/her rival?

4. Start on Section P-37, *Study Questions for Chapter 6*. Do all the questions through question No. 8.

5. Then go to Section P-38, *Encouragement and Recognition*, and discuss first, points 9, 10, and 11 on *"Praise."* Then go over points 1 through 8.

6. Move to Section P-37, *Study Questions for Chapter 6*, Nos. 9 and 10.

7. Return to Section P-38, *Encouragement and Recognition*, and go over the "Do's and Don'ts" of encouragement as presented in that section. Do you remember any of these discouraging things happening to you as a child and how you felt? Discuss together.

8. Finish with points 14 through 17 dealing with training a child in how to handle and use "failure." Mastering this generates considerable courage in children and gives them a "coping skill" for the rest of their lives.

9. Close by pointing out in Section P-3, *Group Outline of Study* for Week 5, the reading assignment in *Effective Discipline in the Home and School*, the study assignment, and the home practice activity for the week.

SECTION P-36
THESE FOSTER COMPETITION

1. Favoring one child over the other.

2. Supporting one child against the other (as in fights).

3. Comparing one child to the other.

4. Praising rather than encouraging.

*When you use words of recognition that acknowledge the act, the thing done, the contribution, the help, the improvement, the effort, the accomplishment, and a positive feeling honestly expressed, you are being **encouraging,** rather than praising.*

NOTE: Competition kills off cooperation. Who wants to cooperate with his/her rival?

SECTION P-37
STUDY QUESTIONS FOR CHAPTER 6

Encouraging the Child

1. According to the authors, how important is encouragement to a child? (Page 34, line 1.)

2. What is the overall conviction of a discouraged child? (Page 34, line 4.)

3. How does a steady diet of discouraging remarks make a child feel? (Page 35, line 8 from bottom to end of paragraph.)

4. Do you ever say any of the discouraging remarks listed, to your child? (Pages 34 and 35.) Individuals think about it and note the acts you want to stop; group members share how such remarks made them feel as a child.

5. If your friend or your spouse made any of these discouraging remarks to you, how would you react? (Individuals think of an example, using one of the remarks. Someone in the group volunteer an example and include one of the remarks. Perhaps some group members could even role play one.)

6. All children have some bad habits, but to encourage their child, for what can parents especially look? (Page 36, line 1 to "appreciated.")

7. What does this encouragement imply? (Page 35, line 2 from bottom.)

8. What are the four dangers of praising a child? (Page 36, line 15 to "doing well.")

9. What five factors distinguish encouragement from praise? (Page 39.) Do you remember praise ever affecting you in these ways? Individuals reflect and use notes page. Group members share.

10. Do you object to any of the encouraging acts listed? Do you do any of them? How about the "do nots?" (Page 36, bottom to page 38, points 2, 13, & 18.)

11. Perhaps this is a good time to look once more in the textbook at Chapter 36, *Change Yourself*, considering again how those ideas might help us encourage ourselves. The more positive and self-assured we feel, the more encouraging we can be to our children and others.

SECTION P-38
ENCOURAGEMENT AND RECOGNITION

Do's and Don'ts

1. Encouragement is a continuous process aimed at giving the child a sense of self-respect and a sense of accomplishment.

2. Encouragement is needed from earliest infancy to help the child find his/her place in the group through useful contribution.

3. Encouragement is more important than any other aspect of child rearing; lack of it is the basic cause of misbehavior.

4. Encouragement is based upon a belief in the innate capacity of humans to overcome the challenges of life.

5. Competition between children does not encourage. Instead, it discourages a child and creates apprehension in the successful child that he/she may not be able to remain ahead.

   It is a killer of cooperation.

6. Smart parents are pleased to recognize *any* partial, positive effort on the part of the child.

   a. By tone of voice and by action, we indicate to the child *if* we consider him/her inept, unskilled, and generally inferior.

   b. Parents should focus on recognition of efforts rather than on accomplishments only.

7. Overprotecting a child is discouraging. Examples are as follows:

   a. Hovering over him/her

b. Protecting the child from any unhappiness or discomfort

c. Not requiring any contribution towards the family welfare

d. Taking care of a child's responsibilities for him/her

e. Rescuing the child from *all* difficulties

8. Unless children learn to tolerate pain, bangs, bumps, and discomforts, they will live with a serious handicap.

   Sometimes, all of us must agree to endure.

9. Praise is not wise.

10. Praise is a reward for something well done, and implies a spirit of competition, while recognition may be given for any effort and result, thus focuses on helping the child feel worthy.

    The reward feature of praise can become the reason for approved behavior, rather than satisfaction in achievement, being useful or making a contribution. No praise or reward— no approved behavior.

11. The child must do something cooperative in order to be encouraged. He/she can be praised for just being pretty, charming, or smart, etc. and grow to feel special, above others, or superior. Thus, if a child sees praise as a reward, then lack of it becomes scorn.

12. Ways to discourage are as follows:

    a. Do not take time to listen to your child or be interested in what he/she is dong.

    b. Dictate to him/her or order him/her around all the time.

    c. Make critical or sarcastic remarks.

d. Make a servant of him/her.

e. Lecture—talk over long on a matter.

f. Say, "Let me do it for you, you're too young or little."

g. Make comparisons with other children or the ideal child.

h. Set too high standards of accomplishment.

i. Be overprotective.

j. Spoil and pamper him/her. (See Section P-22, *Ways to Spoil a Child.*)

k. Praise the child instead of the deed.

l. Pity him/her.

m. Oversupervise your child's activities, efforts, and/or choices.

n. Favor one child over another.

o. Support one child against another (as in settling a fight).

13. Ways to encourage are as follows:

a. Refrain from humiliating the child.

b. Find ways to give the child self-respect through achievement experiences.

c. Show faith in his/her innate capacities and abilities by allowing him/her to practice using them.

d. Allow him/her the chance to cope with dangerous situations, within reason.

e. Allow the child to become responsible by giving him/her responsibility.

f. Refrain from criticizing. Instead, point out and acknowledge any good points, accomplishments, or efforts.

g. When the child is struggling to do something, don't do it better than he/she in front of him/her.

h. Help the child to learn to take pain and discomfort and sorrow in his/her stride.

i. Give the child a chance early in life to learn self-sufficiency.

j. Praise the deed rather than the doer.

k. Turn mistakes into a learning situation.

l. Refrain from doing routinely for the child what he/she can do for himself/herself.

m. Encourage every constructive effort the child makes or talent he/she displays with interest and recognition.

n. Consult with the child about decisions that will affect him/her; seek his/her views.

o. Increase as fast as is reasonable the areas in the child's life where he/she may decide for himself/herself.

14. Failure calls for encouragement.

15. When the child does not perform successfully, parents must help him/her understand that his/her failure in no way reduces his/her value as a person.

a. He/she wasn't at a point of readiness.

b. It wasn't one of his/her talents.

c. One can enjoy participating without being a star.

16. When the child does not meet with success, the parent can say some of the following:

    a.   "I was really pleased to be there as your parent— how are you feeling?"

    b.   "I'm glad you got into this and made the effort."

    c.   "While everything didn't come off as you hoped, it was good that you tried."

    d.   "I can see you have made lots of progress since your last try."

    e.   "A mistake helps us to learn. What can we learn from this?"

17. Courage is found in one who can make a mistake and fail without feeling lowered in his/her self-esteem.

    a.   Mistakes can become learning situations.

    b.   We are not working for perfection, but only for improvement.

    c.   We want the child to be able to accept courageously that he/she can try even if he/she isn't outstanding (or participate).

    d.   The child needs to feel that his/her parents do love and appreciate him/her for his/her own self and his/her own particular set of assets, abilities, qualities, and limitations.

    e.   No matter what, he/she is still O.K. enough and you are glad you have him/her.

NOTE: So, who's discouraged? Parents are learning, too.

SECTION P-39
DREIKURISMS

A child needs encouragement like a plant needs water.

You should never feel sorry for a child. To do so gives him/her justification to feel sorry for himself/herself, and no one is as unhappy as someone who feels sorry for himself/herself.

If mothers can learn to keep their mouths shut, they can learn anything.

So often what we do to correct a child is responsible for him/her not improving.

It is easy to become a father but difficult to be one.

Rearing children is quite similar to the game of bridge. If you overbid your hand, the children will call your bluff and you'll go down in defeat. If you underbid your hand, you cannot be effective.

Nothing is as pathetic as a defeated authority who doesn't know he/she is defeated.

We spend more time with an untrained child then we do in training the child.

We should give the child attention, but not at the times he/she demands it.

Unfortunately, those who need encouragement the most, get it the least, because they behave in such a way that our reaction to them pushes them further into discouragement and rebellion.

When you spank a child, it is because you don't know anything better to do.

We must realize we do not teach children how to take on

responsibility as long as we take on responsibilities for them.

If training were as simple as setting a good example, we would not find so many irresponsible children coming from homes where the parents are so responsible.

It's not the quantity of time spent with our children which is important, but the quality.

If you treat a child according to his/her merit, you make the good child better and the bad child worse.

The fundamental desire of every human being is to belong, to have status in the group of which he/she is part.

NOTE: *Even negative status, if there is no other.*

A striking similarity exists between conflicts within the family and those on the national and international scene, between management and labor, between the white and the colored people, between Gentiles and Jews, between America and Russia.

Most parents are ignorant of methods of child training which do not require punishment or reward.

A bruised knee will mend; bruised courage may last a lifetime.

NOTES
Related to Week 4

SECTION P-40
INDIVIDUAL STUDY PLAN NO. 5

Chapter 7, Pages 40-44

1. First, what happened with the home exercise last week— "Stop All Critical Remarks?" Did you find yourself making very many of them? How did your children react to a critical remark from you? Use the space for notes to take stock of your progress.

2. Having read Chapter 7, play tape No. 3 by Drs. Corsini and Painter on natural consequences if you have access to the tape.

3. Look at Section 42, *Large Mistakes* that parents want to avoid. Because of its importance, we are taking a second look at them. Have any of them become a consistent pattern in your parenting of your children? You cannot stop something of which you are not aware. To become aware of it is the first step. We emphasize the need to eliminate these, because patterns of this kind can hurt your child's self-esteem and self-assurance.

4. Go to Section P-43, *Study Questions for Chapter 7.* Understanding these principles and theories and seeing their validity is important to your successful use of these methods. Turn to Section P-78 and study *Benefits of a Good Relationship* with your child.

5. Next, study Section P-44, *Redirecting Your Child from Misbehavior to Cooperative Behavior.* As you apply these ideas and methods, you can review this section for reassurance and to focus on your *long range goals* with your parenting.

6. For the coming Week 6, look to Section P-2, *Individual Outline of Study,* for your next chapters to read and assignments for study. Your next home practice activity is to help you continue to encourage your child or children more and more. Parents do not perceive how much this

means to these little persons in their charge. Also, our smiling eyes! Many children are, far too often, looking into the angry, disapproving eyes of their parents.

7. Our next reading assignment is going to be covering a group of common problems that parents and children often struggle over. Be sure to read the opening *Preliminary Note*, page 46 of the textbook.

SECTION P-41
GROUP MEETING NO. 5 FORMAT
Chapter 7, Pages 40-44

1. Play tape No. 3 by Drs. Corsini and Painter, if you have it, on natural consequences for 10 minutes.

2. Talk about the home practice for Week 5. Was it hard to stop making critical remarks? How many critical remarks did everyone find themselves wanting to make? This is a deep-grained habit in all of us but one of the chief destroyers of our children's self-esteem and is worth every effort it takes on our part to eliminate it—at least, lessen it. Discuss together how your effort went last week.

3. Look together at Section P-42, *Large Mistakes* parents want to avoid. A *continual pattern* of parental actions of this kind can do the harm.

4. Leader/facilitator, make a list on a separate sheet of any topics group members may want to cover further and go over them now. Review Section P-38, *Encouragement and Recognition,* and contrast praise to encouragement.

5. Everyone take note that this is the last session on theory and principle before moving to more specific answers for particular behaviors. Go to Section P-43, *Study Questions for Chapter 7,* for a detailed overview of what you have been studying the last five weeks.

6. Leader/facilitator, help pace the discussion and leave enough time to study/review Section P-44, *Redirecting Your Child from Misbehavior to Cooperative Behavior.* This is a page all can go back to from time to time to see if you are leaving anything out when you are "retraining." Leaving out a step can nullify your efforts.

7. Close by noting in Section P-3, *Group Outline of Study,* the reading assignment in *Effective Discipline in the Home*

and School, the study assignment in the *Action Guide,* and the home practice activity for Week 6.

8. Everyone should be thinking of and listing on paper which problems they particularly want to get into, using the page for notes. You will now be moving into the area of practical and specific aids and assists for conflicts that arise and cause so much disruption in families.

SECTION P-42
LARGE MISTAKES—
TO BE AVOIDED

1. Over Supervision. (Page 19, your textbook.)

2. Over Protection. (See Section P-38, *Encouragement and Recognition*, this book.)

3. Over Estimation (expecting too much).

4. Over Ambitious (pushing beyond your child's desire or capacity).

5. Spoil and Pamper. (See Section P-22, *Ways to Spoil a Child.*)

6. Foster Competition Between Children. (See Section P-36, *These Foster Competition.*)

7. Neglect to Encourage. (See Section P-38, *Encouragement and Recognition.*)

8. Consistently Reject a Child. Definition: "to reject" is to cast away as worthless, to discard, to leave out, to consider less than . . ., to brush off, to ignore, to repulse, to forget about, etc.

SECTION P-43
STUDY QUESTIONS
FOR CHAPTER 7

General Rules for Child Training, Pages 40-44

1. What are the four necessary rules to follow when using this method of child training? (Pages 40-41.)

2. What are we, the parents, urged to omit in this training? (Page 41, line 11.)

3. What do the authors mean by the word "punishing?" (*Review* page 22, line 14, ff.)

4. What is likely to happen if you are inconsistent about what you have decided to do? (Page 41, line 13.)

5. What about anger in this training method? (Page 41, line 17, ff.)

6. What do you think of the authors' general principles? (Lower part of page 41.) Do you disagree with any of them? Individuals take note of any disagreement and look for more understanding as you continue this study. Group members discuss together.

7. Is it ever possible to use these methods of training if your spouse doesn't agree with them? When? (Page 42, line 8, ff. and line 22, ff.)

8. When is using these training methods not possible under such circumstances? (Page 43, line 1 to end of paragraph.)

9. If you decide to use these training methods, when should you start them? (Page 44, line 1 to end of paragraph.)

10. Does each and every problem you are having with a child have to be solved one at a time? (Page 43, line 7, ff.)

11. Have you looked over the points made in the boxes on pages 43 and 44? Do any of them not make sense to you? Individuals follow advice in question 6. Group members discuss and help each other.

12. What are the characteristics of your new parental attitude? (Page 44, third paragraph, "Attitude.")

13. If you try these methods and fail, what do the authors urge you to do next? (Page 44, fourth paragraph.)

14. What is a second offensive? At such a time, what are you urged to do? (Page 44, second paragraph.)

15. When you have decided to use any of these training methods, do you tell your children? (Page 44, second paragraph.)

16. How does a child become responsible, respectful, resourceful, and responsive? (Page 9, line 5 to "Four R's.")

    a. You let them practice being responsible and resourceful when necessary, using natural and logical consequences to stimulate such practice.

    b. You model being respectful and responsive.

    c. You encourage and reassure them, love them, and respect them.

SECTION P-44
REDIRECTING YOUR CHILD
FROM MISBEHAVIOR TO
COOPERATIVE BEHAVIOR

1. Improve the relationship between you and your child with

    a. positive attention when they are not expecting it or asking for it;

    b. individual time (mother dates and father dates or regular parent-child playtime. See Section P-66, *Characteristics of a Parent Date*);

    c. family fun and family projects (See Section P-78, *Benefits of a Good Realtionship with Your Child*); and

    d. encouragement in its different forms.

    All of the above (a, b, c, and d) will help your children want to cooperate because they love, like, and respect you.

2. Be an example of the behavior you want to see in your child.

    *As you model it, they will copy you **because** they love, like, and respect you and want to be the same as you.*

3. Supply your child with information for each situation once only, as

    a. how the natural order operates;

    b. how the social order operates; and

    c. what your own (changed or otherwise) action is going to be in each situation.

4. Change your own actions, if indicated, using the following guidelines:

    a.   Determine the goal of the misbehavior in each situation. (See Section P-32, *The Discouraged Child's Mistaken Goals.)*

    b.   Armed with this information, decide on an action that:

        (1) will not reinforce your child's misbehavior by supplying it with benefits or payoff.

        (2) will result in discomfiture for your child.

Thus encouraging and stimulating the child to give up the misbehavior and choose a new, more acceptable behavior.

    c.   Be firm and follow through in a friendly manner.

5. Offer the family meeting at a regular time convenient for all.

Model the importance of this meeting by always attending it yourself.

NOTES
Related to Week 5

SECTION P-45
INDIVIDUAL STUDY PLAN NO. 6

Problems of Routine Living

Chapters 8 through 13, Pages 45-90

1. How did your home exercise go? Record the "positive comment" you made in the place for notes. After, look at the note at the bottom of Section P-36, *These Foster Competition.* Look at Section P-38, *Encouragement and Recognition,* and review points 9, 10, and 11 on praise. Was the positive comment you made one of praise or encouragement? If this difference is as new to you as it is to most of us, keep thinking about it, observing yourself and trying to switch more and more into what the authors call encouragement. It will make a difference.

2. Having done your reading, play tape No. 7 by Drs. Corsini and Painter, if you have the tapes.

3. Next, turn to Section P-47, *Adlerian View of Order and Limits,* and read that section. Routine is one aspect of order. If you are a person who gets along quite nicely without much routine, give some thought to the importance of it to your child in this culture. For the child to know at least how a good part of his/her day is going to go is reassuring. Every day, he/she wakes up, gets up, and gets dressed. He/she eats breakfast, and then plays in his/her room, or in a play corner. Then he/she has time with mother, playing, reading a little story, next napping, etc. This rhythm of events gives the child something that he/she knows and can count on. He/she will be easier to live with. (See p. 171, point No. 1, bottom, in your textbook.)

   The matter of what is a parent's business and what is a child's is another viewpoint worthy of some thought. It helps you to begin to see your overall goals as a parent in your child's life. It can serve as a kind of "checklist," and, if you are feeling overwhelmed, remember you have eighteen years in which to get it done. Our favorite Adlerian saying: "We have to have the courage to be imperfect."

4. Do Section P-48 through P-53 chapter questions on the *Problems of Routine Living.* If time is a factor, select those chapters in the textbook that interest you the most. Maybe you are ready to start some more retraining, but go one problem at a time. Do not start work on another one until the first one has been cleared up. Be prepared for a second offensive (see p. 44 bottom, in your book).

5. Have a look at Section P-54, *Four Ways to Learn.* If the child does not learn by the first two, the only ways left to learn are the last two. Like eating and sleeping, it turns out that learning cannot be forced. You have to win them to it.

6. Next, turn to Section P-55, *Training Steps.* This section is provided as a form of shorthand to memorize and mentally refer to when you have need of a consequence to alter your child's behavior. It will help you include all the necessary parts of this method of discipline— a very important factor for the method to work.

7. See Section P-2, *Individual Outline of Study* for Week 7 to identify your reading assignment, your study assignment, and the home practice activity for Week 7. Angry eyes and anger in our voices are much overworked parenting tools. The damage they do to our children's self-esteem and to our relationship with them, we are only beginning to realize. Be sure to read the Chapter 14 Preliminary Note in the textbook. Have you continued the important points in the Preliminary Note most of the time? (Page 92, line 10 and line 3 from the bottom.)

SECTION P-46
GROUP MEETING NO. 6 FORMAT

Problems of Routine Living

Chapters 8 through 13, Pages 45-90

1. Play tape No. 7 by Drs. Corsini and Painter for approximately 10 minutes up to the end of the discussion on chores.

2. Discuss together the home practice for the week, *Watch for Chances to Make Positive Comments to Each Child.* How did your children respond to such comments? Share with the group a description of an incident of this form of encouragement and recognition. What happened? What did they say?

3. Review and discuss together Section P-47, *Adlerian View of Order and Limits.* Consider the value and importance of routine in a child's life and the helpfulness of knowing what areas are clearly the responsibility (or business) of you, the parent, in a child's life, and what becomes the responsibility (or business) of the child. You could well benefit from "pulling out of" some aspects of your child's life in Item 8b, leaving you more relaxed, with more energy and free time to use in other ways.

4. Go to Part 3, Chapters 8 through 13, of *Effective Discipline in the Home and School,* and take a vote (show of hands) on which chapters group members want to discuss first. Record them according to the preference of the majority. Or group members could call out which problems they particularly want to go over. If no seeming preference exists, take the chapters up in order.

5. Leave time to go over together Section P-55, *Training Steps.* It is provided as a kind of mental shorthand to aid you in your retraining with these methods. Discuss how important including all the steps is.

6. Look together at Section P-54, *Four Ways to Learn.* If the child does not learn by the first two, the only ways left to learn are the last two: natural and logical consequences. Like eating and sleeping, learning cannot be forced. You have to provide motivation to win the child to it.

7. Close by looking together at Section 3, *Group Outline of Study,* at the reading assignment in *Effective Discipline in the Home and School,* the study assignment in the *Action Guide,* and the home practice activity for Week 7. Take note this week, which problems you would particularly like to get into. If one of these misbehaviors is a real concern in your family, going into it in detail with the group will get you started on correcting it.

8. Different group members could volunteer to study one of the misbehaviors and present it to the group at the next meeting, if they like. Or two members could offer to work one up together and present it. The more each member involves himself/herself in the group's activities together, the more fun it will be and the more he/she will probably learn and be able to use.

SECTION P-47
ADLERIAN VIEW OF
ORDER AND LIMITS

1. Three kinds of order exist: a natural order, a social order, and a family order.

2. The *family order* is the child's first experience with limits and his/her opportunity to learn that *limits* are necessary for happy living.

3. Children receive assurance from knowing what to expect day by day when there is orderly living or a routine.

   Such a routine is individual to each family.

4. Children receive further assurance from knowing what the limits and regulations are in the family.

   a. As they get older, they cooperate better when they are given a larger and larger part in decisions about the family.

   b. This can be made possible through consultation at a family meeting.

5. In a democratic family of equals, rules of order are set up by all and then observed by all for the benefit of all.

6. Children need to be stimulated and encouraged into voluntarily taking part in the maintenance of order.

7. If they are forced into maintaining order, they will likely develop a dislike for order.

   *What they really didn't like was **the force** that they now connect with order.*

8. In maintaining order, some things are the parents' business and some things are the children's business.

a. The following are the parents' business or responsibility:

   (1) setting up and maintaining a regular routine,

   (2) providing nutritious food,

   (3) making sure car riding is safe,

   (4) preventing offensive company behavior and public behavior,

   (5) forbidding clutter in the common living areas,

   (6) ensuring attendance at school,

   (7) providing opportunity to contribute to family welfare through a choice of chores,

   (8) protecting from life and death situations,

   (9) seeing to legitimate health precautions and recovery care from illness,

   (10) providing for independent time and privacy for parents and children,

   (11) ensuring each child's knowledge of and obedience to civil laws, and

   (12) providing teaching or instruction in the following (Teachers don't teach these—you do.):

      (a) caring for teeth,
      (b) bathing and bathroom habits,
      (c) washing hair and grooming,
      (d) performing household tasks,
      (e) crossing the street safely,
      (f) observing yard boundaries, when small,
      (g) exhibiting manners and courtesy,
      (h) eating skills,
      (i) dressing skills, and
      (j) being ready on time.

b.   These are the children's business or responsibility, once parents have taught them how (Teachers don't teach these, you do.):

   (1)   using allowance, gifts of money, and earnings,

   (2)   care of their own rooms,

   (3)   eating or not eating,

   (4)   washing themselves,

   (5)   care of teeth and grooming,

   (6)   completing school work and homework,

   (7)   getting up and dressing,

   (8)   going to sleep,

         (Can be required to have a room time)

   (9)   choosing clothes,

   (10) choosing friends,

   (11) choosing extra activities,

   (12) forming relationships with others—grandparents, playmates, instructors, etc., and

   (13) getting somewhere on time.

9.   We convince our children of the value and desirability of order by allowing them to experience the discomforts of disorder, through a judicious use of logical and natural consequences.

10. We teach by both instruction and example.

   a.   Time for training (or instruction) is allotted in the daily routine.

b. Training in any skill is repeated until it is mastered.

c. Each skill is learned separately at an appropriate age.

d. Role-playing or "Let's pretend . . ." is a useful means of training.

e. Not taking time for training will result in endless time spent correcting an untrained child.

f. We cannot successfully train at a time of conflict or in public.

g. Choose a time to train when all are relaxed and plenty of time is available.

NOTE: It is easier to do anything ourselves than to teach a child to do it well, but the long range goal is well worth the relatively short term efforts and patience necessary for proper training.

SECTION P-48
STUDY QUESTIONS FOR CHAPTER 8
Getting Up, Pages 47-56

1. When is a child old enough to get himself/herself up? (Page 49, line 9.)

2. What is the suggested solution for a child who will not get up on time in the morning? (Page 49, points 1 through 5.)

3. When a child does not get up in time, instead of calling repeatedly, yelling, lecturing, threatening, grounding, taking away privileges, what are you advised to do? (Let the child face the natural consequences of being late and realize yourself that getting up is the child's business. Page 49, line 1 to end of paragraph.)

4. What about the natural consequences of walking to school in the rain? (Page 50, line 15 from bottom to "Rubbers.") How do you feel about that answer? Individuals record reaction on note page, group members share.

5. If both parents work, how is over-sleeping handled? (Page 54, line 6, from bottom to words, "Dressed himself," page 55.) Is this a natural consequence or a logical consequence? (A logical consequence. It is logically related to the misbehavior, and it is arranged and put into action by the parents. Remember a logical consequence flows out of the social order of things.)

6. Does the exchange between the parent and the school in the example (pages 51 and 52) seem acceptable to you? Individuals reflect and use notes page. Group members share opinions. (If the school takes action, will it be a natural or logical consequence? A logical consequence, because it is arranged and acted out by the school.)

7. What solution is advised for the mother who is a worrier? (Page 55, line 19, ff.) Is this a natural or a logical

consequence? (Natural, if the mother is indeed too ill to be up in the morning, and logical, if she decides to remain in bed as a sure-fire way to stay out of things and let the children handle their own business.) Which of the four R's is the child learning? (Responsibility.)

8. What two parental actions interfere with a child's learning responsibility? (Doing unnecessary service for children and overprotecting them. Page 56, line 4 to end of paragraph.) Why is learning to take responsibility important to the child? Individuals answer on notes page. Group members do the same and share their answers.)

9. Why do you *not* feel the need to feel sorry for your child if he/she must suffer the consequences of his/her actions? (Experience is the best teacher. Page 56, line 12 to end of paragraph.)

SECTION P-49
STUDY QUESTIONS FOR CHAPTER 9

Dressing, Pages 57-62

1. If a child will not dress himself/herself when the child is old enough to do so, what are you advised to do? (Page 57, line 1 from bottom, and page 58, line 8.)

2. If a child leaves his/her dirty clothes lying around instead of putting them in the clothes hamper, what are you advised to do? (Page 59, line 4 to "Mike.")

3. What if the child runs out of clean clothes before washing day? If he/she puts his/her clothes in the clothes hamper, do you wash specially for him/her? (Page 59, line 10 to "Breakfast.") Whom are you respecting? (Yourself, the parent.) Why won't you wash them before washday? (Page 60, line 13.) Is it a natural or logical consequence? (Logical, because it flows out of the social order of the home.)

4. In the solution of the girl wearing warm enough outdoor clothes, is the procedure suggested (page 61, line 16) made up of natural or logical consequences? (Natural, because it flows out of the natural order of things.)

5. In the matter of allowing the daughter to choose what she would wear on Easter Sunday (page 62, line 14), were natural or logical consequences used? (Logical, because they flowed out of the social order.) How would you feel if you were advised to do this with your child? Individuals use notes page and answer. Group members discuss together.

6. Besides letting a child choose what he/she will wear, what other five suggestions about a child and clothes do the authors make? (Page 62, beginning with line 14 from the bottom.) By following these suggestions, which of the four R's are you *allowing* your child to develop? (Responsibility.) Which of the four R's are you practicing with your child? (Respect for your child. Page 62, line

8 from bottom.) You can say, "You've been taught how to dress yourself. You know how to dress yourself and you will when you are ready."

7. If you feel very uncomfortable being with your child in his/her selection of clothes, what can you do? (Page 62, line 6 from bottom, ff.) Which of the four R's are you now practicing? (Respect for yourself, *but* show no anger or resentment. You do not need to feel it; your child is learning.)

SECTION P-50
STUDY QUESTIONS FOR CHAPTER 10

Eating, Pages 63-69

1. Did you find the results of the Davis experiment on feeding newly weaned infants hard to accept? (Page 64, second paragraph.) What findings did you expect? Individuals put answer on notes page. Group members can share their ideas.

2. Though we rightfully do a number of things for our children during certain periods of their development, what are we warned against? (Page 65, line 3 to end of paragraph.)

3. Do you find any of the points listed as a solution to children's eating problems unacceptable? (Page 65, points 1 through 8 on page 66.) If so, what is your objection to particular points? Individuals record objections on notes page and reflect. Group members do the same and share.

4. What kind of a visit do you think their grandchildren had with Grandmother and Grandfather Riggs? (Page 66, starting line 9, ff. from bottom.) Would you call them permissive grandparents? What effect do you think not eating breakfast had on four-year-old William? Remember, he didn't eat breakfast one morning. (Page 67, line 16 from bottom to end of paragraph.) Individuals answer on notes page. Group members can share. Would your answer have been different before studying this material about parenting?

5. According to authors, what reinforces poor eating habits? (Page 68, lines 10 and 6 from bottom.)

6. How is it suggested that you handle snacks? (Page 68, line 1 from bottom, ff.)

7. Do you disagree with any of the authors' general rules about eating? (Page 69, line 14 on.) Individuals reflect and say on notes page. Group members talk it over together.

With older children, you can shop once a week for snack food. When it is gone, everyone (Mom and Dad, too) has to wait until time to shop again. What is working here? (Peer pressure. See pages 140 and 141—"Putting everyone in the same boat.")

Also, you can have "snack-shelf." In refrigerator, with younger children you can have "snack bowls" for each child—"snack sacks" for each child for after school, etc.

SECTION P-51
STUDY QUESTIONS FOR CHAPTER 11
Keeping Clean, Pages 70-75

1. What kind of keeping clean problems are the authors talking about? (Page 71, line 11 to "to do.")

2. What do most parents usually do about them? (Page 71, line 14.)

3. What kind of consequences do the authors suggest you use? (Page 72, line 2 from bottom.)

4. Did it hurt Jeff (in example, page 72, middle, to page 73) more to develop those white pimples under his arm than developing a bad relationship with his mother? How about the rest of the family? (Page 70 to page 71.) If studying individually, answer on notes page. If studying in a group, then discuss together.

5. What kind of a consequence were the parents using with Jeff? (A natural consequence, because cleanliness helps maintain health. Page 72, line 7 from bottom.)

6. Which of the four R's did Jeff also develop, to a larger extent? (Responsibility for himself.)

7. Do our children care about what other children think of them? How would your children react in a situation similar to Nancy's in the example? (Page 73, line 5, ff. from bottom.) Individuals think about it and use notes page. Group members do the same and share.

8. Does it seem logical for the parents to eat elsewhere if their child's body odor offends them? (Page 74, line 17 from bottom, ff.) Could you do it? Notice—the parents told their son of their choice of action only once in a quiet, friendly way, when the family was invited out to eat. (Page 74, line 11 from bottom.)

9. In the matter of their children keeping clean, what obligation do the parents have? (Page 75, line 6 from bottom.)

10. Do you think the television commercial would get your children to regularly brush their teeth if you kept out of it—only doing for them while they are little, and being an example of good dental care yourself? Could your dentist also be an influence on this? Individuals record answers on notes page. Group members can discuss it.

   The notes page can be very useful to group members, too. It helps us to think when we write down our answers. The notes pages are very useful for capturing permanently, any insights we gain as we study alone or in a group.

SECTION P-52
STUDY QUESTIONS FOR CHAPTER 12
School Difficulties At Home, Pages 76-83

1. What three things according to the authors *will not* motivate your child to enjoy learning? (Page 77, beginning line 5 from bottom.)

2. What 16 things do the authors suggest *will* encourage your child to enjoy learning? (Pages 78 and 79, beginning line 1 top of page)

3. According to the authors, what is the sure way for you to fail to get your child to want to study? (Page 79, line 4, ff.)

4. Do you see the logic of not helping a child with his/her homework, except for drilling in spelling or multiplication tables, etc.? (Page 82, line 12 from bottom to "me.") Would someone want to state it? (He will not get in the habit of listening to the teacher and learning from him/her. Also the material being taught will eventually get beyond you. (Page 80, line 10 to "behavior.")

5. What could you tell a teacher who insists that you supervise your child's homework? (Page 80, line 10 from bottom to "for her.")

6. If you are concerned about drugging your young child, unless absolutely necessary, what could you say to a teacher who has requested it? (Page 81, line 1 to end of paragraph.)

7. According to the authors, what responsibilities do belong to the parents in regard to their child's schooling? (Page 81, line 11 to end of paragraph and page 79, line 19, beginning "do however.")

8. Consider this statement, "That year I worked showed me that education is important. But I had to find out for myself." (Page 82, line 14.) Is this not often true? Individuals can make a note of their thoughts. Group members also can share.

SECTION P-53
STUDY QUESTIONS FOR CHAPTER 13

Bedtime, Pages 84-90

1. What is one way parents can show lack of respect for their children? (Page 90, line 6 from bottom to "for them.")

2. How does a child learn how much sleep he/she needs? (Page 86, line 5.)

3. What is the logic of children having a "room time?" (Page 86, line 16.)

4. How do you get a child to stay in his/her room after "room time?" (Page 86, No. 4.)

   And you can tell your child that he/she needs now to be alone and quiet so his/her body can tell him/her when it wants to go to sleep.

5. Why do some children refuse to go to bed? (Page 88, line 3 from bottom.)

6. What procedure may be used for young children's naps? (Page 90, line 1 to end of second paragraph.)

7. If a child leaves own bed and comes into yours during the night, what can you do to stop this? (Page 87, No. 7, and page 88, line 6, ff.)

8. This bedtime training is teaching children which of the four R's? (Responsibility, also Respect for others.) (Page 90, last paragraph.)

SECTION P-54
FOUR WAYS TO LEARN

1. By instruction (give information)

2. By example (model it)

3. By sad or bad experience (the consequences)

4. By good experience Always provide this by preference, if you can think of one.

SECTION P-55
TRAINING STEPS

Think

1. The misbehavior—be specific.

   What is its goal?

Think

2. What natural or logical consequence fits—be specific.

Warn

3. When all are calm and feeling good, give this information (1 and 2 above) to your child, clearly and completely (maybe have him/her repeat it back to you.)

Do

4. Then if the misbehavior occurs, let the natural consequence happen or do the logical consequence you stated in your "I will" message or your "I am not willing to" message.

5. Do this in a friendly, teaching manner in absolute silence.

6. If a "second offensive" happens, continue the consequence in complete silence.

   a. No second information session is needed.

   b. Your child is testing you.

NOTES
Related to Week 6

SECTION P-56
INDIVIDUAL STUDY PLAN NO. 7

Problems of Order and Cooperation

Chapter 14-18, Pages 91-147

1. Your home practice was to "Notice how many times you get angry." Did it help? Actually anger tends to beget anger and resistance unless it is used sparingly. *Righteous anger* could beneficially make a clear imprint. But do we often use anger as a form of punishment, as a means of intimidation, a way to get children to move, to get our way? Look again at Page 25, line 7 from bottom, ff.; page 39, points Nos. 10 and 11; and page 41, line 17 to end of paragraph in your textbook. Anger even interferes with our training. Strong emotion turns off our children's thinking and they are learning nothing, except maybe, "Mommy is mean and frightening." Is anger really a necessary part of training? Do we need to be angry? Our children are not bad yet. They are learning, and we can cheerfully and persistently expect them to adopt better ways of behaving as they become convinced that they want to. This "convincing" we will provide with our training as one of their main teachers. This heavy use of anger, so prevalent in our culture, the Adlerian viewpoint hopes to persuade you to drop.

2. Having done your reading, play tape No. 6 on Routine Problems by Drs. Corsini and Painter if you have it.

3. Did you study Section P-58, *Encouragement for Mom and Dad?* It was written by a mother studying and using these very same ideas and methods as you are. At this point, you are probably breaking away from some old ways of parenting that you are not pleased about, and changing is not easy. However, as this mother points out, we will all be glad we did. Do not get discouraged.

4. Move to Chapter 14 in the textbook on *Cooperation*, pages 93 through 103. Do in the *Action Guide*, Section P-59,

Study Questions for Chapter 14. The concept of compliance with the family's order and limits (obedience) which have been set down by the family council (See Chapter 33, pages 238 through 247) is, of course needed. Study Section P-60, *Effective Obedience When an Order Must be Obeyed,* and Section P-61, *Children Respond To . . .* You need to be as clear as possible on these points to understand the logic and the rationale of this approach to parenting.

5. Next, do the chapter questions, Section P-62 through P-65, for any of the problems of cooperation and order that trouble you most. If the first misbehavior problem you have been working on is beginning to lift, you can start on one of these now. Remember not to be surprised or confused if your child starts a "second offensive." (Page 44, last paragraph.) You know what to do.

6. Now turn to Section P-2, *Individual Outline of Study,* and identify reading assignment in your book, the study assignment in the *Action Guide,* and your home practice activity for Week 8. Two things that will most quickly rebuild or help maintain a good relationship with your children are a regular play time with your little children (see page 171, point 3 in your book) and regular individual parent dates, especially with school age children. (See Section P-66, *Characteristics of a Parent Date.*) Nothing will as surely convince them that they do count with you, that you truly love them, and that you care about them. Their self-esteem will strengthen and their behavior will improve. Try it, you'll like it! This is a promise!

7. Next week's reading will be about problems that arise between parents and children that are highly upsetting. If you have been successful in removing some troubling misbehavior with your children, you could now be ready to work on one of these. Be sure to read the Preliminary Note, page 150 in the textbook.

SECTION P-57
GROUP MEETING NO. 7 FORMAT

Problems of Order and Cooperation

Chapter 14 through 18, Pages 91-147

1. Play tape No. 6 by Drs. Corsini and Painter for 10 minutes. (Routine Problems)

2. What about the home practice for the week where you were to *Notice How Many Times You Get Angry.* Did it help? Will anyone share what they learned about themselves and anger? How did their use of anger affect their children?

3. Review together Section P-58, *Encouragement for Mom and Dad,* in the *Action Guide.* All of us are probably critically in need of this about this time and it is well worth spending time on it. This was written by a mother who successfully studied and used these Adlerian methods and principles. Talk about this together and exchange experiences.

4. Go to Chapter 14 in the textbook on *Cooperation,* page 93 through 103, and do in the *Action Guide,* Section P-59, *Study Questions for Chapter 14.* These points are important to understand clearly and are deserving of emphasis. It involves that word, "obedience."

5. Review together, Section P-60, *Effective Obedience When An Order Must Be Obeyed,* and Section P-61, *Children Respond To . . .* Both sections will give you additional help when doing your training and can quickly be referred to when needed.

6. Spend the remaining time on the problems the group members most want to discuss from this part of the textbook. Try to draw up a list.

7. Close by analyzing Section P-3, *Group Outline of Study,* for Week 8 regarding the reading assignment in *Effective*

Discipline in the Home and School, the study assignment in the *Action Guide*, and the home practice activity for the week. Powerful benefits will occur from this kind of regular encouraging interaction with your children. Nothing can more quickly improve your children's self-esteem. Look together at Section P-66, *Characteristics of a Parent Date*, in the *Action Guide* and discuss. Also, if you choose a regular play time with your young child, look at page 171, point No. 3 in *Effective Discipline in the Home and School* for details.

SECTION P-58
ENCOURAGEMENT FOR
MOM AND DAD

by Mele Fujiwara

To change one's habits of rearing children is difficult. New knowledge comes hard. It involves struggle, effort, and determination. The following are some stages parents go through in learning to change:

NOTE: When you change, your child will change.

1. You use the old ways of child rearing. You think about it and it bothers you.

2. You see and hear yourself making the same old mistakes. You listen helplessly while you stand there talking too much. You look at yourself making the same dumb errors.

3. You are aware you are about to make the same old mistake. You can't think fast enough to act with your new knowledge. Real irritation with yourself sets in. You make a firm mental note to change.

4. Whoops—Goofed again. You feel annoyed with yourself, and you *review* the situation again. You say to yourself, "I should have done . . ." You review it several times. (See Section P-55, *Training Steps.*)

5. Now you are almost eager for a problem to come up so you can use your new approach. You catch yourself as you are about to make the same dumb error. You get your chance! Although a bit awkward, you are prepared, you try something else, and it works! But the method is not quite a part of you yet.

6. You deal with only one problem at a time, becoming more self-assured and more convinced that, "This is the way."

7. Hooray! The children's behavior is becoming respectful, responsible, and resourceful. You aren't bothered as much by certain things any more.

8. Oh! Oh! You are only human. You relax your consistency and make some mistakes. You have some painful moments of feeling helpless and discouraged. (See Section P-78, *Benefits of a Good Relationship with Your Child.*)

9. Back to the book! You evaluate your past behavior step by step. You see and understand why your approach backfired.

10. You recover. You continue to experiment and discover you can be creative in your dealings with your children. Whenever the training method seems difficult, time and energy-wise, or you find yourself concerned with "What will others think?", remind yourself that, "I am investing in the future for smoother family relationships and for my child's maximum growth."

SECTION P-59
STUDY QUESTIONS FOR CHAPTER 14
Cooperation, Pages 93-103

1. What do the authors state can be used to train children to cooperate? (Page 92, line 8 from bottom, ff.) Why is cooperation necessary? (For a family to be happy. Page 92, line 1, ff.)

2. What is the harm of scaring a child into obedience or punishing (meaning spanking, yelling, lecturing, nagging, threatening, depriving) a child into compliance? (Page 94, line 12 from bottom, ff.)

3. Is there any part of the solution offered for getting your child to conform to your wishes (pages 94 through 96) with which you do not agree or do not understand? Individuals write on note page as a record for later reference. Group members discuss together and write conclusions. What about children under three years old? (Page 95, line 10.)

4. What is the difference between an order and a request? (Page 95, line 13, point No. 3.)

5. With what is "little Linda of the kitchen cabinet" being rewarded by her parent? (Page 96, line 15 from bottom.)

6. What two items are vital to any routine of training when using Adlerian methods? (Page 97, line 10 from bottom.)

7. What is part of the "logic of silence" when training? (Page 97, line 9 from bottom to end of paragraph.)

8. If a child is crying and sobbing while we are training, what do we do? (Page 98, line 1 to end of paragraph— could also give him/her a silent hug as you're on to other things.)

9. What is the reason for not looking angry or upset when we are training a child? (Page 100, line 20 and page 97, line 9 from bottom to end of paragraph.)

10. When we are training a child, what is a "second offensive" and when is it apt to happen? (Page 98, line 7 from bottom, to end of paragraph.)

11. What five pieces of advice are we given by the authors about giving orders to children? (Page 103, line 8 to end of paragraph and line 11 from bottom, ff.) Does this method work with teenagers? (Page 103, line 2 from bottom.)

SECTION P-60
EFFECTIVE OBEDIENCE
WHEN AN ORDER
MUST BE OBEYED

1. Give the order once in a low, firm voice.

2. If the child does not comply, make him/her mind with immediate, effective action.

3. Use no more force than it takes to bring about the obedience.

4. Do not repeat the order; doing so dilutes the action.

5. Be friendly but firm and sure.

6. Keep your orders to a minimum (the five areas, page 16, line 16 in the textbook and Section P-29, *Times When a Parent Says "No"* in the *Action Guide.*

7. If you can't think of an appropriate action to make the child obey, do not give the order.

8. Try to think of a way to make the order unnecessary.

SECTION P-61
CHILDREN RESPOND TO . . .

1. the enjoyment of your presence,

2. the discomfort of your "retreating back,"

3. their desire to be older,

4. their sense of fairness and justice,

5. their desire to decide for themselves,

6. their awareness of a person's right to choose,

7. their desire to find out for themselves,

8. consultation—talking it over (from four years on),

9. encouragement for them to consider and search for the best solution,

10. being allowed to practice a responsibility or a skill,

11. smiling eyes,

12. having fun times with you,

13. experiencing their own strengths and abilities,

14. action instead of words,

15. recognition of effort,

16. silent hugs when training, and

17. the satisfaction of accomplishment.

NOTE: With very little ones, when training, it is best to just act, always with a friendly face or, at least, a neutral one.

SECTION P-62
STUDY QUESTIONS FOR CHAPTER 15

Chores, Pages 104-114

1. What do the authors see as one important obligation of parents in regard to their children? (Page 105, line 13.)

2. In this Adlerian view, what is meant by the word chore? (Page 105, line 16 from bottom.)

3. Why does one do chores? (Page 105, line 7 from bottom, and page 113, line 3 from bottom to top of page 114 to "through chores.")

4. What is the general formula offered for the amount of chores a child should do? (Page 106, line 12, ff.)

5. What is the logic of the parents going on strike in the family? (Page 107, line 7 to end of paragraph.)

6. According to the authors, what connection should exist between chores and a child's allowance? (Page 105, line 4 from bottom.)

7. When chores are decided upon, what information has to be established by agreement? (Page 114, line 3, ff., and page 111, line 1 through list.)

8. If a child agrees to be reminded to do his/her chore, when is the best time to remind the child? (Page 112, line 17 from bottom, and page 114, line 8 from bottom.)

9. How did you feel about the children in the Vernon family being treated as a group when the parents went on strike? (Page 109, line 3, ff. to page 110.) What was the logic in it? (Page 110, line 9.) Why did it work? Individuals consider and use notes page for your thoughts. Group members talk it over together and record conclusions.

10. Will this method work with teenagers? (Page 114, line 3 from bottom.)

*When will it work? Answer: When your relationship improves. Look in the **Action Guide** for a point-by-point description of how to accomplish this as given in Section P-77, **Ways to Have a Good Relationship with Your Child.***

SECTION P-63
STUDY QUESTIONS FOR CHAPTER 16

Clutter—Messiness, Pages 115-124

1. What three procedures are offered by the authors to train children to be neat? (Page 117, line 4 through list.)

2. What would be the family areas of the house that are the responsibility of all family members? (Page 118, line 11 from bottom.)

3. What is to be done if the children disagree about whom the clutter item belongs to? (Page 121, line 14 from bottom, and page 120, line 1 to "house looked.")

4. What is unitism? (Page 120, line 13 from bottom.)

5. What is the logic of unitism? (You cannot sort out the argument, they have you! Page 120, line 8 from bottom, beginning "this system.")

6. If parents want their children to be neat, what must they, themselves, be? (Page 124, line 2 from bottom.)

7. What is the logic for taking the time to train children to be neat? (They will make others uncomfortable for the rest of their lives. Page 116, line 10, ff.) Which of the four R's are the children learning? (Responsibility and Respect.)

8. What other procedures are offered by the authors to train children to be neat? (Page 123, line 18, ff.; page 124, line 9; page 122, line 2 from bottom to "nagging"; and page 122, line 5 from bottom to end of example.) When do you not do the last example? (Page 124, line 6 from bottom to end of paragraph.)

9. What point do the authors make about communication? (Page 116, line 7 from bottom to end of paragraph.)

SECTION P-64
STUDY QUESTIONS FOR CHAPTER 17

Own Room, Pages 125-133

1. What is the logic of allowing a child to keep his/her room as he/she wishes? (Page 126, line 5 from bottom, and page 133, line 1, ff.)

2. If a child will not keep his/her room neat, what do the authors suggest? (Page 132, line 3 from bottom; page 126, line 11 from bottom to end of paragraph; and page 129, line 9 to end of paragraph, and line 2, ff.)

3. What is essential in the parents' attitude if the authors' solution for a child's messy room is to work? (Page 127, line 5 to end of paragraph.)

4. How do you handle it if two children share the same room? (Page 127 line 18 to end of paragraph.)

5. What three alternatives are offered if the parents feel they cannot leave the care of this one room to the child? (Pages 127 and 128, points 1, 2, and 3.)

6. When is a child old enough for the responsibility of his/her own room? (Page 132, line 3 from bottom, and page 128, line 8.)

7. If you use the "periodic cleanup" as a solution, about what do the authors advise caution? (Page 128, line 11 from bottom, ff.)

SECTION P-65
STUDY QUESTIONS FOR CHAPTER 18

Money and Property, Page 134-147

1. In what three forms do children receive money? (Page 135, line 9 from bottom, ff.)

2. What is the reason for allowing children to decide how they will spend their money? (They have learning experiences. Page 136, point No. 8, to end of paragraph.)

3. What principles should parents follow with their children in regard to money and property? (Pages 146 and 147, The Summary.) They may also share their knowledge and attitude about money in a friendly, teaching manner.

4. What is the essence of the child training method called "natural consequences?" (The child learns from his/her mistakes. See good example on page 145, line 11 from bottom to end of paragraph.)

5. What do the parents do when children abuse each other's property? (Page 137, line 7 from bottom to end of paragraph.)

6. Some of the parents' property items could be dangerous to a child. How is this handled? (Page 137, line 1, ff., and page 145, line 8, ff.)

7. What do you do if a child does not return a borrowed piece of equipment to its proper place? (Page 137, No. 13.) And what if a child misuses the equipment? (Page 137, No. 14.)

8. What is unitism? (Page 137, No. 15; and starting on page 140, line 8 from bottom to line 5 from bottom of page 141. *Also*, note difference from punishment. Page 141, line 12 from bottom, ff.)

9. What principle of child rearing were the parents using with the boy who wanted to buy a motorcycle? (Letting the consequences of his actions teach. Page 142, line 14 to end of paragraph.)

10. How could you handle a child's demand to own an expensive item—a motorcycle, a musical instrument, etc.? (Page 143, line 10 ff.)

11. Should you loan money to children? (Page 145, line 5 to end of paragraph.)

12. What factors should affect the amount of a child's allowance? (Page 146, line 12 to end of paragraph.)

13. What is the purpose of lengthening the interval between payments of a child's allowance? (Page 146, line 6 from bottom.)

14. When a child does a job for the parent for which he/she will be paid, what is particularly important? (Page 147, line 9 from bottom.)

15. Are any of these ideas about money and property and your children new to you? Do you question any of them? Individuals put thoughts on notes page. Group members discuss together for answers.

SECTION P-66
CHARACTERISTICS OF A
PARENT DATE

You invite your child to have some fun with you that involves

1. making a date at some future time;

2. doing something you both enjoy;

3. going outside away from the house;

4. marking it on your calendar;

5. keeping the date and making sure that nothing will interfere with it (except say, a hurricane, having to check into the hospital, etc.);

6. only the two of you going, so that you have each other's undivided attention;

7. ending up having something good to eat together;

8. talking together—sharing things about yourself that are appropriate, which will encourage your child to share with you.

NOTES
Related to Week 7

SECTION P-67
INDIVIDUAL STUDY PLAN NO. 8

Interactive Problems

Chapters 19 through 24, Pages 149-184

1. Your home practice was to start a regular play time with your little children or arranging a Parent Date with those who are of school age. Have you done it? Even the younger ones benefit from a Parent Date—both Mother Dates and Father Dates. This may be the first time the child has had either Mother or Father all to himself/herself. Your aim is to be together, parent and child, with no one competing for the parent's attention. You want to have fun together and talk with each other, even with your little ones. The benefits come quickly from such interaction with their parents, their most important people. It is as if the child thinks, "There is no one here but Daddy and me and he is having fun. I must be O.K. He must like me." It will always be one of your most vital encouragement efforts in your parenting, especially if you keep it up *regularly.*

2. Having done your reading in your textbook and your study assignment in the *Action Guide,* play tape No. 5 by Drs. Corsini and Painter, if you have it. This one will discuss fighting.

3. Read Section P-69, *Magic Words,* in the *Action Guide.* Are some of these starting to sound familiar to you? Have you used any of them? We call them "magic" because these words so often are amazing in how much they influence your child to move in the direction you want him/her to go. When you are planning and setting up a logical consequence or looking for one to present at the family meeting, a helpful procedure would be to refer to this list. Or if the children's response to your efforts to guide them is not going well, perhaps the way you

are saying it is putting them off. This magic word list and Section P-61, *Children Respond To . . .*, could well be helpful to refer to when you feel backed into a corner and out of ideas.

4. Do the chapter questions, Sections P-70 through P-76, on any of the Week 8's chapters that cover a problem your family is experiencing. Give extra time and thought to Chapters 19 and 20, "Fighting in the Home" and "Fighting in the Car." These two behaviors cause more havoc and harm in families than we realize. If you are ready, pick out one to work on. Maybe, look again at Section P-55, *Training Steps*, in the *Action Guide.*

5. Study Section P-77, *Ways to Have a Good Relationship with Your Child.* Does all this seem like more than you want to do? It does require some self discipline from you and perhaps some changes in your viewpoint and your actions. Change is hard; but someone has to break the way to make things better between children and adults. Perhaps this effort you make will mean your children will absorb some of these ways of doing and thinking and they will more easily have a family life of cooperation and harmony. In Section P-78, *Benefits of a Good Relationship with Your Child*, are provided reasons to make your labors worthwhile. What do you think?

6. Consult Section P-2, *Individual Study of Outline*, for Week 9 regarding reading assignment in the textbook, study assignment in the *Action Guide*, and your home practice activity for the week. About your home practice, if you are enduring a lot of fighting between children in your house, study up on the "fighting" advice and put it into effect. You will be doing retraining, so refer to Section P-55, *Training Steps* for possible assistance. Or if you want to work on "Fighting in the Car" have a look at Section P-72, *Extra Points for Solving Fighting in the Car.* Children tend to resist giving up this "fun thing." If you do not want to tackle either of these problems or do not need to, you can practice "not scolding" or not going into a long or short diatribe about some lapse in behavior. What do the authors urge you to do instead in this system

of parenting? (See page 236, No. 9; page 28, line 12; page 29, line 15; page 31, line 4; page 31, line 10 from bottom; and page 33, line 4, ff.) These three steps are as follows:

a. use appropriate action,
b. wait, and
c. have an information session first, if retraining is needed.

SECTION P-68
GROUP MEETING NO. 8 FORMAT

Interaction Problems

Chapters 19 through 24, Pages 149-184

1. Play tape No. 5 by Drs. Corsini and Painter starting with "I will now take up . . ." for 10 minutes (about fighting).

2. Everyone discuss the home practice for the week. Which one did they do? Plan a regular play time or arrange a Parent Date? What happened? How did they go about it? How did their children respond? Realize this is your most valuable encouragement tool, especially if it becomes a regular part of your children's lives.

3 Look together at Section P-69, *Magic Words*, in the *Action Guide*. The combined experience of parents has built up an awareness of how helpful these ways of telling your child what the situation is, the needs of the situation, and what you, the parent, are going to do or not do. They are called "magic" because a child often immediately responds in a favorable way.

4. Establish together what the preferred chapters to review are, and do them in the order they are called out. Use Section P-70 through P-76, *Chapter Questions for Chapters 19 through 24*. It is urged that you do include Chapter 19, "Fighting in the Home" and Chapter 20, "Fighting in the Car." These two misbehaviors are responsible for a lot of conflict and bad feeling in families.

5. You will need time to look over together Section P-77, *Ways to Have a Good Relationship with Your Child*. Also, stress the "benefits" of such a relationship as provided in Section P-78, *Benefits of a Good Relationship with Your Child*. It will probably sound like your "Dream Family," so——let's do it!

6. End your meeting by looking together at Section P-3, *Group Outline of Study*, and noting the reading assignment in *Effective Discipline in the Home and School*, the study assignment in the *Action Guide*, and the home practice activity for Week 9. All are to be done by the next meeting.

SECTION P-69
MAGIC WORDS

1. You have a choice. You decide.

2. You'll do it when you're ready.

3. Are you old enough now?

4. You'll be ready when you're older.

5. Come back when you're ready to . . .

6. You can try again another day.

7. We'll have to wait until you're older and can act like a big boy/girl.

8. I'm sure you can work it out.

9. When so and so . . ., I will so and so . . . (in a friendly, informative manner).

10. I am not willing to . . . (in a friendly, informative manner).

11. You can try again when you are older.

12. Do you agree this is fair? What would be fair?

13. How about practicing so and so . . .?

14. Johnny (third person) chooses to . . .

15. How do you feel about this (e.g., report card)? What do you want to do about it? How can we help you?

16. You're learning to do that—you're getting it.

17. That's using your mind—great!

18. You have a right to cry (or be angry or whatever feeling you have).

19. I appreciate it when you . . .

20. It's very helpful when you . . .

21. It's fair for Johnny (third person) to . . .

22. You can handle that.

SECTION P-70
STUDY QUESTIONS FOR CHAPTER 19

Fighting in the Home, Pages 151-156

1. According to the authors, what is the real underlying reason for children's fights with each other? (Page 152, line 13 to end of paragraph.)

2. What three ways of handling children's fights are offered? (Page 153, line 1 to end of section.)

3. When a child tattletales about a fight with another child, what can a parent do besides look at him in silence? (Page 154, line 6 to end of section.) (Called "trading complaints.")

4. Why does this view of handling children's fights not see fighting as completely wrong? (Page 152, line 11 from bottom to end of paragraph; page 153, to "problems"; and page 156, line 13 from bottom to end of sentence.)

5. What about a child behaving aggressively with a young baby, pinching him/her, etc. How do you handle that? (Page 155, line 12 to end of paragraph.) What is the rationale behind this advice? (Page 155, line 7 from bottom to "be worse.")

6. What must go with ignoring the misbehavior? (When you cease giving negative attention, you must replace it with positive attention. Page 155, line 16 to end of sentence.)

7. Why do other methods of eliminating fights between children not work? (Page 156, line 4 from bottom.)

8. What about "rights" in regard to fighting? How do the authors view this? (Page 152, line 10 from bottom, ff.)

9. What is a key point for avoiding fights that children need to know? (Page 155, line 5.)

10. Fighting is a prime source of competition and a killer of cooperation, two facts *parents* need to know. Appointing themselves the referee of their children's fights is not as helpful as parents tend to believe. One child sees himself/herself as the winner, one as the loser, and neither of them is getting any practice in solving disputes. This can be a good topic for discussion at a family meeting. Individuals record reactions to Item 10; it is an important subject. Group members discuss together, exchanging reactions.

SECTION P-71
STUDY QUESTIONS FOR CHAPTER 20

Fighting in the Car, Pages 157-161

1. Why is training children not to fight in the car, verbally or physically, especially important? (Page 157, line 2 from bottom, ff. to end of paragraph.)

2. What type of consequence is this training method suggesting? (Page 161, line 3 from bottom.)

3. When does the parent who is training children in safe car behavior begin driving again after having pulled over? (Page 158, line 13 from top, line 13 from bottom, and line 10 from bottom.)

4. How fast do you pull over to the side of the road? (Page 158, line 18 and line 1 on page 159, ff.)

5. When you have pulled over because of fighting and the children beset you with comments or complaints, what else can you do besides ignore them? (Page 158, line 19.)

6. When you pull over because of fighting, *exactly* when do you start driving again? (Page 159, line 8 "driving again"; page 158, line 13 from bottom; and page 160, line 11 to "drive away.")

7. Do you return home? (Yes, it can be an alternate consequence. Page 158, line 4 from bottom.)

SECTION P-72
EXTRA POINTS FOR
SOLVING FIGHTING
IN THE CAR

1. You must go into a "training run" for this to work.

2. You have to plan ahead.

3. You must accept that this training is important—it has priority.

4. During a training run, you set out in the car with your children on jaunts that are not vital, that can be interrupted, or you could have a baby sitter alerted.

5. Should a verbal or physical fight begin, immediately follow through as directed, pulling over to the side of the road and so forth. See page 158 and 159 in the textbook.

6. Or, with a baby sitter alerted, your children can be taken back home. Then you go off without them.

7. If you are planning to pull over to the side of the road, be sure to have an interesting book with you to read.

8. Within the next two days, invite your children to come with you in the car again, following through as before, in complete silence if they misbehave.

9. Never threaten them—only act.

10. Show and feel no anger. Your children are learning, you are teaching them.

11. Keep this up until you and your children have a pleasant outing in the car.

12. If a second offensive occurs, immediately apply the same solution in complete silence without annoyance or anger.

SECTION P-73
STUDY QUESTIONS FOR CHAPTER 21
Behavior in Public, Pages 162-169

1. What kinds of actions are considered by the authors to be unacceptable public behavior? (Page 163, line 13, and page 165, line 14.)

2. How do you end such behavior? (Page 164, line 5 through all 5 points, and page 165, line 9 to "subdued.")

3. How do you handle the situation if only one child misbehaves? (Page 165, line 14 to end of paragraph.) For discussion on "unitism," see page 120, line 13 from bottom, to "separately."

4. What other "out of the home behavior" requires training, besides behavior in public? (Party behavior, visiting behavior. Page 166, the Kent Story.) How do we train children in this? (Page 167, line 14 from bottom, ff. to "our cabin.")

5. What solution is offered for poor restaurant behavior? (Page 167, line 5 to end of paragraph. Or all could go home. An additional solution, the possible cost of the meal, the price of training. See page 167, line 4 from bottom to page 168, ff.)

6. What method of training in table manners is given? (Power of example. Page 168, line 15, ff., from bottom, and page 169, line 10 from bottom.)

7. What general solution is offered? (Page 169, line 12, ff.)

8. Which of the four R's are you teaching your children? (Responsibility and Respect for others.)

9. What additional, important quality are they learning? (Self-control. Page 164, line 1 to end of paragraph.)

SECTION P-74
STUDY QUESTIONS FOR CHAPTER 22
Aggression, Pages 170-174

1. What brings out aggression in a child? (Page 171, line 1 to end of sentence.)

2. What sort of atmosphere along with what types of characteristics in the home seem to produce aggressive children? (Page 171, line 1 to end of paragraph.)

3. What do the authors mean by "order in the home?" (Page 171, line 9 to "lessen.")

4. What three things do parents need to look out for in themselves and, perhaps stop or at least lessen? (Page 171, line 13 from bottom to "the children.") What suggestions do the authors offer for help in this? (Page 171, line 10 from bottom to end of paragraph and point No. 2 on page 172.)

5. What do you think of the five points in the solution given by the authors? (Page 171, bottom to page 172.) Individuals record thoughts on notes page. Group members discuss and share ideas that come to mind.

6. What consequences do they advise if a child hits you? (Page 172, line 10 from bottom to "nice.") What is an additional important part of the consequence? (Page 172, line 2 from bottom to "that day.")

7. What do the authors advise parents to do if their child hits other children? (Page 173, line 7 to end of paragraph.) If they beg for a second chance, what do you do? (Page 173, line 13.)

8. What is the specific solution offered when your child takes up spitting at people? (Page 173, line 7 from bottom, ff.)

9. And if your offspring takes up biting others? (Page 174, line 1 to end of paragraph.) What part of the solution must you be sure to include? (Page 172, point No. 5.) Do you need to feel anger? (Your child is not yet delinquent or heading for jail—your child is learning what is acceptable behavior. Have confidence he/she can learn and become convinced of a better way from his/her training experiences with you.)

SECTION P-75
STUDY QUESTIONS FOR CHAPTER 23

Undesirable Companions, Pages 175-179

1. In what three areas does a child's growing up take place? (Page 176, line 8, ff.)

2. What role does a child's activities and play "on the street" take in the development of a child? (It begins to develop his/her social being. Page 176, line 13, ff. from bottom.)

3. What is the danger in allowing children to play only with screened or approved playmates? (Page 177, line 15 to end of paragraph.)

4. What is the golden rule offered by the authors for handling developments when the child starts to go out playing in the neighborhood? (Page 177, line 16 from bottom.) What are their reasons for this? (Page 177, line 14 from the bottom to "not worry," and page 176, line 9.)

5. If the "neighborhood monster" insists on playing with your child, what might you do as a parent? (Page 178, line 2 to end of paragraph.) Could you do this? Do you think it would work? Individuals think about this and try it out if the situation presents itself. Group members discuss and exchange experiences.

6. What is the rationale behind the advice? (Page 179, line 12 to end of discussion, and line 5 from bottom to "bad.") Which of the four R's would the parent be expressing? (Responsibility and Resourcefulness. Also, Responsiveness.)

SECTION P-76
STUDY QUESTIONS FOR CHAPTER 24

Demanding Too Much Attention, Pages 180-184

1. What do children need to learn about attention? (Page 181, line 2, top to "means.")

2. What is the suggested solution when a child is asking for "undue attention?" (Page 184, line 9 to "behavior.")

3. What could you do if your child will not allow you to talk on the telephone in peace? (Page 181, line 8 from bottom to end of discussion.)

4. What do the authors suggest if your child is consistently engaging in dangerous acts, say, on the playground? (Page 182, line 2 from bottom to end of discussion.) Could you do what is suggested? What would stop you? Individuals reflect about it. Group members talk together and share.

5. What could you do if your child has taken to dawdling in the morning, when getting ready for school? (Page 183, line 4 from bottom to end of paragraph.) What trapped father into not using the advice? (Page 184, line 4 to "herself.") Did he need to feel sorry for her?

6. Do you disagree with any parts of the solution for ending demands for undue attention? (Page 181, line 7, points 1 through 5.) Individuals use notes page and think about it. Group members give reasons if they disagree, and discuss.

7. What important fact should parents remember about "attention" and their children? (Page 184, line 4, ff. from bottom. When you withdraw negative attention you must replace it with positive attention at other times, or you could sabotage your efforts at retraining.)

SECTION P-77
WAYS TO HAVE A
GOOD RELATIONSHIP
WITH YOUR CHILD

1. Encourage them continually in every way possible (never miss the chance).

2. Honestly respect them in your thoughts and with your actions.

3. Trust them to grow, to learn.

4. Have fun times with them:

    a. regular play time (with little children, Page 172 in your textbook, point No. 3);

    b. regular separate "Parent Dates" (See Section P-66, *Characteristics of a Parent Date*); and

    c. family fun and family projects (when old enough).

5. Listen to them when they talk:

    a. seek their views, and

    b. offer your views.

6. Share yourself with them:

    a. your experiences,

    b. your concerns, and

    c. your joys.

7. Help them to discover their talents, their aptitudes, and then to develop them.

8. Offer the family meeting regularly, attending it yourself. (See Section P-99, *Benefits of the Family Meeting.*)

9. Learn what is rightly their business and your business and hold to it. (Section P-47, 8a and b.)

SECTION P-78
BENEFITS OF A
GOOD RELATIONSHIP
WITH YOUR CHILD

1. Your child will acquire a good self-concept and high self-esteem for now and always.

2. Your child will become willing to consider and accept your values.

3. Parenting will be more fun.

4. Family life is more fun.

   Your child becomes a joy to have around, rather than some kind of nuisance or worse.

5. Your child will more willingly say "yes" to a request and obey a command.

6. Family members will more willingly cooperate with each other and be more concerned with the welfare of the family.

NOTES
Related to Week 8

SECTION P-79
INDIVIDUAL STUDY PLAN NO. 9

Special Problems

Chapters 25 through 31, Pages 185-231

1. For home practice you were asked to try "the fighting advice." Did you? Were you able to do it? Did it help? Constant fighting between siblings can be such a blight on a family, it is well worth a good strong period of retraining. If the fighting becomes more fierce and you are becoming afraid they might harm each other, examine whether most of the time you do let them get on with it but you can be induced to intervene. This will cause dangerous fighting because they learn they can get you involved if they get fierce enough. If this is happening, leave and go where you cannot see it and cannot hear it. If you do, no payoff will occur and the "fighting advice" will work. If you chose to practice "not scolding," it is hoped you are having success. This scolding parenting method either hacks away at your child's self-esteem or causes "parent deafness" in the child—neither of which is what you are trying to accomplish. Save all such important teaching for an "information session" or family council meetings or a "one-on-one" time when both of you are feeling good.

2. Having done your reading and your study assignment, play tape No. 9 by Drs. Corsini and Painter if you have the tape. This tape takes up impossible problems.

3. Study Section P-81, *Parental Obligations to Children According to Adlerians.* Perhaps this list of parental obligations is quite different from what you thought. These are seen to be the basic obligations. You may have some additional ones of your own, which is fine if they are not in contradiction to any of these. If they are, we suggest you consider doing some serious rethinking and reconsidering. We cannot be both sides of the coin at the same time.

4. Review again Section P-22, *Ways to Spoil a Child.* If someone ever says to you, "you are spoiling him/her" and you do not know what they mean (this used to happen to me), looking at this list could help you spot what you might still be doing. This kind of parenting mistake could well be serious. Adler felt it was one of two worst things that could happen to a child—being pampered or spoiled by his/her parents; the other one was being rejected.

5. Do Sections P-82 through P-88, study questions for various chapters. If you are short on time, do those that most pertain to you. The authors have identified these as "special problems" because they are highly resistant to change. However, when you are ready to start the retraining, if you go into a "training run" (see Section P-55, *Training Steps*) and follow exactly what the authors advise, you will succeed in eliminating them from your family life.

   "Training run" means that you keep applying the appropriate solution or parenting deterrent until a more acceptable behavior is chosen by the child for his/her own good reasons. See also Section P-72, *Extra Points for Solving Fighting in the Car.*

6. Study Section P-89, *Mistaken Ideas of Parents.* This list is given for you to consider. You have been studying and using a new approach to parenting and you may well see these viewpoints in a different light now. What great credit we give to the spoken word in our culture! Notice how much faith we have in the power of the spoken word. When we must put a training consequence into effect, we can give the child a silent hug before we proceed and when we next see him/her, greet our offspring with smiling eyes (very important). After all, the "lesson time" is over, isn't it? Our children don't have to pay and pay for their misbehavior, all day or all week, do they?

7. You have reached Week 10 with your last reading assignment in your textbook, study assignment in the *Action Guide,* and your home practice activity for the week. Plan some family fun, perhaps, reviewing pages 248 through 250 in your textbook. This would be a good

topic to take up at your first family meeting (pages 239 through 244 in your textbook). Also check out another barometer of progress. How much needless talking are you still doing? Turn a compassionate, honest eye on yourself and watch what happens in this area. If you feel a "talking attack" coming on, consider using a related action, instead, or just withdraw and deal with the misbehavior later.

SECTION P-80
GROUP MEETING NO. 9 FORMAT

Special Problems

Chapters 25 through 31, Pages 185-231

1. Play tape No. 9 by Drs. Corsini and Painter for 10 minutes on impossible problems if you have it.

2. What success was had with the home practice for the week, "The Fighting Advice"? What happened? Did you leave out any steps? (See page 153 in *Effective Discipline in the Home and School.*) How did your children react to this new method? How did that go?

3. Go over together Section 81, *Parental Obligations to Children According to Adlerians.* Have a frank discussion. Some of the "obligations" may be hard for you to accept.

4. Review again Section P-22, *Ways to Spoil a Child.* This can be used as a ready reference to check yourselves on your progress in this important area. Adler held it to be one of the biggest mistakes parents make and a most damaging one.

5. Decide which are the preferred chapters to review, and do them in the order called out or the majority wants, using Sections P-82 through P-88, study questions for various chapters.

6. Consider together the study assignment, Section P-89, *Mistaken Ideas of Parents.* You have been studying the Adlerian viewpoint long enough now to hopefully see these concepts as valid and to be taken seriously. Frankly and honestly express your reactions and discuss together.

7. Close by referring to Section P-3, *Group Outline of Study,* for the reading assignment in *Effective Discipline in the Home and School,* the study assignment in the *Action Guide,* and the home practice for the week—all are found

under "Week 10" and are to be done by next meeting. Two home practice activities are to be done this week. Put in the extra effort to do them both so that all of you can compare notes at the next meeting. This will be the last chance for this type of discussion.

SECTION P-81
PARENTAL OBLIGATIONS
TO CHILDREN
ACCORDING TO
ADLERIANS

1. To teach children the principles and restrictions necessary for group living.

2. To train and guide our children.

3. To set up and maintain a routine—a daily order. (See Section P-47, *Adlerian View of Order and Limits.*)

4. To train our children to cooperate and respect the needs of a situation.

5. To instruct our children in ways, means, and attitudes by which they can cope with life.

6. To establish a family council (See Section P-99, *Benefits of the Family Meeting*) and attend it ourselves, acting in a proper manner.

7. In family happenings, to try to understand the total situation, the goals of children, and the interaction of relationships which will lead to

   a. acceptance of order,

   b. cooperation with the needs of the situation, and

   c. engagement in useful activities.

8. To be consistent in our actions.

9. To offer and make possible family fun times and family projects.

10. To arrange daily individual play time with our little children (see page 172 in your textbook, point No. 3).

11. To arrange regular parent dates with each child when they are old enough. (See Section P-66, *Characteristics of a Parent Date.*)

12. To consciously, actively, encourage our children. (See Section P-38, *Encouragement and Recognition* and in the textbook see pages 34 through 43.)

13. To listen to our children, trying to understand what they think, feel, and value.

14. To help our children understand and become comfortable with their feelings.

15. To become aware of our children's goals and redirect them from mistaken goals into positive goals of cooperation and usefulness. (See Section P-44, *Redirecting Your Child from Misbehavior to Cooperative Behavior.*)

16. To help our children learn how to handle property and money through knowledge and practice.

17. To constantly nourish and maintain a good relationship with each of our children. (See Section P-77, *Ways to Have a Good Relationship with Your Child,* and Section P-78, *Benefits of a Good Relationship with Your Child.*)

18. To improve the quality of our own lives.

SECTION P-82
STUDY QUESTIONS FOR CHAPTER 25

Dawdling, Page 186-190

1. What are some harmful patterns of behavior that can develop from dawdling? (Page 187, line 7 from bottom to end of paragraph.)

2. What solution is given by the authors when your child is slow at eating? (Page 188, line 14, ff.) What must you do first? (Warn him/her what you are going to do. See page 188, line 3; page 188, line 6, ff; and page 189, line 13 from bottom to end of discussion.)

3. Do the authors assure you what will cure slowness in dressing? (Page 189, line 3 from bottom to end of example, and page 188; point No. 3.)

4. Could you apply the solution offered in the example of the child not ready to go to the beach when agreed? (Page 188, line 5 from bottom, to page 189, ff.) Individuals reflect and record answer and why. Group members talk it over, giving reasons for their views.

5. For what is the child being prepared by these methods of handling dawdling? (Page 190, line 13, ff. to "reality.") Is this valid reasoning? Do you see "dawdling" as a critical misbehavior that needs training work by the parents? Individuals put down thoughts on the notes page. Group members exchange views.

SECTION P-83
STUDY QUESTIONS FOR CHAPTER 26

Temper Tantrum, Pages 191-194

1. How do the authors describe a temper tantrum? (Page 192, line 14.) How do they evaluate it? (Page 192, line 3, ff.)

2. If a tantrum occurs in public, what do the authors urge you to do? (Page 192, line 10 from bottom, ff., and page 193, line 7 to "all.") Could you do this? With today's problem of "abducted children," are there some ways you could alter this solution and still use it? Individuals reflect and consider. Group members share their thoughts and creative thinking.

   Most of these solutions and deterrents have been thought up by parents. When it becomes more automatic to think in terms of using connected consequences, you will find yourself doing it, too.

3. What is the best way to react to any temper tantrum, no matter where, or no matter what? (Page 192, line 11 from bottom to "blackmail," and page 194, line 7 from bottom to "yourself.")

4. When your child wails and yells about one of his/her brothers or sisters, what is he/she trying to accomplish? (Page 194, line 8 to end of paragraph.)

5. What is another term for temper tantrums? (Page 194, line 7 from bottom through "negative emotionalism.")

6. What must you also be sure to do? (Page 194, line 2 from bottom.)

SECTION P-84
STUDY QUESTIONS FOR CHAPTER 27

Nightmares—Excessive Fears, Pages 195-201

1. As Adlerian psychologists, what different view about nightmares do the authors hold? (The child purposely scares himself/herself—he/she is not a victim. Page 196, line 7 to "scared" and line 11 from bottom to "night.")

2. Does the solution outlined by the authors mean we ignore the nightmare? (No, but the parents avoid lavishing large amounts of reassurance if a nightmare occurs. Page 197, line 1 to end of paragraph, line 14, and line 10 from bottom to end of paragraph.)

3. What are some ways of conveying our own fears to our children? (Page 199, line 13 from bottom to "overprotection.")

4. Does this mean we cease being watchful of our little children's welfare altogether? (Page 199, line 7 from bottom to end of paragraph.)

5. If your child has become overly fearful about the water, dogs, the playground, etc., how are you urged by the authors to handle it? (Without fanfare and comment, gradually introduce the fearful object or event into the child's experience, expecting him to slowly change his/her attitude on his/her own. Page 200, line 7, ff.; and page 198, line 9 from bottom to page 199, ff. to "the sea.")

6. Does this mean George's parents completely stopped talking to their child while at the beach? (Absolutely not. An important procedure is to remain as usual in all other ways—smiling, exchanging comments, giving a hug, etc.) Why? (This will show that you are in no way displeased with him/her and have confidence in your child's capacity to learn.)

7. At what time would a parent seek professional help about the child's fears? (Page 201, line 2 from bottom.)

SECTION P-85
STUDY QUESTIONS FOR CHAPTER 28

Bad Habits, Pages 202-210

1. What are the five steps usually used by parents in an effort to correct an emerging habit in their child? (Page 203, line 8 to "habit.") What do these five steps have in common? (They don't work. Page 203, line 13.)

2. What is the reward to a child that keeps a bad habit going in spite of all efforts? (Attention. Page 203, line 16, ff. to "giving attention"; page 204, line 12; and page 210, line 3, ff. to "habit.")

3. What is the authors' "essential message" about bad habits? (Page 210, line 8 from bottom and line 3 to end of sentence.)

4. What way do the authors urge you to treat bad habits? (Page 205, line 9, ff. from bottom to "behavior"; page 205, line 9, ff. to "attention"; and page 206, line 5 to "each other.") Provide no interaction; act just as if it isn't happening.

5. At what time do you give your child affection and love? (Page 205, line 12, ff. to "him," and page 210, line 3 from bottom.)

Are these viewpoints about "bad habits" surprising? Do they make sense? Sometimes we have to be absolutely bankrupt and at our wits end to try some of these solutions, but as our successful experiences accumulate, we become more confident. Remember, for these deterrents to work, we have to be sure not to leave out any part of the solution.

SECTION P-86
STUDY QUESTIONS FOR CHAPTER 29
Bed-Wetting, Pages 211-218

1. By what age do most children completely stop bed-wetting? (Page 211, line 4 from bottom.)

2. What is probably the very strongest reinforcer for the continuation of a bed-wetting behavior? (Page 212, line 16 to "it.") What are examples of this attention? (Page 212, line 21 to end of paragraph.)

3. In the authors' view, what parental acts do not stop bed-wetting? (Page 212, line 2 to end of paragraph.)

4. Is any part of the authors' solution for bed-wetting not acceptable to you? (Pages 212 and 213.) Individuals think this over, considering all aspects. Group members talk this over.

5. How is the solution to bed-wetting, offered on pages 212 and 213 by the authors, logically connected to misbehavior? (If you are not ready to stop wetting, you'll be in a wet bed. If you want a dry bed, you can always stop wetting. What you are old enough to do for yourself, you do for yourself.) What benefits to the child is this solution eliminating? (Special attention and concern and special service.) How long should parents allow for this solution to work? (Page 217, line 16 from bottom.)

6. How old must the child be for the parents to put this solution into operation? (Page 212, line 8 from bottom.)

7. If this solution does not work in a year's time, what other method might be considered? (Page 218, line 6 from bottom to end of paragraph.)

8. Ask yourself: Although the natural or logical consequence solution for a problem is often difficult for the parent,

is it as difficult as the unending continuance of the problem for say, until they leave home?

9. While training a child to sleep dry, what two additional acts are important on the part of the parent? (Page 217, line 8 to end of paragraph.)

10. Why is praise for a dry bed a reinforcer? (Page 217, line 6, ff. to "program." To receive praise for a dry bed, there must be a wet bed in contrast.)

SECTION P-87
STUDY QUESTIONS FOR CHAPTER 30
Control of Bowels and Bladder, Pages 219-223

1. If a child was dry and clean but begins soiling himself/ herself again, what has the parent usually begun doing? (Page 220, line 15, ff. to "bowels.")

2. At this point, what are usually the goals of the child with his/her parents? (Page 220, line 12, ff. from bottom to "behavior.")

3. In other Adlerian terms, what else is this called? (A power struggle and, sometimes, revenge. Page 220, line 18, to include the next two sentences.)

4. In the opinion of the authors, what actions on the part of the parent can reinforce a lack of bladder and bowel control in the child? (Page 220, line 9 from bottom to end of paragraph.)

5. What would be a logical consequence in a soiling behavior problem with a child? (Page 220, line 3 from bottom, ff. to "only once," page 221.)

6. What further action on the part of the parent is important when using this logical consequence? (Page 220, line 7 from bottom; page 221, line 5 to "responsibility"; and page 221, line 15, ff. to end of paragraph.) Remember: Don't leave anything out.

7. In this solution, what is helping the child decide to stay dry and free of soil? (Page 223, line 15, ff., and page 221, line 8 to end of paragraph.)

8. What are the sad experiences spoken of on page 223, last paragraph? (When soiled, he/she must clean himself/ herself or be dirty. People move away from the child when he/she is dirty or they tell him/her to leave in a friendly firm manner.)

SECTION P-88
STUDY QUESTIONS FOR CHAPTER 31

Morality, Pages 224-231 (Has to Do With Values)

1. In the matter of morality, the authors see a two-fold problem in teaching values to children—what is it? (Page 225, line 12 to end of paragraph.)

2. What two actions do they warn parents to avoid at such times? (Over frightening the child and over reacting in any form to the morally blameworthy act. Page 225, line 17, ff. to end of paragraph.)

3. In the author's view, what is the best prevention of conduct in children that is offensive to morality? (Page 225, line 8 from bottom, ff. to end of paragraph.)

4. What procedure do the authors urge you to follow if morally offensive conduct occurs in your child? (Page 226, line 1 to end of paragraph.)

5. What reactions in the parent are not likely to help? (Page 225, line 4 from bottom to "denial"; page 225, line 4 to end of paragraph; and page 226, line 8 to end of paragraph.) You are teaching socially "O.K." behavior. Your child wasn't born knowing it. He/she is learning.

6. When a child is chronically stealing, what can sometimes be the cause of it? (Page 229, line 7 to end of paragraph.) Does this make sense to you? Individuals think about it, especially in view of what we have been studying. Group members do the same and talk about it.

7. What is sometimes another cause of stealing in a child? (Page 229, line 13 to end of paragraph.)

8. What do you think of the advice offered by the authors for handling an older child's experimentation with marijuana. (Page 229, beginning with line 11 from bottom to page 230, ff.) Does it make sense? Could you do it? Individuals

think about this. Group members share their views. What could it have become? (A power struggle.)

9. What is a parent urged to do when one child tattletales about another? (Page 227, line 7 from bottom, ff. Trade complaints.)

10. What do the authors advise if your child starts using four letter words. (Page 230, line 6 from bottom to end of paragraph.) If the child switches to another word, what do you do? (Still ignore it—some children don't give up easily.) Of course along with this, at your information session you can say, "Mother/father does not use those words . . . (give your reasons) and from now on, I am not going to hear them if you do. I will be thinking of something else."

SECTION P-89
MISTAKEN IDEAS OF PARENTS

1. A child needs constant, directive orders, and every one of them should be obeyed immediately.

2. A child will be impressed by our anger and be assisted to go in the right way.

3. A child must be observed and reminded constantly of what he/she is learning or the child will never remember it, let alone learn it.

4. If we talk thoroughly to a child about a misbehavior again and again, the child will eventually remove it.

5. The child cannot be trained well, if we are not willing to spank him/her often—at least sometimes.

6. Using an angry, lecturing flow of words is helpful when training a child.

    *Instead we **act** as we warned we would do in an information session.*

7. If you talk long enough, and clearly enough, you can persuade a child to do what you say.

8. Being sure to point out a child's big and little shortcomings will help him/her improve.

9. To impress on a child the error of his/her ways, it is helpful to go around for a while with a sad, disappointed or stern and disapproving face. Or we could hold our "angry eyes" face for an extended period.

10. Out-doing our child in a sarcastic verbal exchange will impress him/her and act as a deterrent.

11. It is essential to win all power struggles between ourselves and our children, or our parental position is imperilled.

12. Parents must referee and settle their children's fights. (See Section 36, *These Foster Competition.*)

NOTES
Related To Week 9

SECTION P-90
INDIVIDUAL STUDY PLAN NO. 10

Building a Cooperative Family

Chapters 32 through 34, Pages 234-253

1. One of the home practices for the past week was to check on how much needless talking you are still doing. What did you discover? Hopefully, you found you have started changing in this area. Many parents cause their children to resort to becoming "Parent Deaf" in self defense or defiance. Our "talk, talk, talking" does have mostly good intentions, but the results are usually far from good. Look at Section P-92, *Times Not To Talk*, and Section P-93, *Acceptable Talk*. A parent has been known to become so fearful about talking that he/she is hardly talking at all, so we have tried to show in more detail what is meant. Especially be aware of when you do want to be talking or interacting with your children. To be talking at these times and in these ways is really as vital as being silent, when that is called for by the situation. The second home practice was to plan some family fun. Did that happen? Fun times together as a family along with family projects help your child to feel like he/she really belongs to the family unit, that he/she is not trying to face this world today all by himself/herself, that he/she is a part of this important group—a family. This greatly contributes to a child's self-assurance and ability to achieve. It doesn't matter what size the family is or who makes up the family so much as that they do these kinds of things together regularly.

2. Now, having done your reading and your study assignment, play tape No. 4 by Drs. Corsini and Painter about the family council, if you have the tape.

3. This is the time to be thinking and learning about some good and more effective ways of communicating with children. As you go over Section P-94, *Communication*, you can see the contrast between our usual ways of

speaking to children and how we are now urged to do. As we bring these ways and these words more and more into exchanges between family members, our children will begin learning them too. Also, would not the first way of communicating be encouraging and the second way discouraging?

4. Move on to Section P-96, *Study Questions for Chapter 32*, on communicating.

5. Next look at Section P-97, *Study Questions for Chapter 33*, on the family council or family meeting (pages 238 through 247 in your textbook). Bringing this event into your family's way of handling matters can be more helpful and beneficial than almost any other change you make. Family meetings are the heart of this system of parenting. The good results are cumulative as you do it regularly. If, you find once a week is not feasible, strike for every other week. However, once you have agreed to a schedule, the parents then demonstrate the importance and value of the meeting by attending it faithfully. You put it in your "top priority list" of things you must do for your children and for yourself. The results listed in Section P-99, *Benefits of the Family Meeting*, cannot happen without this degree of commitment. We urge you to thoroughly study and reflect upon how a meeting of this kind is conducted. Its characteristics are unique and need to be followed *exactly* for it to work.

6. The last vital ingredient needed for building a harmonious, cooperating family to be taken up in this study is that of family fun together. Far too often, planned fun times degenerate entirely into something else. Go to Section P-100, *Study Questions for Chapter 34*, "Fun in the Family" and check Section P-101, *Training to Play Board Games*. Seriously consider this topic. You can train your children to avoid these actions described that sabotage and destroy any chance of having fun together. Review, also, page 165 in the textbook about training for family fun outside the home. Playing and laughing together will nurture and strengthen your family feelings for each other and your faith in yourselves as a family unit. How sad if you are handing each other a steady diet of just the

opposite—family times that are either boring or a disaster. We have all experienced this and it does not have to be. Planning some family fun could be a topic for your first family meeting.

7. We have reached the end of our study time together. May I, as a fellow parent and grandparent who also has traveled this long and sometimes very difficult path, wish you every success in your parenting, whatever methods you use. You will never do anything more rewarding or more important than this.

HAPPY PARENTING!

NOTE: Tape No. 12 is a good summary of all you've been studying.

SECTION P-91
GROUP MEETING NO. 10 FORMAT

Building a Cooperative Family
Chapters 32 through 34, Pages 234-253

1. Play tape No. 4 by Drs. Corsini and Painter beginning with discussion on family council for 10 minutes, if you have the tape.

2. Review together one of the home practices for the week— "Check on How Much Needless Talking You are Still Doing." Have you improved in this area? Are you still talking when you should be doing what you warned you would do? (The consequences.) Are you still repeating yourselves? What is happening there? (Parent deafness?) Did you do the second home practice which was to plan some family fun at a family meeting? Was it successful? Discuss this.

3. At this time go over Section P-92, *Times Not to Talk*, and Section P-93, *Acceptable Talk*. Notice together Section P-93, *Acceptable Talk*. Sometimes parents get so wary of talking at the wrong time that they are not talking at all, and this can be harmful to their children.

4. Go to Section P-96, *Study Questions for Chapter 32*, on "Communicating" and review pages 235 through 237 in the textbook.

5. Follow this with a discussion of Section P-94, *Communication*, and Section P-95, *Criticisms—Helpful and Unhelpful Procedures*.

6. Go to Chapter 33, "The Family Council," in *Effective Discipline in the Home and School*, pages 238 through 247, and do Section P-97, *Study Questions for Chapter 33*. It is important that you understand exactly how a family council operates. Also, go over Section P-99, *Benefits of the Family Meeting*. All parents need all the motivation and encouragement there is. Your family has a vital need to hold these regular family meetings. It could make all

the difference in your succeeding or not succeeding to build a cooperative "glad-to-be-together" family. Remember, it is the heart of this system.

7. If time permits, go over Chapter 34, "Fun in the Family," pages 248 through 253, and use Section P-100, *Study Questions for Chapter 34.* Notice the check list for Section P-101, *Training to Play Board Games.* There is a nourishing role in having fun together in all human relationships and it will help your children to feel they really do belong to this family unit.

8. Wish each other "Happy Parenting" and close with some cake and coffee to enjoy together. You could even consider planning some follow-up meetings now and then for comparing notes and clarifying some topics. Form a kind of parenting support group—a proven helpful stratagem for all endeavors.

NOTE: Tape No. 12 is a good review of all you've been studying.

SECTION P-92
TIMES NOT TO TALK

1. When in conflict.

2. When training.

3. To remind and nag.

4. To repeat information (lecture at length).

5. When you are angry.

6. When the child is angry.

7. When you are critical of or disappointed in your child—
   WAIT.

SECTION P-93
ACCEPTABLE TALK

1. Giving information (one time).

2. Sharing of experiences and feelings.

3. Giving encouragement and recognition.

   When you use words of recognition that acknowledge the act, the thing done, the contribution, the help, the improvement, the effort, the accomplishment, and a positive feeling, honestly expressed, you are being encouraging, rather than praising and discouraging.

4. Discussion of ideas and events. (An opinion is not a fact.)

5. Telling stories and jokes.

6. "I will" messages (one time).

7. "I am not willing" messages (one time).

8. Reflective listening.

9. Brainstorming for ideas.

10. Considering alternatives (problem solving).

11. Considering, with your child, his/her failure or mistaken behavior in a learning and teaching manner. (See last part of Section P-38, *Encouragement and Recognition.*)

SECTION P-94
COMMUNICATION

The "Open Door Policy"

Be available.
    Pay attention.
        Listen carefully.
            Feedback what you think you have heard.

Allow differences of opinion.
    Work toward a resolution, not toward winning or losing.
        Ask for the other's advice.
            Take a "cooling off" break.

Keep a calm, friendly voice.
    Speak as you would to a friend.
        Say what you really mean. Your face will give you away anyhow.

The "Closed Door Tradition"

Never has time to talk.
    Won't take the other seriously.
        Moralizing, lecturing.
            Uses everything to prove a point.

Sees all communications and especially all differences of opinion as "Win or Lose" situations.
Worried about "losing face."
        Feels that parent will lose "Authority" or "Respect" unless he/she is always right.
            Disgraces or shames the other.
            Never asks, only tells.

SECTION P-95
CRITICISM—
UNHELPFUL AND HELPFUL
PROCEDURES

Unhelpful	Helpful
1. charging and attacking	relaxing and going slowly
2. speaking at the wrong time (Whenever either party's emotions are high.)	speaking at the right time (neutral time—us ready and their choice)
3. pouring it on	realizing the impact of criticism
4. using anger for energy	being honest about your own feelings
5. assuming the right to criticize destructively	respecting the feelings of the receiver
6. using criticism as a release	using criticism as information
7. dumping the whole bag of old gripes and hurts or sounding like a broken record	emphasizing the most important points to the situation
8. putting a dent in the doer	speaking to the behavior
9. demanding ("Don't play with your food.")	asking or pointing out ("Do eat nicely.")
10. noticing and pointing up only weaknesses	also noticing and mentioning the strengths (especially at the end)

SECTION P-96
STUDY QUESTIONS FOR CHAPTER 32

Communicating

1. When parents report that they cannot communicate with their children, what do the authors believe they really mean? (Page 235, line 2 to end of paragraph.)

2. According to the authors, for what purpose should talking be reserved? (Page 235, line 10 to end of paragraph.)

3. When should words be avoided? (Page 235, line 5 from bottom to "cool off.")

4. Instead of using an angry, lecturing flow of words as a means of discipline and training, what do the authors suggest? (Page 235, line 4 from bottom to "manner.") Why? (Page 235, line 2 from bottom.)

5. What is an "I will . . . " message? (Page 236, line 6, ff. from bottom.)

6. If positive messages are important, how exactly do you send them to your child? (Page 236, points 1 through 9.)

7. Review the four effective listening skills (page 236 to page 237). All record your opinions of each one, using notes page. Individuals choose one listening technique and commit yourself to trying it for one week. What could using these skills help preserve and nourish? (A good relationship with children.) Parents, learn these, practice them. It will be worth it. These four effective listening skills are needed in our culture today. Learning them from you will stand your child in good stead all of his/her life.

8. What do the authors consider is the most important advice they give to parents? (Page 237, line 4 from bottom, ff.) Why? (Page 238, line 4, ff. to end of paragraph.)

SECTION P-97
STUDY QUESTIONS FOR CHAPTER 33

The Family Council, Pages 238-247

1. Who is eligible to be a member of the family council? (Page 239, line 1 to "included.")

2. What does being invited to be a member of the family council do for even the youngest member of the family? (Page 239, line 5.)

3. How often does a family council meet? (Page 239, line 13.)

4. What does skipping the holding of a family council meeting do to the success of your family? (Page 239, line 10, ff. from bottom.) When would a meeting be canceled? (Page 243, No. 6.)

5. When would you have an emergency meeting? (Page 243, No. 7.)

6. What are some possible hazards to the success of your family council? (Page 244, top, points 1 through 8.) What is the greatest hazard? (Page 244, No. 2.)

7. What is the essence of the family council and its major quality? (Page 242, line 1, ff.) What are some other qualities of a family council? (Page 239, line 8 to end of paragraph.)

8. How is attendance at a family council handled? (Page 239, line 4 from bottom.)

9. Can anyone be expelled from a meeting for any reason? (Page 240, line 6.)

10. Instead, how is a disturbing, misbehaving member handled? (Page 239, line 2 from bottom to "feet.") A most effective

damper on disturbing behavior at a meeting is for all to completely ignore it, if possible.

11. Who can be chairman? (Page 242, line 3.) What are the chairman's duties? (Page 243, line 5 from bottom, Nos. 9b and 9c; page 246, line 7 from bottom; and page 240, line 4 and line 6 from bottom.)

12. Who can be secretary? (Page 239, line 10.) What are the secretary's duties? (Page 239, line 11.)

13. What are the two rules regarding "discussion" at a family council? (Page 240, line 9, ff. to end of paragraph.) What is the wisdom behind this? (Page 240, line 15.)

14. What subjects may be brought up at a family council? (Page 240, line 13 from bottom to end of paragraph.) Also, if a family member has a gripe, he/she can bring it up if he/she agrees to allow the council to consult on it and try to alleviate it. This protects your family council from being used as a gripe session.

15. What is the key qualification for a subject to be discussed? (Page 240, line 10 from bottom.)

16. When discussing a family problem or family concern at the family council, what are you seeking? (Page 240, line 2.)

17. If, after discussion, you cannot reach consensus, what do you do? (Page 241, line 1.) You let things get worse; this could well produce the motivation to solve it.

18. When should you start a family council? (Page 247, line 8 to end of paragraph.)

19. If your children try to sabotage it, how long should you continue? (Page 247, line 5 from bottom to end of paragraph.)

SECTION P-98
PRINCIPLES OF PROBLEM SOLVING

by Dr. Rudolf Dreikurs

These are based on his background in Adlerian Psychology.

1. Mutual Respect

Don't fight and/or don't give in. No one is *obliged* to fight with someone; you disrespect him [or her] by humiliating him [or her] physically and/or psychologically. When *you* give in *you* feel humiliated. Putting oneself in a spot of having to win or fearing to lose is what most of us do. Since this is our real intention—to win, to be on top, to have our way—we don't listen to the other person and only see what he [or she] is doing wrong.

2. Pin Point the Issue

The issue is basically who wins or who loses, fear of humiliation, losing or maintaining status, being morally right, getting one's own way. The particular problem over which one is arguing or fighting is *not* the problem. The problem is the *relationship* between two parties, in particular, the *quality* of the relationship. It is important to realize that an agreement between people is always present. Usually, it is the intention to continue to disagree or to fight, or to insist on having one's own way. This situation can only be changed by *YOU.* You are only able to change or control what *you* do, not what the other person should do. Since continued striving to change the other person, trying to get him [or her] to do or not do something, hasn't worked, realize that the only person you *can* control, influence, or change is YOURSELF. When a person changes his [or her] own behavior, he [or she] *indirectly* influences the behavior of those with whom he [or she] comes in contact. *Their* actions change in response to his [or hers].

3. **Change the Arrangement**

You can only change the agreement by exploring the alternatives to what *you* are presently doing. It may be difficult, but it is essential that one recognize that there are always alternatives in any situation. Generally, one doesn't see them or recognize that they are possible because one's involvement in the conflict may be so intense. Since, at this point, you will have determined to explore the alternatives and decide what *YOU* will do instead of continuing to demand or wait for the other person to change first, you are able to break the deadlock and create a new climate of transaction.

4. **Invite Participation and Share Responsibility**

Anyone who sets himself [or herself] up unilaterally to solve a problem affecting another person, deprives that other individual of his [or her] basic responsibility to contribute to its solution and creates the climate for later rebellion and dissatisfaction. Since the other party doesn't share in contributing towards solving the problem in any way, he [or she] may in no way feel responsible or obligated to cooperate.

SECTION P-99
BENEFITS OF THE FAMILY MEETING

1. Quarrelsome situations can be put off for the time being, until the next meeting.

   a. There is assurance that the problem will be handled.

   b. Tempers have time to cool.

   c. Calm consideration and discussion can be brought to bear.

   d. Some problems solve themselves.

2. Chores can be fairly apportioned, chosen, rotated, and reviewed.

   Consequences can be found, if needed.

3. Family fun and family projects will happen more often.

4. Everyone gets teaching and practice in new and better ways of communicating.

5. Wounded feelings and festering situations can be handled and healed, instead of drifting and harming the family.

6. Children learn how to work together as a group, which is valuable knowledge in this day.

7. Values can be taught during the discussions.

8. Children cooperate more easily with family rules and limits when they have a part in their formulation.

9. Competition between family members lessens.

10. A member's discontent can be aired and remedied.

11. Everyone is encouraged to feel important to the family.

    This in turn nurtures everyone's self-esteem.

12. Everyone in the family has a place where they can go and be heard without fear.

13. Problems of the individual members can be brought to the family group for support and assistance.

14. Children develop more loyalty and love for the family unit.

SECTION P-100
STUDY QUESTIONS FOR CHAPTER 34

Fun in the Family, Pages 248-253

1. What can play, particularly in the family group, teach children? (Page 248, line 3 to end of paragraph.)

2. Could you, as parents, begin a family game as described by the authors? (Pages 248 through 250.) Individuals reflect on family games as children and in own families. How did they go? Is there room for improvement? Group members compare together family game experiences they have had.

3. How long should you play? (Page 249, point 2.)

4. How do the children join in? (Page 249, point 5.)

5. What should you do if quarreling or any disruption starts? (Page 249, point 6 and line 9 from bottom to end of paragraph.)

6. How long should you play the same game? (Page 249, point 8.)

7. What is recommended by the authors after two weeks of playing a game in this manner? (Page 249, point 9.)

8. What do you think of the suggestion about allowing handicaps? (Page 250, line 14 from bottom to end of paragraph.) Do you think it would work? Is it fair? Individuals reflect and record answer. Group members discuss together.

9. What other kinds of fun can families engage in together? (Page 252, line 18 from bottom, ff.)

10. What do the authors recommend in regard to television watching? (Page 253, line 1 to end of discussion.) Can you see sense in this viewpoint? Individuals think about

it, using notes page. Group members discuss and resolve
it.

*If your children are strongly wanting to watch a program
you are against, if you do not think it will frighten them
unduly, you could say: "You can watch it but only if
I can watch it with you and we all agree to talk about
it afterwards." Then the experience could become a teaching
event about values. Movies of this kind can be handled
the same way.*

11. How do you handle a disagreement on which program
to watch if there is only one set? (Page 253, line 8, ff.
Also, this is a good chance for parents to model
unselfishness, fairness, and concern for others.)

12. What different types of outdoor fun do the authors
recommend? (Page 253, line 12 to end of paragraph.)

13. What makes up a large part of the fun and welds the
family together? (Planning it. Page 253, line 15 from bottom
to end of paragraph.)

14. What kind of attitude is needed from the parents? (Page
253, line 7 from bottom, ff.)

SECTION P-101
TRAINING TO PLAY BOARD GAMES

See pages 250 to 252 in your textbook

1. Mother and Father get out a group board or card game and set it up to play.

2. Invite the children to play with them.

3. Review the rules. (No rules, no game.)

4. Start the game and have fun.

5. If any arguing or whining starts or bad feelings erupt, stop and put the game away.

6. Say "We wanted to have fun. It isn't fun now." Say nothing more!

7. Go off and do something else, with a friendly face.

8. The next night, happily get the game out again.

9. Repeat this until the family can play a board game without arguing, fighting, or displaying bad feelings. You are on a "training run."

PART II
Action Guide for Teachers
Related to
Effective Discipline
in the School

ACTION GUIDE FOR "EFFECTIVE DISCIPLINE IN THE HOME AND SCHOOL"

This companion book for the Painter and Corsini book, *Effective Discipline in the Home and School,* allows an individual, parent, or teacher to take this book home, thoroughly study these ideas and methods of "effective discipline," and put them to work for themselves, should they desire. Included are two separate sets of study plans—one for the individual and a second for study group members, working with a leader/facilitator. Also included are study questions for each chapter, with page and line number answers in the text, clarifying summaries and checklists for quick reference when trying out the principles, skills, and procedures. These study questions and practice activities encourage interaction among group members.

SECTION T-1
INTRODUCTION

As in Part I, the "parenting" half of this *Action Guide* for *Effective Discipline in the Home and School,* in Part II all the subject matter pertaining to the needs and concerns of teachers is designed with only their teaching situations in mind. Included is a set of study plans for the individual person who would rather study these ideas and methods on his/her own and a second set with format of group meetings for individuals who prefer to study with others in a group.

Study questions are provided for each chapter, with page and line number answers located in the textbook, *Effective Discipline in the Home and School,* and ways to try out ideas are suggested. Additional sections are offered to augment and help to achieve a clear comprehension of what is meant and intended by the concepts and perceptions of Dr. Alfred Adler, as to the make-up of human beings and what influences their behavior. In addition, Dr. Rudolf Dreikurs' "hands on," specific application of the principles and theories of Dr. Adler is provided. As Adler's associate and student, Dr. Dreikurs' grasp of how to make this information spring to life and fruition in all directions has put him in a special place of respect and esteem in the estimation of Adlerians. As you absorb the conceptions and conclusions of these two social scientists, you also can start thinking creatively in this way with amazing results.

Further helpful information may be found in Part I, Section P-1, *Introduction,* at the front of this *Action Guide,* and could be especially useful for any potential leader/facilitator who is ready to take on the responsibility of a group of persons wanting to consider and try out these ideas together.

Wishing a happy and successful study to all. Let's get down to it!

Margaret K. Cater

SECTION T-2
THINGS TO AVOID

1. Don't Miss a Meeting.

2. Don't Monopolize the Conversation.

3. Don't Expect Miracles Right Away.

4. Don't Expect Instant Change.

5. Don't Expect Perfection.

6. Don't Worry About What Other Teachers Do.

7. Don't Try Everything At Once.

8. Don't Try the Methods Before You Fully Understand Them.

9. Don't Use These Methods as Punishment to Make Your Child Mind.

10. Avoid Talking Psychology to a Child (You're not a therapist).

(Original source unknown)

SECTION T-3
TEACHER'S INDIVIDUAL OUTLINE
OF STUDY

Week 1

Reading Assignment

Textbook: Chapters 37 and 38, pp. 273-276, and Chapters 39, 40, and 41, pp. 279-285

Study in *Action Guide*

Teachers' Attitudes and Ways to Create Respect or Rebellion, Sec. T-12

Topics to be Covered

1. Teacher's dilemma
2. Autocratic and democratic classroom atmosphere

School Practice Activity

1. Do Observe Yourself As a Teacher, Sec. T-7.
2. Observe your own interaction with your students. What happens?

Week 2

Reading Assignment

Textbook: Chapters 42-46, pp. 288-297, and Chapters 47-49, pp. 298-314

Study in *Action Guide*

1. Mutual Respect, Sec. P-19 (Parent's—Part I)
2. Check List for Setting Up Class Discussion, Sec. T-16

Topics to be Covered

1. Classroom discussions
2. Stories for classroom use
3. The class council

School Practice Activity

Notice your eyes this week. How often are they smiling? Angry? Etc.?

Week 3

Reading Assignment

Textbook: Chapters 50-55, pp. 316-338

Study in *Action Guide*

1. Teachers' Attitudes and Acts That Encourage Versus Discourage, Sec. T-20
2. Praise Versus Encouragement, Sec. T-21

Topic to be Covered

Encouragement

School Practice Activity

Try a classroom discussion this week, following guidelines suggested in textbook, pp. 291-292. Refer also to "Checklist," Sec. T-16.

Week 4

Reading Assignment

Textbook: Chapter 56, pp. 339-349, and Chapters 63-66, pp. 414-433

Study in *Action Guide*

Dangers of Praise, Sec. T-26

Topics to be Covered

1. Encouragement examples
2. Centering

School Practice Activity (Try either activity.)

1. Try the encouragement council with a very discouraged student. (Textbook—pp. 331 to 335.)
2. Try some of the words and actions given in textbook, pp. 326-327.

Week 5

Reading Assignment

Textbook: Chapters 57-60, pp. 352-369

Study in *Action Guide*

1. From Negative Interaction to Positive Interaction, Sec. T-35
2. Basic Principles in Dealing with Children, Sec. T-31
3. Needs of Children and Parents, Sec. T-32
4. Basic Causes of Problems, Sec. T-33
5. Positive Bases for Growth, Sec. T-34

Topics to be Covered

1. Goals of misbehavior theory
2. Identifying and revealing goals
3. Correcting mistaken goals

School Practice Activity (Try either activity.)

1. If you like, try a centering exercise.
2. Reword some of your statements from praise to encouragement, Sec. T-21, and in textbook, pp. 328-330.

Week 6

Reading Assignment

Textbook: Chapters 61-62, pp. 372-412

Study in *Action Guide*

1. Teachers and Four Mistaken Goals of Children, Sec. T-43
2. Times When a Teacher Says "No," Sec. T-44
3. How to Muck Up Your Logical Consequences, Sect. T-46
4. When It Is Not a Logical Consequence, Sec. T-45

Topics to Be Covered

1. Natural and logical consequences
2. Applying consequences
3. Teachers' examples of using consequences

School Practice Activity

1. Consider the students in your class or classes and identify those with a mistaken goal, Sec. T-43.
2. Decide the mistaken goal of each.

Week 7

Reading Assignment

Textbook: Chapter 67, pp. 437-448

Study in *Action Guide*

One-Hundred-Six Adlerian Concepts, Sec. T-50

Topics to Be Covered

1. Continuation of teachers' examples of using consequences
2. The C4R Schools

School Practice Activity

1. Try an appropriate consequence for one or more of your students.

2. Use Teachers and Four Mistaken Goals of Children, Sec. T-43.
3. Refer to material on logical consequences, Sec. P-31 in Part I, and Sec. T-45 and Sec. T-46.

SECTION T-4
TEACHERS' GROUP OUTLINE OF STUDY

Week 1

Reading Assignment

Textbook: Chapters 37-38, pp. 273-276, and Chapters 39, 40, and 41, pp. 279-285.

Study in *Action Guide*

Teachers' Attitudes and Ways to Create Respect or Rebellion, Sec. T-12

Topics to Be Covered

1. The teacher's dilemma
2. Autocratic and democratic classroom atmosphere

School Practice Activity

1. Observe Yourself as a Teacher, Sec. T-7
2. Observe your own interaction with your students. What happens?

Week 2

Reading Assignment

Textbook: Chapters 42-46, pp. 288-297, and Chapters 47-49, pp. 298-314

Study in *Action Guide*

1. Checklist for Setting Up Class Discussion Meetings, Sec. T-16
2. Mutual Respect, Sec. P-19, Part I.

Topics to be Covered

1. Classroom discussions
2. Stories for classroom use
3. The class council

School Practice Activity

Notice your eyes this week. How often are they smiling? Angry? Etc.?

Week 3

Reading Assignment

Textbook: Chapters 50-55, pp. 317-335

Study in *Action Guide*

1. Teachers' Attitudes and Acts that Encourage Versus Discourage, Sec. T-20
2. Examples of Praise Versus Encouragement, Sec. T-21

Topics to be Covered

1. Encouraging students
2. Encouragment versus praise
3. Encouragement council
4. Principal-student encouragement

School Practice Activity

1. Try a classroom discussion this week, following guidelines suggested in the textbook, pp. 291-292. Refer also to "Checklist," Sec T-16.
2. Review the guidelines on pp. 291-295

Week 4

Reading Assignment

Textbook: Chapter 56, pp. 339-349. and Chapters 63-66, pp. 414-433.

Study in *Action Guide*

Dangers of Praise, Sec. T-26

Topics to be Covered

1. Encouragement examples of teachers
2. Centering

School Practice Activity (Try either activity.)

1. Try the encouragement council with one of your very discouraged students. (Textbook, pp. 331 to 335.)
2. Try some of the encouraging words and actions given in textbook, pp. 326-327.

Week 5

Reading Assignment

Textbook: Chapters 57-60, pp. 352-369

Study in *Action Guide*

1. Negative Interaction to Positive Interaction, Sec. T-35
2. Basic Principles on Dealing With Children, Sec. T-31
3. Needs of Children and Parents, Sec. T-32
4. Basic Causes of Problems, Sec. T-33
5. Positive Bases for Growth, Sec. T-34

Topics to be Covered

1. Goals of misbehavior theory
2. Identifying and revealing goals
3. Correcting mistaken goals

School Practice Activity (Try either activity.)

1. If you like, do some of the centering exercises.
2. Reword some of your statements from praise to encouragement, Sec. T-21, and textbook, pp. 328-330.

Reading Assigment

Textbook: Chapters 61-62, pp. 372-412

Study in *Action Guide*

1. Teachers and Four Mistaken Goals of Children, Sec. T-43
2. Times When A Teacher Says "No," Sec. T-44
3. How to Muck Up Your Logical Consequences, Sec. T-46
4. When It Is Not a Logical Consequence, Sec. T-45

Topics to be Covered

1. Natural and logical consequences
2. Applying consequences
3. Teachers' examples of using consequences

School Practice Activity

1. Consider the students in your class or classes and identify those with a mistaken goal, Sec,. T-43.
2. Decide the mistaken goal of each.

Week 7

Reading Assigment

Textbook: Chapter 67, pp. 437-448

Study in *Action Guide*

One-Hundred-Six Adlerian Concepts, Sec. T-50

Topics to be Covered

1. Continued teachers' examples of using consequences
2. The C4R Schools

School Practice Activity

1. Try an appropriate consequence for one or more of your students.
2. Use Teachers and Four Mistaken Goals of Children, Sec. T-43.
3. Refer to Characteristics of a Logical Consequence, Sec. P-31, Part I and Sec. T-45 and Sec. T-46.

SECTION T-5
TEACHER'S INDIVIDUAL
STUDY OVERVIEW

1. You are going to be studying the use and application of Adlerian theories and principles when teaching children in a school setting. It is perhaps, a new viewpoint for you. Hopefully, you will find some help with your sobering, crucial task through these insights and suggested methods and techniques. The further we have moved into the twentieth century and approach the twenty-first century, the teaching profession has become increasingly difficult, sometimes hazardous. As has often been observed, little children arrive at school all alight, wide-eyed, and expectant, wanting to learn. However, many educators are noticing that, for a lot of these children, somehow that light goes out. Society needs to know what is putting out that light and how we can re-light it. A growing number of teachers and parents believe that a large share of the answers can be found in this Adlerian System of ideas and methods.

2. At the beginning of Part II of this book, look over Section T-3, *Teacher's Individual Outline of Study.* You will note the material is divided into separate blocks of study with accompanying material for deeper study.

3. A school practice activity to be done with your students is included in every block of study, which will help you put this information to practical use in your teaching work, should you desire to do so.

4. Areas are provided for your own individual notes and insights as you pursue this study, under the heading of "Notes."

5. Look over Section P-11, *Basic Adlerian Concepts,* in Part I of this book. Even though it is addressed to parents, its aim is to give a capsulized picture of Dr. Alfred Alder's theories and principles and Dr. Rudolf Dreikurs' practical elaborations of them. They apply to the development of children and will give you a quick view of the Adlerian

approach. A great deal of Dr. Adler's first work with children was done in schools with teachers and their students. He felt that the teacher's role was very influential.

6. Do Section T-7, *Observe Yourself as a Teacher.* It will help you when doing the school practice activity for the coming week.

7. Move on to Section T-8, *Teacher's Individual Study Plan No. 1.*

SECTION T-6
ORGANIZATIONAL MEETING
FOR GROUP STUDY

1. As the teachers come in, everyone buys a textbook and an *Action Guide.*

2. When sitting down, each person introduces himself/herself, starting with the leader/facilitator. Also go around saying how you got interested, and so forth. (As in Part I, Section P-5, *Organizational Meeting for Group Study* of this book.)

3. On 3 x 5 cards, each participant should write his/her name, address, home phone number, business phone number, and grade of the class he/she is presently teaching. On the back of the card, state how he/she learned about this study class and what he/she hopes to gain by attending the sessions. If a chalkboard is available, the format may be shown. The cards could then be filled out as participants arrive and are waiting for the session to begin.

4. Establish together the ground rules for the group. (See Part I, Section P-5, *Organizational Meeting for Group Study* in this book)

   a. Select day or night and time of meeting, and the number of meetings. Usually seven study meetings are held after the organizational meeting.

   b. Will you start on time?

   c. Will you have coffee during a mid-break, or made available when wanted individually?

   d. Will it be a closed group after the second study meeting? (This is strongly urged.)

   e. Will baby-sitting be available? Where? Costs? Sitters?

   f. Anything else important to your group?

5. Give attention to Section T-4, *Teachers' Group Outline of Study,* in the *Action Guide.* Become aware of the four headings in *Action Guide:* The Reading Assignment, the Study Assignment, the Topics to be Covered, and the School Practice Activity. Notice that each meeting deals with one week's material to be studied and done by the next meeting.

6. As with your students, all of you know that taking part in the discussion of the subject matter being considered will increase what you gain from these study sessions. The more you take part, the more likely you will continue all the way through the seven sessions and receive the value in them.

7. Notice the pages provided for taking notes and recording insights, conclusions, and so forth.

8. If time remains, look together and discuss Part I, Section P-11, *Basic Adlerian Concepts* in the *Action Guide.*

9. Take note together of Section T-7, *Observe Yourself as a Teacher.* It will help you take note of your ways of interacting with your students—your school practice activity for the coming week.

10. Look again at Section T-4, *Teachers' Group Outline of Study,* for your reading assignment in the textbook, *Effective Discipline in the Home and School,* the study assignment in the *Action Guide,* and your school practice activity for the coming week which are to be done by the next meeting.

SECTION T-7
OBSERVE YOURSELF AS A TEACHER

For one week, observe yourself in the act of teaching. Look at your own behavior relative to the following:

1. How do I act towards my pupils? Is my attitude friendly, courteous and encouraging?   Yes ___   No ___

   Or is it critical, nagging, impatient?   Yes ___   No ___

2. Do I use bribes (promises of rewards) as incentives?
                                                   Yes ___   No ___

3. Do I continually issue orders, directives, and commands?
                                                   Yes ___   No ___

4. Do I accompany instructions and demands with threats of punishments?   Yes ___   No ___

5. Do I berate or put the child down when I disapprove of his/her actions?   Yes ___   No ___

6. Is my attitude that of trying in a friendly and kindly manner to educate each child?   Yes ___   No ___

7. Are my pupils "disciplined" (punished, that is) as I think other adults expect me to, rather than treated in ways that actually benefit him/her?   Yes ___   No ___

8. Do I humiliate my pupils by publicly scolding them when they "let me down" by failing to say "please," "thank you," or failing to shake hands, etc.?   Yes ___   No ___

9. Do I insist on adult standards and manners from my pupils (such as forcing children to sit still too long with nothing interesting to do or to exhibit perfect manners?   Yes ___   No ___

10. Do I jump on my pupils for faults that I accept or ignore in myself?   Yes ___   No ___

11. Do I talk so much (lecture, moralize, correct, nag, "bitch," scold, complain, criticize) that my pupils become "deaf" to my words?   Yes ___   No ___

12. As a teacher, do I regard respect, consideration, and friendly cooperation as something to be earned rather than demanded?   Yes ___   No ___

13. Do I show more approval than disapproval of my pupils?   Yes ___   No ___

14. Do I find things to like about each child?   Yes ___   No ___

15. Do I build each child up, encourage, and boost his/her confidence?   Yes ___   No ___

16. Am I more interested in helping each child be right than proving to him/her how wrong he/she is?   Yes ___   No ___

17. Do I show partiality or favoritism and negatively compare my pupils with other children, either in or out of the class?   Yes ___   No ___

NOTES
Related to the Organizational Meeting

SECTION T-8
TEACHER'S INDIVIDUAL
STUDY PLAN NO. 1

Chapters 37 through 41, Pages 272-285

1. Having read Chapters 37 and 38 in the textbook, do Section T-10, *Study Questions for Chapters 37 and 38*. The answers can be read in your textbook by following the directions in Section P-1, *Introduction*, of the *Action Guide*, regarding Page No." and "Line No." locating. Just count the lines up or down on the page designated.

2. Using the notes page (following Section T-12), consider if you are having any experiences similar to those in the textbook, either milder or worse ones and make a note of it, along with how you felt at the time and what you did about it. Also, jot down anything of this sort that you noticed this week (your school practice activity for the week). Check again Section T-7, *Observe Yourself as a Teacher*. Was there anything there that surprised you and you want to change?

3. If you have not already done it, look now at Section P-11, *Basic Adlerian Concepts*, in Part 1, *Action Guide.* Notice the descending scale of discouragement. The worse the child's discouragement becomes, the worse his/her behavior becomes. The Adlerian view stresses the value of a steady diet of encouragement from parents and teachers, as a counteractant to this discouragement. This subject will receive a lot of emphasis in this study, along with many suggestions.

4. Complete study questions for Chapter 39 in Section T-11. Were you surprised at the exception taken to some of the methods you are accustomed to using? Which ones do you think are especially discouraging to a child? Make a note in the textbook or on the notes page in this *Action Guide*. Reflect about whether you tend to do some of them at times. If they have become a habit, think of

what ways you could use to lessen them, should you want to do so.

5. Do questions for Chapters 40 and 41 in Section T-11.

6. When looking at the two leadership style characteristics, Figure 41.1 in the textbook, page 285, it is interesting to remember that the leadership style in most businesses and industries is also changing along these lines. Managers and foremen are being required to take company classes about their style of leadership. Equality is becoming almost a "given" in America today. In many places and areas, doing so is to a large extent an ideal and a goal but the feelings and demands are becoming increasingly intense. Even the little countries want to be considered equals of the big countries. Equality might even be called contagious, and the children have caught it.

7. Look at and study Section T-12, *Teachers' Attitudes and Ways to Create Respect or Rebellion in the Classroom.* A recognition of effort is especially helpful to a child who is having trouble. The accomplishment could be a long time in coming while he/she gets more and more discouraged. Little increments of effort can be noticed and recognized, offsetting the further discouragement. Also, smiling eyes—how often do some children see these kinds of eyes? Apparently, they are very reassuring as well as nourishing from both parents and teachers. On the rebellion side, check off things you do not do. Fill in any additional traits on both sides that you are aware of from your own experience and your reading.

8. Something wants to be said about the use of your textbook, and your *Action Guide.* Teachers, rightly so, are solicitous of careful protective handling of books. But these two books are yours. You have bought them and you are urged to use them to help your study in every way. For instance, a personal index on the back inside cover of your books is very useful for any points that you feel are particularly significant and you want to be able to easily re-read for yourself or to share. These can be listed with the page number, plus, you can place a little mark

in the margin on the correct page at the beginning of the line or paragraph which will lead you right to it. This is mentioned in case you have not formed the habit. Any marks, underlining, paper clips, and so forth, that would assist your study of this material is recommended. Any help that will aid us in our effort to teach today's children more effectively is in order.

9. Follow Section T-3, *Teachers Individual Outline of Study*, in the *Action Guide*, even though you are doing this on your own. It will pace your study and use of these ideas and methods. Think about these concepts, views, and methods during the week; reflect on them.

10. Do the school practice activity for each week as listed in Section T-3. This will start you testing the validity and applicability of these ideas. Doing so is an important part of your success with this system of teaching and influencing children. Be sure to give it a try and monitor the results. For the coming week, look for directions given for Study Week No. 2 in Section T-3, *Teacher's Individual Outline of Study*.

SECTION T-9
TEACHERS' GROUP MEETING
NO. 1 FORMAT

Chapters 37 through 41, Pages 272-285

1. Having done your reading for the week, look together at Section T-10, *Study Questions for Chapters 37 and 38*. The answers can be read in your textbook, following the directions in Section P-1, *Introduction*, which provides information regarding "Page No." and "Line No." locating. These are provided with that Section under the heading *To Leaders/Facilitators*. Just count the lines up or down the page designated.

2. Consider together whether you are having any similar incidents in your classrooms of a milder or worse form, as the teacher describes. Exchange with other group members any experiences you are willing to share, including how you felt and what you did. There needs to be no embarrassment or reproach here; we are considering together how we might eliminate this sort of thing. Use your notes page for any insights and possible answers you garner from the discussion and from completing Section T-7, *Observe Yourself as a Teacher*.

3. If you have not already done so, look now at Section P-11, *Basic Adlerian Concepts* in Part I. Notice the descending scale of discouragement. The worse the child's behavior becomes, the more discouraged the child becomes. The Adlerian view stresses the value of a steady diet of encouragement from parents and teachers as a counteractant to this discouragement. This subject will receive a lot of emphasis in this study, along with many suggestions.

4. Complete together study questions for Chapter 39 in Section T-11. Are you surprised at the exception taken to some of the methods most everyone is accustomed to using? Do you see any of them as possibly very discouraging to a child? Talk about it and exchange your reactions.

Also, discuss ideas that could help teachers give up the use of those methods when teaching.

5. Do together the study questions for Sections 40 and 41 in Section T-11.

6. When looking at the two leadership style characteristics, Figure 41.1 in the textbook, page 285, an interesting point to remember is that leadership style in most businesses and industries is also changing along these lines. Managers, supervisors, and foremen are being required to take company classes on styles of leadership. How can we be surprised at children when women, races, work groups, the handicapped, and countries are all demanding equal treatment and equal respect. It is in the air and must be contagious. Discuss this together.

7. Examine Section T-12, *Teachers' Attitudes and Ways to Create Respect or Rebellion in the Classroom.* The recognition of effort is especially helpful to a child who is having trouble, as is the recognition of improvement. The "accomplishment" could be a long time in coming while the student gets more and more discouraged. Also, smiling eyes are important. How often do some children see these kinds of eyes? Apparently, smiling eyes are very reassuring as well as nourishing from both teachers and parents. On the rebellion side, check off the things you do not do. Consider the validity and usefulness of any you are doing. Fill in any additional traits on both sides that you are aware of from your own experience and reading. Talk about this together.

8. Something wants to be said about the use of your textbook and your *Action Guide.* Teachers, rightly so, are solicitous of careful protective handling of books; however, these two books are yours. You have bought them and you are urged to use them to help your study in every way. For instance making a personal index on the inside of the back cover of your text is very useful for noting any points that you feel are particularly significant, and you want to be able to easily re-read for yourself or to share with others. The key word can be recorded along with

the page number, plus you can place a little mark in the margin of that page at the beginning of the line or paragraph that is pertinent, and then quickly find it when you want it. This is mentioned in case you have not formed the habit. Any marks, underlining, paperclips, and so forth that would assist your study of this material are recommended. Any helpful "tricks" for memory or recall to augment your efforts to teach today's children more effectively are in order. Your job is a tremendous one and vitally important.

9. Turn to Section T-4, *Teachers' Group Outline of Study*, and locate the reading assignment in the textbook and the study assignment in the *Action Guide* to be done by the next meeting. Also, recognize the school practice activity to be done this coming week. Try to be faithful with your school practice activity. It will help you decide on the validity of these ideas and help you make them a part of your teaching skills, if you like. To make any difference, they have to find their way out of the books and into your teaching day.

SECTION T-10
STUDY QUESTIONS FOR
CHAPTERS 37 AND 38

Chapter 37, Example

1. What do children get out of "tricking" and upsetting adults as in the example of the teacher, Mr. Ray? (Pages 272 through 274.) Individuals write your answer on notes page. Group members discuss and give your views.

2. How did Mr. Ray's students seem to react to his efforts to shape the class into a teachable group? (They got worse.) What were his ways of influencing their disrespect and rebellion? (He yelled and tried to intimidate with anger; he threatened, deprived them of recess, only to get visibly upset, even ill, and was at a loss as to what to do. To his credit, he still valiantly kept trying to teach. Page 274, line 1 to end of chapter.)

Chapter 38, Moving Towards Democratic Discipline

1. Today we have a society that accepts social equality as an ideal and as a goal. How does this differ from the not-too-distant past? (Page 275, line 2 from bottom to end of paragraph.)

2. What reactions have we seen to these "old days?" (Page 276, line 10 to end of paragraph.)

3. According to the authors, what will children no longer accept? (Page 275, line 6 to end of paragraph.)

4. What do children tend to think today? (Page 276, line 18, "In a democracy" to "all the responsibilities.")

5. What method will not handle this classroom situation any better than the old autocratic method? (The permissive method, page 276, line 9 from bottom to "develops.")

6. What method does the Adlerian viewpoint see as the answer for teachers today? (Page 276, line 5 from bottom to end of paragraph.)

SECTION T-11
STUDY QUESTIONS FOR
CHAPTERS 39, 40, AND 41

Chapter 39, Autocratic Methods

1. Why do teachers usually use autocratic ways in dealing with children? (Page 279, line 4 to "the children.")

2. What are eight of these autocratic methods of teachers? (Pages 279 and 280 through " . . . no shared responsibility.") Individuals try to give an example of each from your own school days; note them on notes page. Group members share examples of each one.

3. What are some problems that can develop from the use of rewards? (Four are listed. Page 280, No. 4, a through d.)

4. What do these autocratic methods seem to do to children besides not making them behave and learn? (Page 280, line 13 from bottom to end of sentence. They discourage them.)

5. If they are getting discouraged, why is this serious? (Page 280, line 6 from bottom, to end of sentence.) How about this? Individuals consider, reflect, and record thoughts. Group members discuss, recording their conclusions.

6. What would make teachers use these discouraging methods? (Page 280, line 10 from bottom to "techniques." They don't know any other methods.)

7. Why are these autocratic methods difficult to stop? (They are a habit. Page 280, line 8 from bottom to "discard.")

8. What else makes discouraging teaching methods harmful to children? (Page 280, line 5 from bottom to end of paragraph.)

Chapter 40, Democratic Methods

1. How are democratic teaching methods described? (Page 281, line 1 to end of sentence.)

2. What makes the democratic method a stronger form of discipline? (Page 281, line 2 to "measures.")

3. In a democratic class system, when a student misbehaves, whose problem is it? (Page 281, line 4 to end of paragraph.)

4. What is another important characteristic that describes a democratic classroom? (Unified. Page 281, line 6 from bottom to end of paragraph.)

5. Can you see yourself doing what the teacher did in the example? (Page 281, line 3 from bottom to page 283, line 8.) How do you think it would go? Individuals note ideas. Group members share their views and record their conclusions.

6. If you had been with a group of people whom you barely knew—say, in a workshop—and you experienced such a friendly exchange while planning some guidelines together, how would you have felt about that group? (Pages 281 through 283.) Individuals reflect about it and answer. Group members share conclusions.

7. How is planning and discussing together helpful to the cohesiveness of a group? Individuals reflect and use notes page. Group members discuss. How could it hurt?

Chapter 41, Autocratic and Democratic Leadership Styles

1. What would exposure to the democratic attitudes and skills do for children living in our democratic society? (Page 284, line 4 from bottom to end of paragraph.) How would they differ from our present day children in a classroom? (Page 285, line 4 from bottom to end of paragraph.) If you would apply this to the classroom

situation, how would it help? Individuals record on notes page. Group members discuss together.

2. What is really different about the methods and ways of a democratic leader? (Instead of forcing, he/she influences and leads.) How would a teacher learn to do them? (Page 285, Figure 41.1. Study and practice.)

3. Of what do autocratic parents and teachers deprive children? (Page 285, line 6 from bottom to "equality.") How does this hurt our democracy? (Page 284, first paragraph.)

4. Considering leadership styles in the textbook on Page 285, Figure 41.1, how would a teacher who has the attitude and ways of a democratic leader handle students in a classroom? What would be different? Is there anything under an autocratic boss you would want to give up? Individuals think and make notes. Group members give ideas and discuss.

SECTION T-12
TEACHERS' ATTITUDES AND WAYS TO CREATE RESPECT OR REBELLION IN THE CLASSROOM

RESPECT

Class Discussion
   Mutual Problem Solving
Firm and Kindly Manner
   Privacy
Use of Consequences
   Full Attention Offer
Choices
   Treat as an Equal
Express Confidence
   Recognition of Effort
Smiling Eyes
   Others: _____
   _____
   _____

REBELLION

Arbitrary Rules
   Dictatorship
Cross and Threatening Manner
   No Consistency
Favoritism
   Never Offering Help
Constant Criticism
   Sarcasm
Labeling
   Nagging
Angry Eyes
   Others: _____
   _____
   _____

Which will it be in your classroom—**Respect or Rebellion?** People seldom rebel unless they feel there is no other way to get a fair shake. *Fill in more examples from your own experience.* (What about how it was when you were growing up and in school? What made you feel like rebelling? What made you respect your teacher and fellow students?) Individuals write answers. Group members discuss.

NOTES
Related to Week 1

SECTION T-13
TEACHER'S INDIVIDUAL STUDY PLAN NO. 2

Chapters 42 through 49, Pages 288-310

1. What about your school practice activity in the classroom, Section T-3, for this week? How did it go? What did you notice? Were your eyes often shining with acceptance and approval or were they more often dark with disapproval and angry frustration, even close to rage? In our culture, anger has long been used as a legitimate and useful means of influencing others and is felt to be natural. If it was really helpful in spurring our students on to do better, we could continue to do it more and more, even search for ways to be more overpowering and confounding. However, such anger is coming under question today as to how helpful it really is. Some anger is righteous, but that is something else and probably rather rare. Most anger tends to beget anger and conflict, which is not a climate for learning and growth to take place. The physical stress it engenders is also becoming a concern. We could ask ourselves two things. First, do we need to be angry, especially in the teacher role? Our charges are still learning and becoming convinced about a lot of things; they still are testing and finding out how they want to go. Our courts of justice punish adults because they have had time and opportunity to know what they are doing or not doing. Children are still learning. They are not bad yet. The second question for our consideration is, what is the purpose of our anger? Is it a punishment? Or are we hoping to impel the person to do what we want by the very energy force of anger? Or could we be hoping to threaten them into compliance by the fierceness of our anger? Our intention could be good, but more often today, it seems only to set children against us and what we have to teach them. A neutral face or a friendly, encouraging face, seem to be the most effective. We will be exploring this further. Be thinking about it and keep noticing what happens between you and your students along this vein.

2. Having done your reading in the textbook, pages 288 through 293, do the study questions for Chapters 42, 43, and 44, beginning with the Preliminary Note, in Section T-15. Be sure to take time to reflect and think about the questions and their answers. If you have an objection or a doubt, note it. As you go along with your study, be mindful of it. Some later statement or further explanation of this viewpoint could clear it up.

3. To see that in some ways a young person, even a child, could be equal to an adult seems arguable, perhaps unacceptable. To be able to take a more democratic position with your students, it is crucial that equality be seen as plausible. Turn to Section P-19, *Mutual Respect Between Parents and Children* in Part I of the *Action Guide*. It is to help clarify this aspect of Adlerian thinking. Have a look at it.

4. Do the study questions for Chapters 45 and 46 in Section T-15.

5. Look at Section T-16, *Checklist for Setting Up Your Class Discussion Meetings.* Use it as a reference when you are in a hurry.

6. Go to Chapter 47, pages 298 through 310 in the textbook, and take time to consider the use and value of stories in classroom discussions. Questions are included in Section T-15 in the *Action Guide* so as to highlight how and where such stories help form children's attitudes.

7. Consider the idea of a class council or a class government while doing the study questions for Chapter 48 in Section T-15.

8. Be aware of the many sources available for "discussion stories" listed in Chapter 49. Turn to Section T-3, *Teacher's Individual Outline of Study,* for the coming week's reading and study assignments and your school practice activity. You are being urged to get your feet wet; hold a class discussion this week. If you have never been a part of any such thing, do it anyway and see what happens. Refer to the textbook, page 291, first paragraph for suggestions.

SECTION T-14
TEACHERS' GROUP MEETING
NO. 2 FORMAT

Chapters 42 through 49, Pages 288-314

1. Any new members can be asked to introduce themselves. The leader/facilitator reminds everyone that, from now on, the group is a closed study group. Any additional members can be placed on a waiting list for the next study group session.

2. Everyone shares what happened with the school practice activity. Were you surprised how many times you found yourself frowning or troubled? Did you catch yourself very many times with a smile on your face? A little smile will do. What shows up in the eyes is what really counts. If you think about it, a smile in the eyes has the warming effect of the sun, while anger antagonizes or frightens— neither of which assist the learning process. Everything shuts down, especially with younger children; they cannot even think, let alone hear you. Talk about it together. What did you observe happening? We will be thinking more about this later in this study.

3. Go to the study questions for Chapters 42, 43, and 44. pages 288-293 doing first the Preliminary Note, Section T-15. This major use of a class discussion may be new to you, but it does seem to have a good effect on young ones today. They want to be encouraged to think, to understand what is happening around them, and to help form rules and limits that are going to affect them. It helps them to feel more cooperative.

4. To see that in some ways a young person, even a child, could be equal to an adult seems arguable, perhaps unacceptable. To be able to take a more democratic position with your students, a crucial point is that equality be seen as plausible. Turn to Section P-19, *Mutual Respect Between Parents and Children* in Part I of the *Action Guide*. It is to help clarify this aspect of Adlerian thinking. Have a look at it.

5. Do the study questions for Chapters 45 and 56, Section T-15.

6. Look together at Section T-16, *Checklist for Setting Up Your Class Discussion Meetings.* Use it as a reference when you are in a hurry.

7. Do together the study questions for the stories to be used during a class discussion, Section T-16, Chapter 47. They could be quite useful in getting children to start thinking more deeply about how they want to behave and why.

8. If time permits, talk about the value of having a class government, as is discussed in Chapter 48, pages 311 and 312 in the textbook. The study questions on it are at the very end of Section T-15.

9. Before closing the group meeting look together at Section T-4, *Teachers' Group Outline of Study,* the reading assignment in *Effective Discipline in the Home and School,* the study assignment in the *Action Guide,* and the school activity for the coming week. All of these are to be done by the next meeting. Actual use of some of these ideas and methods will help you to evaluate them better and learn if they could assist you with your arduous responsibility of teaching today's children.

SECTION T-15
STUDY QUESTIONS FOR
PRELIMINARY NOTE AND
CHAPTERS 42 THROUGH 48

Preliminary Note, Pages 288 and 289

1. Why is a democratic form of government thought by most Americans to be the best form of government? What is difficult about it? (Page 288, line 2. It is a challenge to make it work.) Individuals consider and try to answer. Group members discuss together.

2. How is democracy helpful in a classroom? (Page 288, line 2 to "work.") What can be used to help democracy work in a classroom? (Page 288, line 5 to end of paragraph.)

3. How does a teacher usually view each child in the classrooms? (Someone whom " . . . they must single-handedly teach, correct, and control . . .," page 288, line 11 to "Class.")

4. How does a teacher who is a skilled group leader regard each child? (Page 288, line 20 to end of paragraph.)

5. What does Dr. Dreikurs urge teachers always to keep in sight and why? (Page 288, line 11 from bottom, beginning with "the total" to end of paragraph.)

6. How does using the cooperation of the group for the correction of behavior help the misbehaving child? (Page 288, line 6 from bottom, "the misbehaving child," to " . . . the behavior.")

7. How does the class benefit? (Page 288, line 3 from bottom, " . . . The group . . ." to end of paragraph.)

8. What worries teachers about using the group leader method? (Page 289, line 1, to " . . . discussions . . .") However, what actually happens? (Page 289, line 3, to " . . . lessen.")

9. How do children feel about regular class discussions? (Page 289, line 10 to "belonging.") What is another benefit? (Page 289, line 13 to end of paragraph.)

10. What else bothers teachers about regular classroom discussions? (Page 289, line 19 to "church.") What about this? Is the teacher, as the authority, based on a set of values? How do the authors feel about this? (Page 289, line 21 to end of paragraph.) If studying as an individual, reflect and try to think this through. Group members discuss and consider.

11. How is a classroom discussion different from conversation? (Page 289, line 9 from bottom to end of paragraph.)

12. What about children having a deep need to discuss issues that really matter to them? What value is in it for them? (See page 289, last paragraph.) Individuals note your own thoughts on this. Group members discuss and exchange views.

Chapter 42, *What Children Learn in Classroom Discussion*, Page 290

1. What do regular classroom discussions aim to do for children? (Page 290, list of 12 points.) How would such skills be helpful to them now and in the future? Individuals use notes page for answer. Group members discuss and use notes page. Social scientists are beginning to believe that a child's conscience begins to develop as he/she identifies with the feelings of others.

Chapter 43, *Guidelines for Classroom Discussions*, Pages 291-292

1. Look in the textbook, Chapter 43, at the sixteen "Guidelines for Classroom Discussions." Take time to evaluate this kind of classroom discussion. What do you like about it? What troubles you about it? Individuals use notes page. Group members do the same while sharing ideas.

Chapter 44, *Ground Rules for Classroom Discussions*, Page 293

1. What do you and other group members think of the ground rules? How well do you feel they will work? What do you like about these rules? Not like? Individuals consider and reflect. Group members also discuss. Would these ground rules help a lot of discussions that take place in life?

Chapter 45, *Topics for Classroom Discussions*, Pages 294-295

1. What kind of subjects could students in a class discuss? (Page 294, line 1 to "discussions.") What are some early topics they take up? (Page 294, line 2 to end of paragraph.) What are some additional topics? (Page 294, line 8 to end of paragraph.)

2. What sort of questions are good and why are they good? (Page 294, line 5 from bottom, ff.) Think about it and record answers. Group members also discuss. Being skilled with open-ended questions is important.

Chapter 46, *General Structure of a Classroom Discussion*, Pages 296-297

1. What is thought by the authors to be a good way to initiate your first class discussion? (Page 296, line 1, to 297, line 3.)

2. What are you urged to persevere, even though your first efforts may not be successful? (Page 297, last paragraph.) If this classroom discussion effort could improve your experience as a teacher and improve your opportunities to teach your students, it could well be worth the work involved.

Chapter 47, *Stories for Classroom Use*, Pages 298-310

1. What is helpful about using stories to start discussions in a classroom of children? (Page 298, line 3, "Reading . . . personally.")

2. When using stories for discussion, how does the teacher handle questions? (Page 300, line 7 from bottom to "answers . . .") What is your evaluation of the use of stories in this manner? Individuals answer. Group members discuss and share answers.

Story A, *The Fox and the Grapes,* Pages 298-300

1. What insight on behavior is illustrated in the story *The Fox and the Grapes?* (Page 300, line 10 to "anyway.")

Story B, *Consequences vs. Punishment,* Pages 300-303

1. What did the mother of Jim (the first boy) teach him with her reaction to his disobedience and her form of discipline? (To lie. Page 301, line 2 from bottom to page 302, line 2.) If you had been Jim, how would you have felt? (Angry? Apprehensive?) What would you have thought? (Parents are mean and don't care about me. Page 302, line 6 to end of paragraph.) What made him lie?

2. What was missing in the reaction of Seth's mother? (Anger and loud voice. Page 302, line 17). What did Seth feel that was different? (Page 302, line 15 from bottom to end of sentence.) What did his mother stress besides the danger and the disobedience? (Not keeping his agreement. Page 302, line 13 from bottom to end of paragraph.) Which of the 4 R's was he neglecting? (Being responsible.)

3. How do you feel about Seth's being involved in setting his own unpleasant consequence (logical consequence)? How would it serve as a deterrent and a teaching experience? (Loses a share of his self direction. Page 303, line 1 to end of second paragraph.) Individuals write your reactions. Group members discuss and share.

Take special note of the last paragraph at the bottom of page 303. Keep referring to it while your skills at leading this kind of discussion are growing.

Story C, *The Bully,* Page 304

1. What do you, as an adult, think six-year-old Don's mother and father could do about Bill's behavior? (Report it to his parents.) How would it help? (Page 304.) How about their own son, Don? What does their son, Don, need to learn? (Not to be provocative himself? Walk away from any of Bill's provocative actions?) Individuals give answers and take notes. Group members discuss and record conclusions.

Story D, *Forgetful Jessy,* Page 305

1. How could Jessy's forgetting and procrastinating handicap him as an adult? (Get fired from a job for not being thorough and reliable.) According to the authors, how was the outcome logical and also a learning experience for Jessy? (Page 305, line 9 from bottom.)

2. What was the logical connection? (Page 305, line 13 from bottom to end of paragraph.)

Story E, *The New Classmember,* Page 306-308

1. How do you feel about how the second teacher handled Ronald's arrival as a new student in her class? (Page 307, line 8 to end of paragraph, and page 307, line 16 to end of paragraph.) What made Ronald feel he was a part of the group by the time he was having lunch? (People valued him enough to meet him and hear about Minnesota. Page 308, line 1 to end of paragraph.) Compare this, if possible, to your first day at a new school as a child. What happened and what did you feel? Individuals use notes page. Group members discuss and take notes.

2. What do you think about the first half hour of class each Monday that his teacher instituted? (Page 308, line 10 to end of paragraph.) What could be good about it? What's bad? Did the teacher have benefits in these procedures? (Page 308, line 20, ff.)

Story F, *Getting Up*, Pages 309-310

1. See questions in Section P-48 in this *Action Guide* about "Getting Up."

Chapter 48, *Class Council*, Pages 311-312

1. What form could a class government take? (Page 311, line 3, starting with "the form" to end of sentence.) What makes it hard for children to do well with this project at first? (Page 311, line 5, starting with "Children" through line 8, "peacefully.")

2. What is really crucial to the eventual success of a class council? (Page 311, line 8 to "at it.") What are the benefits that make such efforts worthwhile? (Page 311, line 12 to "alone.") What helps or hinders the successful development of a class council? (Page 311, line 2 from bottom to end of sentence.)

3. How are the members of the class council selected? (Page 312, line 1 to "Council.") What is the role of the teacher? (Page 312, line 4 to "restless.") What two factors are especially important? (Page 312, line 5 from bottom.)

SECTION T-16
CHECKLIST FOR SETTING UP
YOUR CLASS DISCUSSION MEETINGS

1. The class discussion meeting is not a "gripe session." It is the class' best (maybe only) opportunity to work cooperatively on planning things and resolving difficulties.

2. The teacher and every student is to help set up the class discussion format. The best seating arrangement is for everyone to sit in a circle or a semi-circle, if possible.

3. Using a democratic procedure, have everyone agree on a specific day of the week and time. Stick to it! First meetings should probably be short.

4. No one person may run things all the time. Teacher rotates the leadership as soon as students have learned how. This gives everyone a chance to feel important and learn to be responsible to the class as a democratic group.

5. All meetings are always open to everyone in the class.

6. During the meeting, make sure everyone gets an equal say. Always be sure everyone is allowed input. Students resist following a decision about which they were not consulted.

7. Once a decision is reached, everyone should stick to it. If it is a bad decision, then it offers an experience all can learn from. Decisions should be followed until the next meeting. By that time, any problems in the decisions will be clear to all and can be changed.

8. Let the class discussion agreements become the authority in the class. This gets the teacher off the hook. Relieved of the role of authoritarian, the teacher can become friends with the students and become their mentors.

9. Start the class discussion meetings around something positive, as described on page 294, line 2 to end of

paragraph; and page 281, line 3 from bottom to page 283, ff. to end of discussion. Use the first meeting to plan something fun. Doing so will help students to feel good about class discussions and will set a confident orientation towards the whole idea. Later, you can move into problem solving.

10. If a decision cannot be reached, at least agree that you do not agree! This gets things out in the open and the students will be less likely to step on each other's toes, or the teachers.

11. Remember, the goal is not perfection, but simply to improve a little each time. Class discussion meetings will never solve all your problems. But they surely can help reduce these problems to a manageable size.

12. Keep in mind that this is a new approach for most students. Children who have been conditioned to being treated as inferiors may think that this is just another trick to manipulate them. Over time, they will come to accept class discussions as a forum for their participation.

NOTES
Related to Week 2

Action Guide for Effective Discipline in the Home and School

SECTION T-17
TEACHER'S INDIVIDUAL STUDY
PLAN NO. 3

Chapters 50 through 55, Pages 317-338

1. Did you hold a class discussion this week with your students? How did they react? Use your notes page to record what happened, what you thought of the experience, and any areas on which you want to work. Becoming skilled at engineering these kinds of events can do more for your students' schooling and you as a teacher than any one thing you can do. This encourages them to think, evaluate, and learn to help with projects and problem solving. This in turn will aid them to feel good about being in your class and will result in your having a happier time teaching them. Such seems to be the usual outcome and is why it is urged that you adopt the use of class discussions.

2. Do Section T-19, *Study Questions for Preliminary Note and Chapters 50 through 55.*

3. Go over Section T-20, *Teachers' Attitudes and Acts that Encourage Versus Discourage.* Discouraging ways are so prevalent in our culture that it takes a lot of effort to change, so we offer more practice and thought.

4. Do next Section T-19, the questions for Chapter 54 entitled "Encouragement Council." This could be a valuable tool for you to have at hand for some of your students.

5. Look now at Section T-21, *Examples of Praise Versus Encouragement,* in the *Action Guide.* The concept of a difference between praise and encouragement may be hard to implement. However, doing so is particularly important to your being an encouraging teacher. Praise has long been thought of as an encouraging act but the Adlerian view finds it harmful in many aspects.

6. Do study questions for Chapter 55, "Principal-child Encouragement Process," in Section T-19.

7. Go to Section T-3, *Teacher's Individual Outline of Study*, to see what the coming week's reading assignment, study assignment, and school practice activity are. If you are ready, put the Encouragement Council, Chapter 54, to work. It can slowly but surely bring results with sometimes difficult, even impossible students. If you are not ready for that or do not have such a deeply discouraged student, try some of the words and actions given on pages 326 and 327 in the textbook that maybe you are not presently using.

SECTION T-18
TEACHERS' GROUP MEETING
NO. 3 FORMAT

Chapters 50 through 55, Pages 317-335

1. Regarding the class discussion you held this week with your students, how did it go? What were your topics for discussion? How did your students react to this new experience? Discuss together and evaluate what happened and what you might want to do differently next time. Being encouraged to think and express thoughts helps all persons think better of themselves, especially young ones. To become adept at consultation or discussion is an invaluable tool of managing in our culture today. Also, in some seemingly mysterious way, as you invite students to assist with setting up the class rules and limits, students become more willing to go along with them. Even should you feel awkward at first, you are urged to keep doing it. Practice will increase your skill and the results will be that you are glad you continued it.

2. Do Section T-19, *Study Questions for Preliminary Note and Chapters 50 through 55.*

3 Look at Section T-20, *Teachers' Attitudes and Acts That Encourage Versus Discourage.* Talk over the shifts in attitude that are being recommended. Do they make sense according to what you have studied so far? What about the use of criticism so freely dispensed in our society with good intentions? Is it really that helpful? Is recognition of effort and improvement important? Discuss together and use notes page for any conclusions.

4. Try role-playing a class discussion meeting, drawing on your experiences of last week, along with incorporating some of these encouragement ideas you have been going over. One person volunteer to be the teacher and the rest be students, each of you with one particular teacher or student characteristic of a cross section of participants. For instance, have a shy one, a talker, a clown, a belligerent

one, etc. Perhaps you could choose a story to generate discussion or decide on a field trip from a list and agree to the rules to be followed while on the trip. Another idea might be to prepare for a coming Parents' Night, what to display, how to decorate the room, and what about students serving as greeters, etc. Take turns being the teacher.

5. Do next, Section T-19 on the Study Questions for Chapter 54, "Encouragement Council." This can be a tool of real value with any highly discouraged student, even an impossible one. Discuss your opinions of it when you have finished the questions.

6. Look together at Section T-21, *Examples of Praise Versus Encouragement.* Acquire a clear understanding of the difference between praise and encouragement, and be able to make use of the idea. Praise seems to speak to the individual's ego and develops a need to be always superior to others. Encouragement assists the student to feel like an "OK" person who is likable and capable, who is an achieving and contributing person.

7. Do in Section T-19, *Study Questions for Chapter 55* on the "Principal-child Encouragement Process." Discuss whether this could be important additional means of encouraging a student who is misbehaving.

8. Close by all checking Section T-4, *Teachers' Group Outline of Study,* for the reading assignment in your text, the study assignment in the *Action Guide,* and the school practice activity for this coming week. We are spending two sessions on aspects of encouragement because of the vital importance given to it by the Adlerian view.

SECTION T-19
STUDY QUESTIONS FOR
PRELIMINARY NOTE AND
CHAPTERS 50 THROUGH 55

Preliminary Note, Page 316

1. How do the authors describe the word "encouragement?" (Page 316, line 6, ff.)

2. What does Dr. Dreikurs say is the basic cause of misbehavior? (Page 316, line 14 to "child.")

3. How does Dr. Dreikurs say teachers can discourage children in the classroom? (Page 316, line 15, from "children" to "discouragement.")

4. What does Dr. Dreikurs say encouragement is? (Page 316, line 14 from bottom, to "achievement.")

5. What can overprotection do to a child? (Page 316, line 11 from bottom to end of paragraph.)

6. What else can cause people to lose their courage? (Page 316, line 7 from bottom to "might be.")

7. What is encouragement aiming for in children? (Page 316, line 3 from bottom to end of paragraph.) Psychologists have been known to say that the adults from every walk of life and calling who fill their offices are the "perfectionists." They keep themselves unhappy and everyone around them unhappy.

Chapter 50, *Becoming an Encouraging Teacher,*
Pages 317-319

1. What about teacher's self-esteem? (Page 317, line 1, ff. to end of paragraph.)

2. What often can be discouraging us without our realizing it? (Our negative beliefs. Page 317, line 6 to "changed.") What could we do about these negative beliefs? (Page 317, line 8 ff.)

3. What is the flaw in the belief that we must control the classroom? (Page 317, line 2 from bottom to page 318 top, to "days.") What would classroom discussion contribute? (Page 318, line 1 to end of paragraph.)

4. What can we do about viewpoints that differ from our own? (Page 318, line 10 to end of paragraph.)

5. And so here we are, imperfect! What can we do about that? (Page 318, line 15 to "perfect.") How does this help with our students? (Page 318, line 18 to "teachers.") And how does it help us? (Page 318, line 19, ff.)

6. What else do we fear? (Page 318, line 14 from bottom to "challenged.") How does it hurt us? (Page 318, line 13 from bottom to end of paragraph.)

7. "But I can't keep friends. I must be inadequate." (Page 318, line 6 from bottom to end of paragraph.)

8. What will help with children who do not seem to like us? (Page 318, line 2 from bottom to end of paragraph.) And when they do not trust us? (Page 319, line 6, ff.)

9. What could be going on when children will not treat us fairly? (Page 319, line 10 to end of paragraph.)

10. How can we help rid ourselves of negative beliefs? (Page 319, line 17 from bottom to end of paragraph.) Everyone think of an example in himself/herself. Can you think of an alternative idea? Individuals record on notes page and group members discuss.

Chapter 51, *How We Inadvertently Discourage Students*, Pages 320-322

1. If we give in and respond to undue bids for attention from our students, how does it end up discouraging them? (Page 320, line 5, ff. to end of paragraph.)

2. How does it make children feel if we are always pointing out their mistakes? (Page 321, line 2, ff.) Why does telling the child he/she can do better, not really help? (Page 321, line 6 to end of paragraph.)

3. How can we encourage children who tend to end up being victims? (Page 321, line 6 from bottom to end of paragraph.)

4. What other actions and words of teachers tend to discourage students? (Page 321, paragraphs 4, 5, and 6.)

5. Do you think you ever use words like the ones listed on page 322? Do you remember how the children reacted when you did? (Dropped heads, downcast eyes, hurt expressions.) Probably the intent was to motivate the child? But did it? (Page 322.) Think back to when you heard some of these words as a child. How did you feel? Individuals use notes page. After discussion, group members do the same.

Chapter 52, *How to Encourage*, Pages 323-327

1. Do you especially like any of the encouragement procedures suggested on pages 323 to 326? Have you ever done any of them and do you remember how it went? Do you object to any of these suggested procedures? Individuals reflect and use notes page. Group members share with each other.

2. How many of these encouraging words and actions have we been doing with our students? Anyone remember an example? (Pages 326 and 327.) Individuals write it down. Group members talk with each other and exchange.

Chapter 53, *Encouragement Versus Praise,*
Pages 328-330

1. Look at the dictionary definition of the word "praise." (Page 328, line 8.) Why is praise used in this sense a risky form of encouragement? (Page 328, line 6 from bottom to end of paragraph.) What about the self-centeredness, conceit factor? Is that something to concern ourselves about? Individuals and group members consider and answer.

2. How could telling a child that he/she did very well at something backfire? (Page 328, line 5 from bottom to end of paragraph.)

3. What else does praise tend to do to children? (Page 329, line 6, "praise" to "success.") What do we want to generate in children instead? (Page 329, line 8, ff.)

4. What is the discouraging flaw in statements of praise found on page 329, points 1 and 2? (1. Overstated—child sees it as insincere or as stupid. 2. Puts child under great pressure that he/she must do wonderfully or is not good enough.)

5. When do children need encouragement most of all? (Page 330, line 1, ff.)

6. What causes a child to feel that highly complimentary remarks must follow the completion of every task? (Page 330, line 6 to end of sentence.)

7. What handicapping message can children get from always hearing this kind of praise? (Page 330, line 11 to end of paragraph.)

8. What is handicapping about it? (They are dependent on the spoken approval of others to feel "OK" about themselves and people do not always oblige. On the other hand, they can always decide to help or contribute and feel good about that.) Everyone think and reflect whether they have ever fallen vicitm to such reactions.

Chapter 54, *Encouragement Council,*
Pages 331-335

1. What could help when a teacher and a student have a bad relationship that only grows worse? (The Encouragement Council. Page 331, line 4 from bottom to page 333, line 4 from bottom.) How does it work? How would you describe it? Individuals try to state it in your own words, using notes page. Group members take turns describing it.

2. Why would some students not be able to answer questions 3, 4, and 5 on page 332? (Page 332, line 8 from bottom to "O.K.") What does the teacher do in this case? (Page 332, line 6 from bottom to end of paragraph.) What does the teacher not do? (Show any concern. Instead, project "We can work this out together. Page 332, line 4, ff.) And how does the session end? (Page 333, line 1 to end of paragraph.)

3. How is each subsequent session handled? (Page 333, line 3 from bottom to end of section on page 335.) What else can you do to encourage this student and improve your relationship with him/her? (Page 335, line 14 from bottom, ff.) What could be the result? (Page 335, line 11 from bottom to end of paragraph.)

4. How does the teacher use the "Encouragement Council" with an "acting out" student? (Page 333, Acting Out Child, ff.)

Chapter 55, *Principal-child Encouragement Process,*
Pages 336-338

1. What do you think of the "Principal-student Encouragement Process" covered by Dr. John Platt on pages 337 and 338? How would it have helped in some similar situations you remember in your experiences? Everyone reflect and answer. Individuals can use notes page.

SECTION T-20
TEACHERS' ATTITUDES AND ACTS THAT ENCOURAGE VERSUS DISCOURAGE

ENCOURAGING	DISCOURAGING
Show faith in the child.	Act as if he/she is "only a kid" or "too small," etc.
Accept failures as learning experiences.	Come down hard on his/her failures.
Accept him/her as he/she is, so far.	Don't recognize achievements that he/she is proud of (even if they seem small to us).
Reinforce his/her independence and self-respect.	Build him/her up with too much praise.
Acknowledge improvement.	Set standards too high.
Give recognition for effort. (Effort involves a risk.)	Use criticism to gain improvement.
Have the whole class remark on his/her achievement.	Correct or chastise him/her in front of the whole class.
Talk to him/her like an adult.	"Baby" the child who is no longer a baby.
See him/her as a unique individual with his/her own set of talents.	Concentrate on the child's character or personality, rather than the task at hand.
Allow experimentation.	Show partiality to a few "special" students.
Have smiling eyes.	Have angry eyes.
Add others: _____ _____	Add other: _____ _____

Encouragement is not praise or rewards. It helps a child learn about himself/herself and like himself/herself better. Encouragement is words of recognition that acknowledge the act, the thing done, the contribution, the help, the improvement, the effort, the accomplishment, and any positive feeling of your own, accurately and honestly expressed.

SECTION T-21
EXAMPLES OF PRAISE
VERSUS ENCOURAGEMENT

PRAISE	ENCOURAGEMENT
Aren't you wonderful to be able to do this?	Isn't it nice that you can help?
I am so pleased with you.	We appreciate your help. The way you did the billboard is eye catching.
That's my best boy/girl.	How nice this paper looks.
I am happy with you for taking care of the rabbits.	Thanks for taking care of the rabbits. It was a big help.
You did this so well.	I like your drawing. The colors are so pretty together.
You are such a good boy/girl.	How much neater the reading corner looks now that the books are put away.
I like you being so smart.	How nice that you could figure that out for yourself. Your skill is growing!
I'm so proud of you for getting good grades this term. (You are high in my esteem.)	I'm so glad you enjoy learning (adding to your own resources).
I'm proud of you for behaving so nicely on the field trip.	We all enjoyed being together at the school picnic.
I'm awfully proud of your performance in the recital at the school assembly.	It is good to see that you enjoy playing. We all appreciate the job you did. I have to give you credit for working hard.
Add other examples: _____	Add other examples: _____

NOTES
Related to Week 3

SECTION T-22
TEACHER'S INDIVIDUAL STUDY
PLAN NO. 4

Chapter 56, Pages 339-349, and 414-433

1. What about your school practice activity when you used encouraging words and actions with a particular student? How did it go? If you felt a little awkward with it, that is probably because our culture has not taught us to feel and act in those ways. So often we are relying instead on correcting, criticizing, reproving, or lecturing—sometimes, in strong, angry terms. Record on your notes page what you did and the outcome. If you actually put to use the "Encouragement Council," record how that went. Or make note of the results if you used the encouraging words and actions recommended.

2. Do Section T-24, *Study Questions for Chapter 56.* Go over the questions for each situation provided in the textbook, pages 339-349. These are describing actual "in class" experiences of teachers, putting to work these methods of encouragement, and could assist your understanding of their usefulness with your difficult students. If any of the examples are similar to one of your own experiences, make a note of it.

3. In the *Action Guide,* go over Section T-26, *Dangers of Praise.* The difference between encouragement and praise can be illusive. To help with this changeover to the use of only encouraging statements, which are seen by the authors as vital as well as helpful, we are providing in Section 26 an Adlerian view of the effect of praise.

4. Go to Section T-25, *Study Questions for Chapters 63 through 66,* on centering, beginning with the Preliminary Note. Possibly you are using some exercises of this nature with your students, or maybe you have never even considered such an idea. This method is viewed as outstanding by the authors. Take a look at it.

5. Turn to Section T-3, *Teacher's Individual Outline of Study,* to identify the reading assignments in the textbook, the study assignments in the *Action Guide,* and your school practice activity. If you are intrigued and convinced about the centering exercises, have a go! If you would rather wait, try to reword your previous praise statements into encouragement and use them with your students this week. Notice how they respond.

SECTION T-23
TEACHERS' GROUP MEETING
NO. 4 FORMAT

Chapter 56, Pages 339-349, and
Chapters 63 through 66, pages 414-433

1. Compare experiences with group members about your school practice activity of using encouragement techniques with your students this week. Discuss which ones you chose to do and how it went. Especially share any new insights you might have gained. If some of these ideas are new to you, discuss what you are thinking as to their usefulness. Did these ideas and methods make any difference with any of your students so far?

2. Do Section T-24, *Study Questions for Chapter 56*, which has questions for each situation provided in the textbook of examples where teachers used encouragement. These are included for you to see how some teachers have applied these ideas and actions, and with what results. Discuss together your evaluation of the results reported by the different teachers.

3. Review again Section T-21, *Examples of Praise Versus Encouragement* and Section T-26, *Dangers of Praise*. The Adlerian outlook sees the employment of praise as seriously harmful to the healthy development of self-esteem in young persons. Are you finding yourself agreeing with this assessment? Whether this differentiation between praise and encouragement is new to you or not, what do you think of it now? Do you see it as a valid view and worth making some changes in your methods of handling your students? Do the suggested dangers of praise give you pause? Compare reactions and conclusions. Use the notes page to record any insights.

4. Do Section T-25, *Study Questions for Chapters 63 through 66*. These exercises are offered as one additional way to augment the ego strength of your students. If any of you have had experience with similar relaxation and

meditation procedures, your sharing of your reactions with the group could be helpful. Talk it over. These ideas are receiving more attention today. The authors are favorably impressed with what these processes can accomplish. They give you a detailed guide of how to apply them.

5. Review together Section T-4, *Teachers' Group Outline of Study,* for the reading assignment in your textbook, the study assignment in the *Action Guide,* and the school practice activity to be done for Week 5. Do one of the suggested encouragement techniques. It is hoped you will find them valuable and helpful. If your students feel better about themselves and about life as they are finding it usually it leads to more cooperation on their part.

SECTION T-24
STUDY QUESTIONS
FOR CHAPTER 56

Pages 339-349

In each situation, what seemed to encourage the young person described?

Situation 1, Pages 339-340

Being able to feel better about his writing. (Page 340, line 5, "I think . . . encouraged him.") What did not help him? (Page 339, line 4 from bottom, ff. "I used to . . . doing wrong.") Comparing his wrong letters to the teacher's correct ones.

Situation 2, Page 340

Having a friend and the acceptance and interaction with the others. (Page 340, line 15 from bottom to end of paragraph. "Soon Chuck was . . . prestigious friend.")

Situation 3, Pages 340-341

Having a chance to share knowledge that his peers valued and meeting role models he valued. (Page 340, line 3 from bottom to page 341, " . . . from them, too.")

Situation 4, Page 341

Doing something he liked to do and did well that the other students accepted and appreciated. (Page 341, line 13, "He seemed . . . listened quietly.")

Situation 5, Pages 341-342

Learning that her peers did like and value some things about her. (Page 341, line 6 from bottom to end of paragraph on page 342.)

Situation 6, Page 342

Learning that her thoughts were O.K. and would not be laughed at. Also, learning ways to get started to think of a thought to write about. (Page 342, line 16, "I also" to "many ideas.")

Situation 7, Pages 342-343

Hearing her mother say she was smart and could learn her spelling words. Then seeing herself in the mirror say that she was "terrific." (Page 343, line 1 through first two paragraphs.)

Situation 8, Page 343

Finding that someone would spend time with just him alone and help him and acknowledge what he did know. (Page 343, total last paragraph.)

Situation 9, Page 344

Getting him interested in his own care and progress, pointing out to him his gifts and talents, arranging contact with other children with his same physical problem, and helping him realize he was responsible for and in charge of how his own life went. (Page 344, point 1 to "of self involvement," and all of points 2 and 3.)

Situation 10, Page 345

Finding he could do things by doing them, being noticed for doing so, being asked to help another to do better, and having his strong qualities sincerely pointed out to him. (Page 345, line 7 to end of paragraph.)

Situation 11, Page 345

Finding a friend who seized on any good thing he did and spoke of it in a positive context. (Page 345, line 10 from bottom to "each other.")

Situation 12, Pages 345-346

Finding out that she could be entrusted with an important job in the care and guidance of younger children and that other people knew of it, and appreciated it, and also appreciated her. (Page 346, line 3, ff. to "helpful.")

Situation 13, Page 346

Learning how really well they were doing with their particular difficulties. (Page 346, line 13, ff. to "any situation.")

Situation 14, Page 346

Having one-on-one fun with her in play time and listening with interest and appreciation during show-and-tell time. (Page 346, line 8 from bottom to end of paragraph.)

Situation 15, Page 346-347

Having his strengths emphasized and then being helped to learn that how things turned out for him was primarily his responsibility. Helping him learn to identify a smart and sound decision. (Page 347, line 5, ff. to "further encouragement.")

Situation 16, Pages 347-348

Being encouraged to read to the younger children and help them, and have them see him as older and capable. Also, arranging to have him read to someone in his family regularly and to read aloud to the class gave him a place and recognition. (Page 347 to page 348, points 1 through 5.)

Situation 17, Page 348

Having someone take an interest in her who really wanted to help her and who believed in and spoke appreciatively of her progress. (Page 348, line 14 from bottom, ff. to "be capable.")

Situation 18, page 349

Seeing some positive things that peers said about them. (Page 349, line 1, ff. to end of discussion.)

Situation 19, Page 349

Having someone really interested in him and giving at least some positive feedback and honest comments about himself. (Page 349, line 8 from bottom to end of discussion.)

SECTION T-25
STUDY QUESTIONS FOR
PRELIMINARY NOTE AND
CHAPTERS 63 THROUGH 66

Preliminary Note, Page 414

1. What are many of us, children included, experiencing in our lives today? (Page 414, line 7 to end of paragraph and line 3 from bottom.)

2. What does Dr. Painter feel helps to lower this stress level? (Page 414, line 5 from bottom.)

3. What is centering, the Relaxation Response? (Page 414, line 4 from bottom to ". . . a procedure to quiet the body and mind.")

Chapter 63, *New Classroom Dimensions*, Pages 415-418

1. With what psychological perspective are educators becoming increasingly concerned? (Page 416, line 1 to "of life.")

2. What is complicating the teachers' task of imparting knowledge to their students? (Page 416, line 8 to end of sentence, and page 417, line 9 to end of sentence.)

3. What do these authors believe would help teachers increase their influence on the motivation of their students? (Page 416, line 12 to end of sentence.)

4. What could help improve the relationship of teachers and their students? (Page 416, line 1 from bottom to end of paragraph.)

5. According to the authors, what else helps students be better students? (Page 417, line 17 to "naturally.")

6. And what can help everyone (children, too) become more creative, perceive more clearly, and find needed solutions with more ease? (Page 418, line 1 to end of paragraph.)

7. What is involved in teaching pupils to "lead out from within?" (Page 417, line 18 from bottom to end of paragraph, and page 418, line 1 to end of paragraph.)

8. What two kinds of education then, should be taught by teachers in their classes? (Page 418, line 5 from bottom, ff.)

Chapter 64, *Centering Process*, Pages 419-422

1. According to Dr. Painter, how can we prepare our children for today's challenges? (Page 419, line 2 to "intuition.")

2. What kind of stressful conditions are a part of children's lives today? (Page 420, line 3 to "acceptable.") How can this high stress be alleviated? (Page 420, line 8 to end of paragraph.)

3. What are centering exercises? (Page 419, line 8 to "of us.") What can they do for us? (Page 419, line 1 from bottom to end of sentence.)

4. How does centering help us contact our inner wisdom? (Page 420, line 11 to "certainty.")

5. What does Dr. Painter believe regarding centering and children? (Page 420, line 17 to end of sentence.) When should it happen? (Page 420, line 18 to "minutes.")

6. What results do children report? (Page 420, line 14 from bottom to "parents now.") How do teachers like it? (Page 420, line 9 from bottom to ". . . participation.")

7. When teaching centering, what is the first step? (Page 421, line 1 to end of sentence.) What suggestions are given to accomplish this? (Pages 421-422, including *Safe Space, Positions,* and *Rules.*)

8. Since closing their eyes is difficult to achieve, how do you persuade children to do this? (Page 421, line 14 to end of paragraph.)

Chapter 65, *Exercises in Centering*, Pages 423-429

1. What do you think of the exercises in centering? Have you any favorites? Have any of you ever done this? Would you share your experiences? Individuals reflect and record conclusions on notes page. Group members share thoughts and record any insights.

Chapter 66, *Life Purpose Fantasy*, Pages 430-433

1. What task as an educator does this life purpose fantasy assist you to accomplish? (Page 432, line 15 from bottom to end of sentence.)

2. What is stated about the life purpose fantasy by its originators? (Page 430, line 5 to "life purpose.")

3. How do you prepare your young students for this powerful life purpose fantasy? (Page 431, line 1 to "to them.")

4. After experiencing the "guided fantasy," how do the students' comments differ about their life purposes? (Page 431, line 9 to end of paragraph.)

5. Describe in your own words, the procedure to be followed when leading your students through the life purpose fantasy. (Review page 431, line 15 to end of paragraph on page 432, ending with "of three.")

6. Why can this fantasy be especially helpful to adolescents? (Page 430, line 9 to end of paragraph.)

7. What do you think of the responses of students to this experience described on page 432, beginning with line 13 to end of paragraph? How valuable does this suggest the exercise is and why? Individuals record thoughts. Group members discuss together and record answers.

8. Of what do the originators of this exercise caution teachers? (Page 432, line 13 from bottom to "cookbook.") Instead, what do they suggest? (Page 432, line 11 from bottom to end of paragraph.)

9. What do the authors feel is a necessary addition to the children's education now? (Page 433, line 1 to "complicated situations," and page 433, last paragraph.)

10. How do they see centering exercises helping with this? (Page 433, line 5 to end of paragraph.) Do you tend to agree with this or not? Individuals use notes page for answer. Group members discuss and do the same.

SECTION T-26
DANGERS OF PRAISE

The dangers of praise are that it can produce a person who

1. is egocentric, conceited;

2. is angry, distrustful and who has set such high standards that praise sounds insincere and he/she then thinks you cannot be very smart;

3. is dependent on expressed approval and appreciation to feel O.K.;

4. equates love with approval;

5. sees life as unfair if he/she is not praised for what he/she does; and/or

6. does not feel he/she should have to perform if there is no praise.

Another danger is that of never helping the really discouraged person, in spite of all efforts.

NOTES
Related to Week 4

Action Guide for Effective Discipline in the Home and School

SECTION T-27
TEACHER'S INDIVIDUAL STUDY
PLAN NO. 5

Chapters 57 through 60, Pages 352-369

1. What second encouragement class practice activity did you do? Use your notes page to write how it went. If you introduced a centering exercise to your students, what was their reaction? Did they like it? Were you comfortable doing it? Or if you chose changing praise statements into encouragement ones, were you satisfied with your new wording? Did your students seem happier with what you said to them?

2. This week, you will be studying some other ideas and methods which are possibly new to you. These principles and theories about what human beings are like and how they develop are central to this Adlerian viewpoint. Give your study some extra time and work, if needed. The reward will be worth it to clearly understand what is being stated. Having done your reading, do Section T-29, *Study Questions for Preliminary Note and Chapters 57 through 59.*

3. Turn to Section T-35, *From Negative Interaction to Positive Interaction,* in the *Action Guide.* The circles are to illustrate how the action of adults can affect those of the child, either in one direction or another. Realizing this helps motivate adults to make the effort to change usual reactions. Be assured that to make such changes is an effort because these actions usually have the force of a habit. In the diagram, the line starts with the student over to the teacher, and the teacher comes back to the student with a reaction. It is the teacher's reaction that can change to one that gives the student no "payoff," thus making it less and less worth the effort of the student to keep doing it. Meanwhile, the teacher can start new actions of his/her own that can begin to bring about new reactions and actions in the student (see second circle). Take some time to study this diagram, seeing what is involved. This

is quite an interesting and usually helpful viewpoint. You may never have thought before of the student/teacher interplay in this light. Put any conclusions on the notes page.

4. Do Section T-30, *Study Questions for Chapter 60*, for more details on how to change the behavior of misbehaving students with these Adlerian methods.

5. Go over the observations about the Adlerian view as it applies to children that you find in Section T-31, *Basic Principles in Dealing With Children*, by Dr. Rudolf Dreikurs. He spoke so clearly and to the point on these ideas, it will help your understanding of the Adlerian concepts and their practical application.

6. Also have a look at Section T-32, *Needs of Children and Parents*, which points out what parents and children are often needing today. Section T-33, *Basic Causes of Problems*, could help you spot what might be going on in a home and Section T-34, *Positive Bases for Growth*, could assist you in your parent/teacher conferences. Use your notes page for any insights that come to you as helpful.

   Some schools have had a great deal of success, sponsoring parenting study groups which are then available for teachers and counselors to urge some parents to attend. You might suggest this to your school principal. Perhaps offering to lead it if you feel so minded.

7. Look at Section T-3, *Teacher's Individual Outline of Study*, for your reading assignment in your textbook, and your study assignment in the *Action Guide* for the coming week. You are going to be looking at ways to change your students' misbehavior with other means than the usual rewards and punishments. For your school practice activity, consider your students and locate those with mistaken goals— identifying which mistaken goal they have chosen.

SECTION T-28
TEACHERS' GROUP MEETING
NO. 5 FORMAT

Chapters 57 through 60, Pages 352-369

1. Share this week's encouragement experiences. Have those group members who did the centering exercises share experiences. Having them share will probably be interesting to the others. Converting praise statements into encouragement statements, what happened with that? Role-playing encouragement versus praise, even using one of the actual accounts of one of your members would be good. Someone could take the part of the teacher, another, that of the student. At first, use a praise kind of comment. The second time, for the same incident, use an encouragement statement. The person who took the role of the student then reports how it made him/her feel each time. This kind of activity often helps us to see the difference between praise and encouragement more quickly. If the student role is that of a young child, have the teacher stand on a chair and/or maybe have the student kneel.

2. Do together Section T-29, *Study Questions for Preliminary Note and Chapters 57 through 59.*

3. Go to Section T-35, *From Negative Interaction to Positive Interaction,* to the diagram of the two circles. This is included to highlight the part one's own behavior plays when a student starts misbehaving. If we satisfy their goal, giving them a payoff, they will keep doing it. The arrow is meant to go from the student to the teacher, carrying the offending behavior as a bid for undue attention. The teacher then comes back to the student by supplying the attention— even negative attention will do—then the circle of action-interaction continues. If the teacher stops his/her end of it, noticing in the meantime how he/she is feeling to learn which goal it is, the behavior will lose its appeal

for the student and the motivating energy to keep it up will dwindle. Then the teacher has the chance to start a new circle. Now, he/she is acting, not reacting.

Consult together about how true this is. Have you noticed anything of this nature happening? Does it have the feel of familiarity? How about a power circle? Talk it over.

4. Do together Section T-30, *Study Questions for Chapter 60.* You are beginning to get more details on how the Adlerian viewpoint assists you to change and end a lot of difficult misbehavior; you can apply the methods with more conviction and sureness as you absorb the theory and principles upon which they are built.

5. If time permits look at Section T-31, *Basic Principles in Dealing with Children,* by Dr. Rudolf Dreikurs. His observations are clear and concise, and can shed additional light on the meaning of these principles and methods. Share your reactions to what he had to say.

6. Look together at Section T-32, *Needs of Children and Parents.* This points out what parents and children are often needing today. Section T-33, *Basic Causes of Problems,* could help you spot what might be going on in a home and Section T-34, *Positive Bases for Growth,* could assist you in your parent/teacher conferences. Consider these sections together. Are there ways these could help you?

Some schools have had a great deal of success, sponsoring parenting study groups which are then available for teachers and counselors to urge some parents to attend. You might suggest this to your school principal. Perhaps offering to lead it if you feel so minded.

7. Close by looking together at Section T-4, *Teachers' Group Outline of Study,* for your reading assignment in your textbook, your study assignment in the *Action Guide,* and the school practice activity for the coming week. All are to be done by the next meeting.

SECTION T-29
STUDY QUESTIONS FOR
PRELIMINARY NOTE AND
CHAPTERS 57 THROUGH 59

Preliminary Note, Pages 352-354

1. Instead of *cause*, with what is Adlerian psychology concerned? (Page 352, line 8 to end of sentence.)

2. How do children form their belief systems? (Page 332, line 17 to "system.")

3. What else do children need? (Page 352, line 16 from bottom to end of paragraph; page 353, line 13 to end of paragraph; and page 353, line 13 from bottom to "their peers.")

4. How could we describe children's efforts to belong through disturbing behavior? (Page 353, line 10 from bottom, ff. to "my power.")

5. What is important to understand in Adlerian Psychology? (Page 353, line 3 from bottom to end of paragraph.)

6. What part do parents and teachers play in children's continued misbehavior? (Page 354, line 1 to "the child.")

**Chapter 57, *Goals of Children's Misbehavior,*
Pages 355-360**

1. How could apperception be defined? (Page 352, line 17, ff. to "belief systems," and page 355, line 1, ff. to "with others.")

2. When is the child's goal one of cooperation? (Page 355, line 8 to "cooperation.")

3. According to this theory, when does a child start to misbehave? (Page 355, line 6 from bottom to "their place.")

4. How else could children's misbehavior be understood? (Page 355, line 2 from bottom, ff., to page 356 "purposes.")

5. What does Dr. Dreikurs identify as the four goals of children's misbehavior? (Page 356, line 3, ff. to "of age.")

6. Besides the first four goals of misbehavior, what additional goals do adolescents have? (Page 356, line 18, ff. to "and so forth.")

7. With the adolescents, what additional element has entered the picture? (Page 356, line 13, ff. to "them.")

8. In a descending scale of four mistaken goals, what does the goal of displaying inadequacy indicate? (Page 356, line 2 from bottom.) How do children first show that they are getting discouraged. (Undue attention. Page 356, last paragraph.)

9. What in today's culture tends to cause children to seek undue and negative attention? (Page 357, line 3 to end of paragraph.)

10. What do children usually first do to gain undue attention? (Page 357, line 17 from bottom to "so forth.") Why are these thought to be useless misbehaviors? (Page 357, line 15 from bottom to "not to cooperate.")

11. According to this viewpoint, what are some other forms of useless attention-getting behavior? (Page 357, line 8 from bottom to end of paragraph.)

12. *When do* children go to even more negative misbehavior? (Page 357, line 12 from bottom to end of paragraph.)

13. What can children (in fact, all of us) not tolerate? (Page 358, line 6 to "being ignored.") What makes being ignored so intolerable? (We become a "nothing." We don't exist.) Do we recall ever feeling this as a child? What did we do about it? Individuals reflect and use notes page. Group members discuss and share.

14. In what way do teachers (and parents) unknowingly reinforce and perpetuate these attention-getting behaviors? (Page 358, line 9 to end of paragraph.)

15. What is the next goal of misbehavior and when does it start to occur? (Page 358, line 13 to "attention.")

16. How does the goal of power differ from the goal of undue attention? (Page 358, line 15 to end of sentence.)

17. What do power-seeking children want? (Page 358, line 14 from bottom to end of sentence.) What is their faulty logic? (Page 358, line 15 from bottom to end of paragraph.)

18. What two kinds of power can children seek? (Page 358, line 11 from bottom.) What are examples of each? (Page 358, line 10 from bottom to end of paragraph.)

19. Who else are involved in the power struggle? (Page 358, line 6 from bottom to end of paragraph.) Even if the adults win temporarily, what have they lost? (Page 359, line 1 to end of sentence.)

20. What advantage do children have in a power struggle? (Page 359, line 4 to "will think.") What other message does such a power struggle teach children? (Page 359, line 9 to end of paragraph.)

21. As the power struggle grows worse, what goal do children seek next? (Page 359, line 15 to end of sentence.) How is it described? (Page 359, line 17 to "destructive.")

22. What do delinquent children believe? (Page 359, line 12 from bottom to end of sentence.)

23. How do adults usually respond to revenge? (Page 359, line 9 from bottom to end of paragraph.) What first has to be done to lift the participants out of revenge? (Page 359, line 2 from bottom.)

24. What needs to be realized about revenge-seeking behavior? (Page 359, line 3 from bottom to end of sentence.)

25. In Goal 4, displaying inadequacy, what has happened to the child? (Page 360, line 1 to end of paragraph.) What happens to the adult involved with the child? (Page 360, line 11 to end of paragraph and line 1 from bottom.)

26. To help a discouraged, misbehaving child move from negative to positive behavior, what must you first do? (Page 368, line 14 from bottom.)

Chapter 58, *Identifying Goals*, Pages 361-362

1. What is the identifying behavior of a child seeking undue attention? (Page 361, line 7 from bottom to end of paragraph.) What is the identifying feeling of the adult? (Page 361, line 1 from bottom.)

2. What behavior identifies a child who is seeking power? (Page 362, line 1 to end of paragraph.) And what is the identifying feeling of the adult for power? (Page 362, line 5.)

3. In revenge, what is the child's behavior? (Page 362, line 6 to end of paragraph.) Following this, how does the adult feel? (Page 362, line 9.)

4. What are the behavior signs of assumed inadequacy? (Page 362, line 10 from bottom to "misbehavior.") Why are these children often not seen as misbehaving? (Page 362, line 8 from bottom to "others.") However, why do the authors see it as misbehavior? (Page 362, line 6 from bottom to end of paragraph.) What is the identifying feeling of the adult? (Page 362, line 4 from bottom.)

5. Why is an effort made to understand the goals of children's misbehavior? (Page 361, line 1 to end of sentence.)

Chapter 59, *Revealing the Goal to the Child*, Pages 363-364

1. What else can a trained adult do when they want to know a child's misbehaving goal? (Page 363, first sentence in first paragraph.) Should parents ever try to do this? (Page 363, line 3 to end of paragraph.)

2. What action that most adults do with children is said to be futile? (Page 363, line 7 to "motives.") What could the adult do instead? (Page 363, line 6 from bottom to end of paragraph.) How is this helpful to the child? (Page 363, line 4 from bottom to end of paragraph.)

3. When should a discussion of a child's goals not take place? (Page 364, line 1.) When could such a discussion take place? (Page 364, line 2 to "privately.") When could such a discussion take place as part of a class discussion? (Page 364, line 5 to end of paragraph.) What would be the value? (Page 364, line 13, last sentence of paragraph.)

4. Describe the recognition reflex technique (page 364, line 14 from bottom to end of discussion) that Dr. Dreikurs taught his students. What signaled that a suspected mistaken goal was correct? (Page 364, line 10, ff. to "downward.")

5. What does the recognition reflex do? (Page 364, line 13, and Page 363, line 4 from bottom to end of paragraph.) How does this technique strike you? Individuals record thoughts on notes page. Group members discuss and do the same.

SECTION T-30
STUDY QUESTIONS FOR CHAPTER 60
Pages 365-369

1. What are we told is best to do with undue, inappropriate, constant attention seeking? (Page 365, line 2 from bottom to "annoyance.")

2. What makes a child continue the misbehavior of undue attention seeking? (Page 366, line 1 to end of sentence.)

3. What special technique did Dr. Dreikurs teach to teachers for correcting undue attention seeking? (Page 366, line 2 to end of description of example.)

4. When is it important to give children attention? (Page 366, line 11 from bottom to end of sentence.) What is an example of encouraging constructive attention by a teacher? (Page 366, line 10 from bottom to end of paragraph.) What kind of consequences can be used as a deterrent of undue attention seeking? (Page 366, line 7 from bottom.)

5. In a power struggle between a child and a teacher, who will win? (Page 366, line 5 from bottom.) What about anger? (Page 366, line 4 from bottom.) Do these two statements surprise you? Reflect and think of some experiences of your own with power struggles and students. How did it go? Individuals use notes page. Group members discuss.

6. What is the best thing to do in a power struggle? (Page 366, line 2 from bottom.) What is one good way to do it? (Page 366, line 1 from bottom to "I can't.")

7. What is one characteristic that you can work with to turn a child away from power? (Page 367, line 3 to "life.") Read in the textbook some suggestions of how a teacher could do this. (Page 367, line 5 to end of paragraph.)

8. What kind of consequences are effective in power driven children, and what kind are not? (Page 367, line 10 to end of paragraph.)

9. What is important to remember when a teacher is faced with a child who is into revenge? (Page 367, line 13 to "staff members.") How can you help them? (Page 367, line 10 from bottom to end of paragraph.)

10. What makes this kind of child worse? (Page 367, line 13 from bottom to "this game.") What else helps? (Page 367, line 10 from bottom to end of paragraph.)

11. What is an example of a game of encouragement that can be used in a classroom situation? (Page 367, line 3 from bottom to page 368, end of paragraph.)

12. How can a teacher use kindness to deflect a child who is into revenge? (Page 368, line 7 to end of paragraph.)

13. What kind of consequences can be used with a child who is into revenge? (Page 368, line 13 to end of paragraph.)

14. How could a child who displays inadequacy be described? (Page 368, line 15 to "trying.") How does it make the adult feel? (Page 368, line 17 to "give up.")

15. How can this child, who is discouraged to the point of despair, be helped by adults? (Page 368, line 16 from bottom, ff. to "worthwhile.") How must the teacher perceive the situation in order to be able to help? (Page 368, line 10 from bottom to end of sentence.)

16. In what simple way can the teacher start? (Page 368, line 7 from bottom to end of paragraph.) What are some other encouraging techniques? (Page 369, line 1 to end of paragraph.)

17. Can you use logical consequences, as well as natural consequences, with a child who is discouraged? (Page 369, line 7 to end of sentence.)

18. When we know the goal of our misbehaving student, what is our goal in regard to his/her behavior? (Page 369, line 10 to end of sentence.) Is such a goal a new idea for you? In the past, what would your goal have been? Individuals reflect and use notes page. Group members think together and exchange answers.

SECTION T-31
BASIC PRINCIPLES IN
DEALING WITH CHILDREN*

Dr. Rudolf Dreikurs—June 30, 1960
*(Minor editorial changes have been added)

Golden Rule: "Do unto others as you would have others do unto you." This is the basis of democracy, since it implies equality of individuals.

Mutual Respect: Based upon the assumption of equality, it is the inalienable right of all human beings. No one should take advantage of another—neither adult nor child should be a slave or a tyrant.

Encouragement: Implies faith in the child as he [or she] is, not in his [or her] potentiality. A child misbehaves only when he [or she] is discouraged and believes he [or she] cannot succeed by useful means. The child needs encouragement as a plant needs water.

Reward and Punishment are outdated: A child soon considers a reward his [or her] right and demands a reward for everything. He [or she] considers that punishment gives him [or her] the right to punish others, and the retaliation of children is usually more effective than the punishment of adults.

Natural Consequences: Utilizing the reality of the situation rather than personal power, can exert the necessary pressure to stimulate proper motivation. Only in moments of real danger is it necessary to protect the child from the natural consequences of his [or her] disturbing behavior.

Action Instead of Words in times of conflict: Children tend to become "mother-deaf" and act only when raised voices imply some impending action and then respond only momentarily. Usually the child knows very well what is expected of him [or her]. Talking should be restricted to friendly conversations and not used as disciplinary means.

Withdrawal—Effective Counteraction: Withdrawal is not surrender and is most effective when the child demands undue attention or tries to involve one in a power contest. He [or she] gets no satisfaction in being annoying if nobody pays attention.

Withdrawal from the provocation, not from the child: Don't talk in moments of conflict, but friendly conversation and pleasant contacts are essential. Have fun and play together. The less attention the child gets when he [or she] disturbs, the more he [or she] needs when he [or she] is cooperative.

Don't interfere in children's fights: By allowing children to resolve their own conflicts they learn to get along better together. Many fights are provoked to get the adult involved and, by separating the children or acting as judge, we fall for their provocation, thereby stimulating them to fight more.

Take time for training: Teaching the child essential skills and habits. If a mother and/or father does not have time for such training, she will spend more time correcting an untrained child.

Never do for a child what he [or she] can do for himself [or herself]: A "dependent" child is a demanding child. Most adults underestimate the abilities of children. Children become irresponsible only when we fail to give them opportunities to take on responsibility.

Understanding the child's goal: Every action of a child has a purpose. His [or her] basic aim is to have his [or her] place in the group. A well-behaved child and well-adjusted child has found his [or her] way toward social acceptance by conforming with the requirements of the group and by making his [or her] own useful contribution to it. A misbehaving child is still trying, in a mistaken way, to gain social status.

The four goals of a child's misbehavior: The child is usually unaware of his [or her] goals. His [or her] behavior, though illogical to others, is consistent with his [or her] own orientation.

1. Attention getting . . . . wants attention and service.

2. Power . . . . wants to be the boss.

3. Revenge . . . . wants to hurt us.

4. Display of inadequacy . . . . wants to be left alone.

Our reactions to a child's misbehavior patterns:

1. Feel annoyed . . . . want to remind and coax.

2. Feel provoked . . . . "you can't get away with this!"

3. Feel deeply hurt . . . . "I'll get even!"

4. Feel despair . . . . "I don't know what to do."

Fallacy of first impulse: By acting on our first impulse, we tend to intensify the child's misbehavior patterns rather than to correct them.

Minimize mistakes. Making mistakes is human. We must have the courage to be imperfect. Build on strength, not on weakness.

Danger of pity: Feeling sorry for the child, while natural, often adds harm to an already tragic situation, and the child may be more harmed by the pity than by the actual tragedy. Life's satisfactions depend on one's ability to take things in stride. Feeling sorry for someone leads to his [or her] self-pity and to the belief that life owes him [or her] something.

Don't be concerned with what others do: Instead accept responsibility for what we can do. By utilizing the full potential of our own constrictive influence, we do not have to worry about what others may do to the child. Compensation for the mistakes of others is unwise and over-protection may rob the child of his [or her] own courage and resourcefulness.

A family council: Through a family council, every member of the family has a chance to express himself [or herself] freely in all matters pertaining to the family as a whole and to participate in the responsibilities each member of the family has for the welfare of the family. It is truly education for democracy and should not become a place for parents to "preach" or impose their will on children, nor should it deteriorate into a "gripe" session. The emphasis should be on "What can WE do about the situation?"

Have fun together: Help to develop a relationship based on mutual respect, love and affection, mutual confidence and trust, and feeling of belonging. Playing together, working together, sharing interesting and exciting experiences lead to the kind of closeness which is essential for cooperation.

NOTE: *These statements are adaptable to teachers' activities and interactions with their students, also. M.K.C.*

SECTION T-32
NEEDS OF CHILDREN AND PARENTS

1. Children have the need to

be fed
run
make noise
explore
choose their own friends
have school be theirs
receive positive attention
help
participate
have encouragement
have consistency/security
have transportation
have acceptance and trust
make choices (where appropriate)
make mistakes
have independence
let off steam
have individual time with their parents
live relaxed in their own homes
have friends in to share their homes
have their own relationships with peers and other adults
be allowed the responsibility of their successes AND failures
have privacy at times
have the choice of activities
experience the "hurts" of life
contribute to the family
solve their own problems
get help from the family

2. Parents have the need to

have peace and quiet
have help and cooperation
have social experiences
have lack of interruptions
have a full night's sleep
have a life of their own
feel useful, not used
enjoy parenting
have positive attention
know being imperfect is OK
share encouragement
be able to make choices
have faith and trust in themselves
live relaxed at home
do their own activities
have confidence in setting limits
have individual time with each child

SECTION T-33
BASIC CAUSES OF PROBLEMS

Power struggles
Nagging
Hollering, Preaching
Punishing
Rewarding
Laying down the law, Ordering (constantly)
Threatening
Interfering
Becoming a slave
Hurrying
Criticizing
Sarcasm
Our own expectations
Thinking child is incapable
Double messages
Overprotection
False praise
Generating dependency
Not allowing experimentation
Dominating child

SECTION T-34
POSITIVE BASES FOR GROWTH

Cooperation
Mutual respect
Firmness
Understanding
Encouragement
Action, not words
Use of consequences
Withdrawing from conflicts
Routines and training time
Allowing independence
Avoiding the first impulse
Family council
Parent dates with child
Staying out of fights
Fun time
Separation of home/school
Separation of home/street
Relaxing—taking it easy
Listening/talk it over
Tone of voice—awareness of and avoidance of
    body language and double messages
Honest feelings—it will show anyway
Being willing to say "I am sorry," "I goofed,"
    "I was wrong"
Follow through/consistency
Use situations for learning/growing
Refrain from overprotection
4 R's

SECTION T-35
FROM NEGATIVE INTERACTION
TO POSITIVE INTERACTION
(BETWEEN TEACHER AND STUDENT)

NEGATIVE INTERACTION

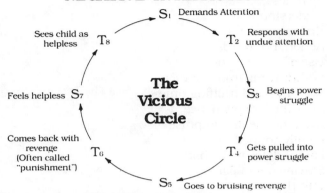

S_1 Demands Attention

T_2 Responds with undue attention

Sees child as helpless T_8

The Vicious Circle

S_3 Begins power struggle

Feels helpless S_7

Comes back with revenge (Often called "punishment") T_6

T_4 Gets pulled into power struggle

S_5 Goes to bruising revenge

Who Can Break This Circle? Who is the "Big One"? Who's aware of what is happening? Who is the one with information of what's going on and the self-control to stop it?

How to Break This Circle: This Circle feeds on itself. Simply stop your part in it and watch it starve to death.

Build a New Relationship Circle: Restrain and teach by not only breaking this vicious circle but by also starting a new circle of Mutual Respect, Cooperation, and Friendship with the student and yourself and his/her fellow classmates.

POSITIVE INTERACTION

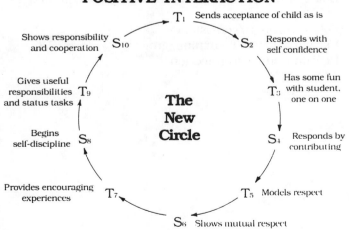

T_1 Sends acceptance of child as is

S_2 Responds with self confidence

Shows responsibility and cooperation S_{10}

Gives useful responsibilities and status tasks T_9

The New Circle

T_3 Has some fun with student, one on one

Begins self-discipline S_8

S_4 Responds by contributing

Provides encouraging experiences T_7

T_5 Models respect

S_6 Shows mutual respect

NOTES
Related to Week 5

SECTION T-36
TEACHER'S INDIVIDUAL STUDY
PLAN NO. 6

Chapters 61 and 62, Pages 372-412

1. Were you successful in locating some students operating from mistaken goals? Were you able to decide with some certainty which goal? On your notes page, record which students you located with mistaken goals and your reasons and clues that helped you decide. Next week, with one of these students, you can try some corrective actions.

2. Having done your reading, do Section T-38, *Study Questions for Preliminary Note and Chapter 61.*

3. Study in the textbook, page 377, Figure 61.1 which can assist you in identifying differences between punishment and consequences. Note the point made about the use of anger in No. 4. Remember our discussion in Sections T-13 through T-16, Study Plan No. 2, about the possible purposes of anger and their effect. You might look at them again now. Other comments by the authors about the use of anger and its results are found in the textbook on page 25, line 5 bottom; page 37, No. 10; page 97, line 9 from bottom ff.; and page 100, line 20 to end of paragraph. Consider further, the differences listed between punishment and consequences. Realize that this concept lies at the heart of the Adlerian viewpoint on "Deterrents" and is why Adlerians urge you to shift from the old to these new deterrents. The make up of today's humans, young and old, almost seems to demand it. Especially, freedom to decide within limits.

4. Take note of Section T-44, *Times When a Teacher Says "No."* This is a crucial point when using the Adlerian system. On these points the students must comply and obey. They are not open to negotiation. Think of some examples of this kind of absolute limits that would apply in a school setting. Use notes page.

5. Study and reflect about the differing *long range* effects of punishment and consequences, as stated and listed in the textbook, Figure 61.2, page 378. The long range effects are gaining a pivotal importance in the eyes of educators and government leaders, as well as business leaders. Our young people's attitudes are showing up badly today and affecting many aspects of our present and future society. Finding ways to influence this alarming development would seem to put teachers on the right track. This is also a large concern of the authors, in addition to the difficult and painful experiences many teachers are having in their classrooms. Think and reflect about these long range effects for their validity. If you see these conclusions as sound, you will have added motivation and energy to change some of your attitudes in regard to your students and the methods you use to influence their behavior. As stated already, you are being urged to do something that is probably accomplished only by a tremendous amount of work over a period of time. But the nice part is that it does not have to be accomplished all at once. Changes that come about little by little seem to be the ones that last.

6. Look at Section T-43, *Teachers and Four Mistaken Goals of Children*. Notice especially the column titled "Teacher's Corrective Procedures." This will be useful for next week's school practice activity. Of course, you already realize how important it is to decide first which goal is serving the student's mistaken purpose. With all mistaken goals, you can avoid your first impulse and do the unexpected, withdraw from the situation, and/or make use of natural consequences. However, logical consequences must be used judiciously and only when they will not be perceived as punishments. (See page 379, line 6 to end of section in your textbook.) Remembering another critical point " . . . anger doth burn the liver; avoid (it) . . . as you would a lion" (*Divine Art of Living*, compiled by Mabel Hyde Paine, 1970, Ed. page 58) is crucial during the process of effecting a change in a student's behavior. Anger begets anger or increases it. Calmness and a neutral or friendly face are best.

7. Start on Sections T-39 through T-42, study questions of Chapter 62. These examples of using consequences in the classroom will assist you to see their valuableness to teachers as at least an alternate measure. Their continued application to situations that arise could well place them in your regard as a preferred method. Go as far as you can with these examples this week. We have only one more week of structured study.

8. Look at Sections T-45 and T-46 about logical consequences. These are seen as important because, for a logical consequence to be successful, it must be applied in the exact form described or it will only have the effect of another punishment. These thumb-nail lists (Sections T-45 and T-46) are to help you check yourself before you proceed and, also, if or when the logical consequence seems to backfire. Consequences as deterrents are a broad departure from traditional punishments and are sometimes more tricky than at first thought.

9. Turn to Section T-3, *Teacher's Individual Outline of Study.* Identify the reading assignment in your textbook, the study assignment in the *Action Guide,* and the school practice activity for the coming week. You are to use an appropriate consequence for a student's behavior you would like to see change. Refer to Section T-43, *Teachers and Four Mistaken Goals of Children,* and Sections T-44 and T-45 about logical consequences, while you are thinking it out. Then, at the next opportunity, use it. Good luck! Start with a fairly easy behavior. Do not start with your most troublesome student.

SECTION T-37
TEACHERS' GROUP MEETING
NO. 6 FORMAT
Chapters 61 and 62, Pages 372-412

1. What happened with looking for students with mistaken goals? If you spotted some, share with the others, describing the students and why you think that they are operating on a mistaken goal and which mistaken goal you assess it to be. Other group members do the same. Did you see these students in a different light before you considered them from the mistaken goal viewpoint? Discuss together your thoughts and ideas about this.

2. Having done your reading, do Section T-38, *Study Questions for Preliminary Note and Chapter 61.*

3. Go in your textbook to Figure 61.1 on page 377. Talk over the differences shown between punishment and consequence. Realize that the authors are not recommending the elimination of all deterrents, but a change in the kind of deterrent you use when trying to influence the behavior of your students. When you look at these lists of differences between the two kinds of deterrents, think of the developed and stimulated young person of today, who is very mindful of the value of freedom of choice (within limits). Which column of characteristics would more likely dissuade him/her? Figure 61.1 lies close to the heart of the Adlerian System. Consider this together.

4. Notice point No. 4 about anger in Figure 61.1. In Section T-13, *Teacher's Individual Study Plan No. 2,* the use of anger when disciplining is discussed at length. If referring to it would be helpful, please do so. Also, the authors speak about anger in your textbook on pages 25, line 5 from bottom; page 37, no. 10; page 97, line 9 from bottom, ff.; and page 100, line 20 to end of paragraph.

5. Start doing Sections T-39 through T-42, study questions for Chapter 62. Do as many of these together as you

can, discussing as you go. These examples drawn from actual class experiences of teachers could assist your understanding of what this kind of deterrent can do for you in the classroom. As you try these methods yourself, you could well become convinced of their usefulness, and become more and more proficient as you go. Practice— ah—practice, isn't that the idea behind homework? We adults get our training while on the job, it seems. At least, it is faster that way!

6. For further assistance in choosing how to influence a misbehaving student to change to a more acceptable behavior, consider *Sections T-43 through T-46*. Section T-43, *Teachers and Four Mistaken Goals of Children*, will help you go about altering the misbehavior of a student. Taking up one goal at a time, you first are helped to spot the child's mistaken logic. Next you are assisted in becoming aware of how you usually react to this kind of misbehavior. (See pages 365-369 in the textbook.) Then you will find listed some other more helpful reactions to misbehaving goals. (See pages 355 through 360 in the textbook.) And lastly you review what a teacher says when looking for a "goal recognition reflex." (See pages 363 and 364 in the textbook.)

7. Section T-44, *Times when a Teacher Says "No,"* is an important part of the Adlerian system of training a child. Naturally, no child may play on the freeway or in the street at all, in order to find out for himself/herself that it is dangerous. Limits do exist which the student must accept and obey. These limits are not open to negotiation, only explanation, if needed. As a group think of examples of these kinds of absolute limits that would apply in a school setting.

8. Sections T-45 and T-46, about logical consequences, are there as checklists. If you are wondering whether a consequence is really a "logical" one, check it against Section T-45, *When It is Not a Logical Consequence*. For a logical consequence to work, it cannot contain any of these elements. Section T-46, *How to Muck Up Your Logical Consequences*, is to help you not spoil your logical

consequences, once you have chosen one, by the way you put it into effect. It could be helpful to check out these points before you act. The only way to test this new way of thinking and doing is to try it out but in an accurate and complete form. If you leave out any parts or add any extraneous ones, it probably will not work.

9. All look at Section T-4, *Teachers' Group Outline of Study*, for your reading assignment in your text, the study assignment in the *Action Guide*, and your last school practice activity. The next meeting will be your last structured meeting together. This coming week you will be putting to work the concept of a consequence as a deterrent. Be sure to think it out. Have a plan which in effect says, "If he/she does so-and-so, I will do so-and-so." Do it only if you feel you understand why it will be a workable deterrent without accompanying negative side effects (which punishment has with students.) Teachers are using these principles and methods in the classroom with a great deal of success and satisfaction and with the wonderful bonus of a "teaching atmosphere" in their classrooms. Good luck! Don't start with your most difficult student. Choose an easier one!

SECTION T-38
STUDY QUESTIONS FOR
PRELIMINARY NOTE AND
CHAPTER 61

Preliminary Note, Page 372

1. How do consequences teach children to decide to be obedient and cooperate with the teacher's rules for the classroom? (Page 372, line 4 to end of paragraph.)

2. How early can this training begin? (Page 372, line 8 to end of sentence.)

3. What goes along with planning and allowing a consequence for it to be able to work? (Page 372, line 8 to "eating" and line 13 from bottom to "a smile." In training, words from an adult are always a payoff to a child.)

4. Of what else must adults remind themselves? (Page 372, line 5 from bottom to "two.")

5. What attitude must the adults be able to take? (Page 372, line 4 from bottom to end of paragraph.)

Chapter 61, *Natural and Logical Consequences,* Pages 373-379

1. What is a one sentence description of a natural consequence? (Page 373, line 1 to "intervention.") And a logical consequence? (Page 373, line 10 to end of sentence.)

2. What is the best way to establish order and discipline in a classroom, according to the authors? (Page 374, line 4 to "year.") When should you start it? (Page 374, line 5 from "at the" to "year.") Can you do it at any other time? (Page 374, line 6 to end of sentence.)

3. In a classroom discussion about rules, how do you arrive at some consequences? (Page 376, line 5 from bottom to "arise.")

4. Which kind of consequence will always work and can always be applied? (Page 379, line 1.) However, what two characteristics must this consequence have? (Page 379, line 1 to "happen.")

5. Why doesn't an adult need to be sorry for a child while the child is experiencing a consequence? (The child is learning how to be a happy, productive, cooperative individual. Page 379, line 15 from ". . .it is" to end of paragraph.)

6. What is crucial to the selection of a logical consequence? (Page 379, line 7, ". . . must be . . ." to "child.") What else must be true about a logical consequence? (Page 379, line 11, " . . . planned" to "in life" in line 16.)

7. Why would this cause the child to learn, rather than become resentful and rebellious? (Page 379, line 13 from bottom to end of paragraph.) Is there anything that does not make sense to you about this? Individuals consider and use notes page for future reference. Group members discuss together, using notes page for conclusions.

8. When can logical consequences not be used? (Page 379, line 3 from bottom to end of paragraph.)

9. With all misbehaviors, what is a good general rule to remember? (Page 365, line 7 to "readily.")

10. Also, what is an important procedure to keep in mind? (Page 365, line 5 from bottom to the end of paragraph.)

11. Here, the importance of mutual respect is emphasized. Why would it be important? (Child will not become resentful because he/she feels discounted. Many people feel discounted today, not just children. Workers, minority races, women—even teachers—do not feel valued fairly, and rightly so.) Individuals record reactions to the concept of mutual respect on notes page. Group members discuss and do the same.

SECTION T-39
STUDY QUESTIONS FOR
CHAPTER 62—ELEMENTARY SCHOOL
NATURAL CONSEQUENCES

Situation 20, Pages 380-381

1. What natural consequence was used? (Page 380, line 2 from bottom to end of paragraph on page 381.)

2. How did the consequence flow naturally out of what was happening? (If you don't wash yourself and your clothes, you will begin to smell and look dirty. (Page 381, line 5 to "stinky.")

3. What choice did the fourth grade girl have? (She could eliminate what her worthwhile friends disliked so much about her that they wouldn't play with her or sit next to her. Page 381, line 14 to end of paragraph.)

4. Why did it work? (She wanted to belong to the group and be accepted and valued by them. Page 381, line 11 to "situation.")

5. What part did an adult play, if any? (Page 381, line 1 to end of paragraph and line 14 to end of paragraph.)

Situation 21, Page 381

1. What natural consequence was used to motivate the child's change of behavior? (A discussion on the harm stone and concrete can do to a human body. Page 381, line 11 from bottom to "dangerous."

2. Did the consequence flow naturally out of the existing situation? How? (The school walls, stairs, and floor were made out of concrete, so rules exist in order to protect the children from injury. Disobedience risked injury.)

3. In this case, why didn't it work immediately as a deterrent? (Some children insist on proving things for themselves and will only learn from experience. Page 381, line 9 from the bottom to "his head.") See Section P-54, *Four Ways to Learn*, Part I, *Action Guide for Parents*.

4. What did the injured child learn? (Page 381, line 6 from bottom to end of paragraph.) What additional learning probably took place? (Vicariously, the other children took note and began to accept offered information and rules much more seriously.)

Situation 22, Pages 381-382

1. What natural consequence came to bear on this little girl's penchant for pinching? (She got pinched back. Page 382, line 2 to end of paragraph and page 382, line 5 to end of the paragraph.)

2. Did the consequences flow naturally out of what was happening? (If you pinch, you are very likely to get pinched back.)

3. Why did it work? (Aggression usually begets aggression.)

4. What part did an adult play? (The teacher might have warned the pinching child one time. After that, you wait for the consequence to teach. Pinching hurts.)

Situation 23, Page 382

1. What natural consequence taught the boys playing ball that playing near buildings was risky? (High kicked balls can end up on high roofs. The result is no ball to play with. Page 382, line 14 to end of the paragraph.)

2. Did it flow naturally out of what was happening? (Yes, see answer above.)

3. What choice did they have? (Plenty of room to play was available far away from the buildings. Page 382, line 10 to "buildings.")

4. Why did it work? (They couldn't play ball and they knew it was their own fault. Page 382, line 14 to end of the paragraph.)

5. What part did an adult play? (The teacher warned them. The custodian didn't feel sorry for them and run around madly to get the ball down right away. He got it when he had time.)

Situation 24, Page 382

1. What natural consequence was used to motivate a change in behavior? (Running indoors risks falling and getting a painful rug burn. Page 382, line 9 from bottom to "carpet.") Did it flow naturally out of the situation? (Yes.)

2. It's easy to get hurt on furnishings indoors if you run or roughhouse. How? (The body is a bit fragile—not made of iron.)

3. What choice did the boy have? (To run or not to run indoors.)

4. Why did it work? (Page 382, line 7 from bottom to the end of the sentence.)

5. What part did an adult play? (The boy had been given the information. Page 382, line 13 from bottom to end of the paragraph.) How about the reminders? Were they needed or was it a form of undue attention?

Situation 25, Pages 382-383

1. What was the natural consequence used to motivate a change of behavior? (Hunger from going without lunch helped the boy take his lunch money along with him to school. Page 383, line 11 to end of paragraph.)

2. Was there a logical consequence here as well? Who? (Page 383, line 7 to "to me.") What was the logical consequence? (The teacher politely felt it was fair for her to be reimbursed forthwith. Page 383, line 7 to end of paragraph.)

3. Did everyone have a choice? (Yes.)

4. Why did it work? (For the boy, physical discomfort. For the mother, the nuisance, discomfort of the loss of time.)

5. What part did the adult play? (The teacher had to plan it out. Page 383, line 3 to end of paragraph.) Did anyone need to be angry? Was it an honest difference of opinion? Was the teacher involved in teaching her student anything of importance? How about responsibility?

Situation 26, Page 383

1. What was the natural consequence involved in this happening? (Brine shrimp die in too salty water. Page 383, line 16 from bottom to "not hatch.")

2. Did it flow naturally out of what was happening? (It is a natural law. Just the right amount of salt in the water or brine shrimp cannot live.)

3. What choice did Shannon have? (She decided how much salt to put in, in spite of instructions. Page 383, line 14 from top to "salt in.")

4. Why did it work? (Page 383, line 14 from bottom to end of sentence.)

5. What part did an adult play? (Page 383, line 14 from top to "and stir" and line 18 to "what happens.") If the teacher didn't get angry, why would that be? (The child was learning; she wasn't bad yet.)

Situation 27, Pages 383-384

Using the following questions, formulate your answer to each.

1. What natural consequences were used to motivate the young person's behavior?

2. Did it flow naturally out of what was happening? How?

3. What choice did he/she have?

4. Was there an information time?

5. Why did it work?

6. What part did an adult play, if any?

SECTION T-40
STUDY QUESTIONS FOR
CHAPTER 62—ELEMENTARY SCHOOL
LOGICAL CONSEQUENCES

Situation 28, Page 384

1. What logical consequence was used to motivate a change in the three students' misbehavior? (Page 384, line 12 from bottom to "floor.")

2. How was the consequence logically connected to the misbehavior? (They messed up the lavatory; they cleaned it up. Page 384, line 12 from bottom to "floor.")

3. What choice did the students have? (They could choose to mess up the lavatory, which, as third graders, they knew was misbehavior, or choose not to do it.)

4. Did anything else influence the situation? (The misbehaving students were more embarrassed than antagonized by their peers supervising the cleanup. (Page 384, line 10 from bottom to "the class.") Also, the use of a class council or class discussion to examine the event and influence the three boys' future behavior along such lines, using peer pressure and class accepted reasons why such conduct was not O.K. (Page 384, line 7 from bottom to end of sentence.)

5. Why did it work? (Other than setting up the logical consequence and the class discussion, the teacher stayed out of it. No anger was employed. The logical consequence seemed logically fair.)

6. What part did an adult play? (The teacher chose and employed the logical consequence, having first determined who the culprits were.)

1. What logical consequence motivated Mary, the student, to change her behavior? (She was to pay back all of her friends from whom she had either stolen money or whom she had pressured to buy things for her, promising to reimburse them. Page 385, line 16 to "weekly allowance.")

2. How was the consequence logically connected to Mary's misbehavior? (Mary took money, and pressured her peers to purchase items for her. Mary then had to repay her loans out of her allowance. Page 385, line 16 to end of sentence.)

3. What choice did she have? (Mary could steal or otherwise extract money from her friends or she could decide that was a poor idea. She decided to try stealing. Page 385, line 5 to "she didn't.")

4. Did aything else influence the situation? (First, Mary was confronted with the accusations of which she allowed she was guilty. Page 385, line 10 to end of paragraph. Also, a conference was held by the teacher, the principal, and Mary's parents, who decided together she should right the results of her misbehavior by restitution. Page 385, line 16 to "weekly allowance." Also, the teacher did not involve herself in checking up on her but, instead, learned from her friends that Mary was paying everybody back. Page 385, line 17 and 18.)

5. Why did it work? (Having to pay everyone back seemed fair to Mary, and the teacher stayed out of checking up on her and, instead, let peer pressure exert its influence. This made it hard for Mary to blame the teacher for her predicament.)

6. What part did an adult play? (Page 385, line 13 to "matter." Also, Mary's parents faced up to the situation and cooperated in bringing the logical consequence to bear on their daughter's misbehavior.)

Situation 30, Pages 385-386

1. What logical consequence motivated the student to make a behavior change? (If during class reading, he could only distract and disturb, he could find something else to do. Page 385, line 6 from bottom to page 386, "stopped.")

2. How was the consequence logically connected. (If you do not like to read, do something else.)

3. What choice did the student have? (Read with the rest of the class or choose something else to do that is not disturbing. Page 385, line 2 from bottom.)

4. Did anything else influence the situation? (The teacher stopped all anger and, in a friendly manner, gave him the choice to do something else. The result was that all the fun was gone. He just felt out of things. Page 385, line 7 from bottom, ff.)

5. Why did it work? (See response in question No. 4)

6. What part did an adult play? (The teacher gave up his/her anger, because it did not work and, in a kindly manner, gave Kevin a choice to do something else. Mainly, he lost his power to upset the teacher and just felt left out, which was uncomfortable.)

Situation 31, Page 386

1. What logical consequence motivated a behavior change in the students? (When they could not get a "tardiness excuse" note from their homeroom teacher, the two boys had to write an "excuse note" themselves. Page 386, line 14, ff. to "their problems.")

2. How was it logically connected to the misbehavior? (Bennie and Casey were late to class, which required a tardiness excuse note. They had to get such a note from somewhere, so they ended up writing one themselves, which was tedious and uncomfortable. Page 386, line 19 to "compose it.")

3. What choice did they have? (Be on time or write a tardiness excuse note.)

4. Did anything else influence the situation? (No one did anything interesting like get angry or agitated and Bennie and Casey were invited to think of a solution.)

5. Why did it work? (There was no payoff, only discomfort for them, and they were invited to discuss the problem. Page 386, line 19 to "problems." Also, they were informed ahead of time that they would need a tardiness excuse note. Page 386, line 11 to end of sentence.)

6. What part did an adult play? (The teacher planned the logical consequence, warned everyone ahead of time of the tardiness excuse note and he/she did not get angry or agitated. Also, the tardy students were offered a chance to discuss the situation.)

Situation 32, Pages 386-387

1. What logical consequence motivated the student to make a behavior change? (Page 387, line 1 to end of second paragraph. Also the class group consulted and came up with some very effective consequences as listed on page 387, line 3 to end of paragraph.)

2. How was the logical consequence connected logically to the misbehavior? (The four listed consequences at the top of page 387 all related to how lateness of any student would be handled by the teacher and the other students.)

3. What choice did Tommy have? (To be late and endure the consequences, or be on time. He was informed of these consequences at the time of the class discussion and the decision about being late to the class.)

4. Did anything else influence the situation? (Tommy's peer group, with himself there to consult, also came to these solutions, not just the teacher deciding for himself/herself and then issuing an edict.

5. Why did it work? (Tommy got no payoff of undue attention or power by arriving late. He just missed out, had to exert extra effort and miss recess making up the work. Page 387, line 10 to end of paragraph.)

6. What part did an adult play? (The teacher elected to ask the class to discuss the situation of lateness and decide how to best handle it. He/she also took part in the discussion in an encouraging manner. Page 387, line 1 to end of sentence.)

Situation 33, Pages 387-388

1. What logical consequence motivated the student to make a behavior change? (Page 387, line 7 from bottom, ff. to "at recess.") This consequence seems more punitive than logical. However, it was a consequence that *was uncomfortable for the students and required them to give up their highly valued recess time, which was good.*

2. How was this logically connected to the misbehavior? (The connection to the misbehavior was in that it happened close to the classroom in which the tardiness occurred, but it does not logically flow out of the misbehavior as, say, clothes you want washed but do not bother to put in the designated "dirty clothes" hamper, end up not being washed and you have only dirty clothes to wear. Dirty clothes remain central to the whole process. This consequence is more like being required to sit on a "punishment chair" at home, when you have misbehaved. But if you look at Section T-45, *When It Is Not a Logical Consequence*, only No. 4 seems to apply. It was used as a teaching/learning tool, not for the teacher to get his/her way. It was discussed and decided in a class discussion with the offending students present.)

3. What choice did the students have? (To be late or not be late.)

4. Did anything else influence the situation? (The fact that the class of students decided how to handle the problem made even the not-so-logical consequence more acceptable

to the misbehaving students. Page 387, line 12 from bottom to "at recess.")

5. Why did it work? (Because students involved, not the teacher, decided what action needed to be taken and what the consequence would be.)

6. What part did an adult play? (The teacher, instead of taking unilateral action on his/her own, invited the class to take part by discussion and a vote. Page 387, line 12 from bottom to "if they were not.")

Situation 34, Page 388

1. What logical consequence motivated the student to make a behavior change? (Page 388, line 16 from bottom to end of paragraph.)

2. How was it logically connected to the misbehavior? (The consequence is logically connected in that it flows out of the actions of the other child towards Jay. It happened in the midst of the children's interaction and the offending behavior is specifically mentioned as Jay pinches her cheek. That aggression tends to beget aggression is the message.

3. What choice did he/she have? (Jay's cousin, Alice, could continue to harass Jay or she could stop. Page 388, line 15 from bottom to end of paragraph.)

4. Did anything else influence the situation? (Jay's parents gave him information about how to handle aggression extended towards him from others. Then the mother stepped back and gave her son space in which to put this knowledge into effect, should he so choose. Page 388, line 15 to end of paragraph.)

5. Why did it work? (No anger entered into the application of the consequence. The adult kept out of it. Jay and his mother continued to be friendly to Alice after the teaching/learning experience. Page 388, line 15 from bottom to end of paragraph.)

6. What part did an adult play? (See answer to question 4.)

Situation 35, Pages 388-389

1. What logical consequence was used to motivate a change in the student's misbehavior? (The pointing system was used. Page 388, line 10 from bottom to page 389, line 4.)

2. How was it logically connected to the student misbehavior? (When a story was read to the group, disrupting behavior during that time resulted in the logical consequence, because disrupting behavior at story time kept the other children from hearing the story. The teacher's required remedial action flowed out of the needs of the situation of all the students at story time. Page 388, line 10 to "listen.")

3. What choice did the student have? (To sit quietly at story time or move away from the group. Page 388, line 10 from bottom to end of paragraph.)

4. Did anything else influence the situation? (When putting the stated consequence into effect, the teacher was firm but not angry, and the child could return to the group as soon as he/she was ready to give up the misbehavior. Also, the child was given this information ahead of time. Page 389, line 1 to end of paragraph.)

5. Why did it work? (No anger in the interaction, the student had a choice, he/she had been forewarned of the consequence, and no payoff was received from the teacher for the misbehavior, so only discomfort resulted for the student from not being a part of the group's activity.)

6. What part did an adult play? (The teacher arranged the consequence and the manner in which it would be put into effect. Page 388, line 10 from bottom, ff.)

Situation 36, Page 389

1. What logical consequence motivated the student to make a behavior change? (Page 389, line 12 to "parents.")

2. How was it logically connected to the misbehavior? (The child is misbehaving at school so, when this happens, the student cannot stay at school and must go home. Page 389, line 14 to "home.")

3. What choice did he/she have? (To behave in school or go home and try again tomorrow.)

4. Did anything else influence the situation? (No arguments and no anger occurred. They just went home. No pay-off was received to make it worth the energy. Page 389, line 16 from bottom to "teacher.")

5. Why did it work? (They were warned. The consequence happened immediately in silence and the children knew they could stop the consequences from happening whenever they chose to.)

6. What part did an adult play? (The teacher arranged the consequence and the parents cooperated. Page 389, line 12 ending with line 20, "child home.")

Situation 37, Pages 389-390

1. What logical consequence motivated a change in the misbehavior? (Page 389, line 11 from bottom to end of paragraph.)

2. How was the consequence logically connected to the misbehavior? (The chair was the source of the misbehavior, so to not have the chair when he misbehaved with it was logical. Page 389, line 10 from bottom to end of paragraph.)

3. What choice did he/she have? (To rock in the chair or sit properly.)

4. Did anything else influence the situation? (The teacher included all the parts of a logical deterrent.)

5. Why did it work? (The student was warned and agreed it was a logical consequence. No payoff was received to make the discomfort of standing and working at his desk worthwhile.)

6. What part did an adult play? (The teacher thought up the consequence, talked it over with John, warning him; he agreed to it. The teacher put it immediately into effect in silence, when the misbehavior occurred, showing no disappointment or disapproval of his choice of behavior.)

Situation 38, Page 390

1. What logical consequence motivated the student to make a behavior change? (If Michelle lost her lunch money, she went hungry. Page 390, line 8 to "the money.")

2. How was it logically connected to the misbehavior? (If you lose your money, you cannot buy lunch. Page 390, line 13 to end of sentence.)

3. What choice did Michelle have? (To watch out for her money or be careless and lose it.)

4. Did anything else influence the situation? (The teacher had a conference with Michelle and her mother together. Michelle felt a part of the solution when she was a part of the discussion and given a chance to agree. This helped her to cooperate. Page 390, line 5 to "her mother.")

5. Why did it work? (Michelle was consulted and warned. It seems as if there was no more talk about it—warnings, reminders, etc. No anger was felt or expressed. Michelle was allowed to learn.)

6. What part did an adult play? (The mother asked for a conference and the teacher complied, arranging for Michelle to be there also and suggested the logical consequence. Page 390, line 5 to "the money.")

Situation 39, Page 390

1. What logical consequence motivated the student to make a behavior change? (Page 390, line 11 from bottom to "was over.")

2. How was it logically connected to the misbehavior? (It had to do with his mathematics class work; he was coming late to his math class and getting a late start on his class work.)

3. What choice did George have? (He could arrive late to math class or get there on time. Page 390, line 12 from bottom and line 2 from bottom.)

4. Did anything else influence the situation? (The consequence gave George discomfort but did not in any way inconvenience the class. Page 390, line 5 from bottom to "this situation." Also, the consequences involved "peer pressure," which is always a good deterrent to bring to bear.)

5. Why did it work? (George was given a private warning of the new result of being late that was going to be put into effect. He was told quietly with no anger or disapproval. It was completely logical and brought in peer pressure. Page 390, line 10 from bottom to "homeroom class.")

6. What part did an adult play? (The teacher thought up the consequence, warned George calmly, and put it faithfully into effect in a neutral, friendly, manner with no extra talk.)

Situation 40, Page 391

1. What logical consequence motivated the student to make a behavior change? (Page 391, line 9 to "in recess.")

2. How was it logically connected to the misbehavior? (The misbehavior occurred during recess; during the next recess Mark had to take time out from playing and taking part. Page 391, line 5, to "the rules.")

3. What choice did he have? (He could choose to break the recess rules for the play period or follow them. Page 391, line 9 to end of sentence.)

4. Did anything else influence the situation? (Mark was a part of the process of setting up the rules with the other children. Today's children cooperate with rules and the consequences of breaking them much more readily if they have had a part in setting them up. Page 391, line 1 to "in mind.")

5. Why did it work? (Page 391, line 13 to end of paragraph.)

6. What part did an adult play? (The teacher gave the students the opportunity to discuss and decide together how recess time on the playground should be handled, etc. Page 391, line 1 to "in mind.")

Situation 41, Page 391

Using the following questions, do Situation 41.

1. What logical consequence motivated the student to make a behavior change?

2. How was it logically connected to the misbehavior?

3. What choice did he/she have?

4. Did anything else influence the situation?

5. Why did it work?

6. What part did an adult play?

SECTION T-41
STUDY QUESTIONS FOR
CHAPTER 62
INTERMEDIATE AND
HIGH SCHOOL
NATURAL CONSEQUENCES

Situation 42, Pages 391-392

1. What natural consequence was used to motivate a change in the student's behavior? (If you don't bother to listen to instructions, you will not know accurately what to do. Page 392, line 4 to end of sentence.)

2. How did it flow naturally out of what was happening? (Cooking instructions, both visual and auditory, were given. When you don't listen, you don't know, and you get poor results. Page 392, line 5 to "warm water.")

3. Was there an information session? (The one reminder in a neutral or friendly voice held an implied warning. Page 392, line 1 to end of sentence.)

4. What choice did he/she have? (To listen or not to listen.)

5. Why did it work? (It is disastrous and embarrassing if cooking goes wrong. Also, an important procedure for the teacher is to not say anything further, just show a mild concern. Page 392, line 9 to end of sentence.)

6. What part did an adult play? (The teacher provided an instruction and demonstration session. He/she also gave only one reminder and did no further admonishing, etc. When the student got poor results, the student's attention could then remain on the fact that he/she had decided not to bother to listen, instead of digressing into anger at the teacher.)

Situation 43, Page 393

1. What natural consequence motivated the student's behavior change? (They witnessed that rocked chairs can fall over in an alarming fashion. Page 392, line 13 from bottom to end of paragraph.)

2. How did it flow naturally from what was happening? (Chairs were being rocked and one of them did fall over with a resounding crash.)

3. Was an information session held? (Page 392, line 11 to end of paragraph.)

4. What choice did he/she have? (To rock the chair or not to.)

5. Why did it work? (A chair finally did go over and convince everyone that maybe chair rocking wasn't that great an idea. Page 392, line 13 from bottom to "at him.")

6. What part did an adult play? (The teacher gave the students a thorough information session—they knew about rocked chairs. Page 392, line 11, ff.) Why didn't the first natural consequence work? (Giving even one verbal warning provided enough payoff to keep things going. They had involved the teacher considerably in their antics and had become the center of attention of the whole class. If the teacher finds a way to not talk at all about the subject after the information session and uses only some firm action, this seems to work best. Page 392, line 13 to "each other.")

Situation 44, Pages 392-393

1. What natural consequence motivated the student's behavior change? (Page 392, line 4 from bottom to end of paragraph.)

2. How did the consequence flow naturally out of what was happening? (If you don't listen to instructions, you don't know the correct thing to do.)

3. Was an information session held? (Before working on a car, during the very thorough instruction session, the

importance of bending their energies towards listening to what is being said could be stated in a neutral manner. Page 392, line 7 from bottom to end of paragraph.)

4. What choice did the students have? (To listen or not to listen.)

5. Why did it work? (Having such disastrous results when using those kind of skills and knowledge is very embarrassing in front of his/her peers and others. Page 392, line 2 from bottom to end of paragraph.)

6. What part did an adult play? (The teacher stayed out of it. He/she did not admonish, remind, or react strongly at the results, so the students had to direct their anger at themselves for not listening.)

Situation 45, Page 393

1. What was the natural consequence that motivated the students' behavior change? (Page 393, line 14 to end of paragraph.)

2. How did the consequence flow naturally out of what was happening? (When your body is busy trying to digest a lot of food, you cannot ask it to make an all-out effort physically in another direction. It will stop you by jamming, so to speak.)

3. Was an information session held? (Page 393, line 5 to "game time.")

4. What choice did Billy have? (To eat a light meal four hours before the game or not to.)

5. Why did it work? (What had gone wrong was very clear. He had been warned, and the devastating effect of the peer pressure was felt. The perception of having let his team and his school down was an unpleasant experience. Page 393 line 10 from bottom to end of paragraph.)

6. What part did an adult play? (No adult accompanied him to the locker room, admonishing or lecturing him along the way. He had only his own part in the event to concentrate on.)

Situation 46, Pages 393-394

1. What natural consequence was used to motivate a change in the student's behavior? (Since she didn't pay attention to the class presentation of the subject material, she got a failing grade in the quiz that followed. Page 394, line 7 to end of paragraph.)

2. Did the consequence flow naturally out of what was happening? (If you don't listen and absorb subject information at the time it is being given, how can you answer the quiz questions? Page 394, line 13 to "the quiz.")

3. What choice did the student have? (To pay attention at the subject presentation time or to busy herself with something else. Page 394, line 7 to "autographs.")

4. Did anything else influence the situation? (The teacher's decision to not warn or admonish the student any further, and instead, to let matters take their course. Page 394, line 9 to end of paragraph.)

5. Why did it work? (The teacher was friendly but firm, and he/she was not willing to warn the student any further, letting the student learn from the results.)

6. Why didn't the student resent the outcome of her behavior in class? (Because she had been clearly and amply warned and given her right to be wrong and learn from the results. No one took her to task or put her down while she was having this learning experience. Page 394, line 17 to end of paragraph.)

Situation 47, Pages 394-395

1. What natural consequence was used to motivate a change in the student's behavior? (If you don't keep track of

the cookies' baking time, they can burn and not taste good. Page 394, line 4 from bottom to "themselves.")

2. Did the consequence flow naturally out of what was happening? (Yes. If you don't watch the baking time of cookies, they can bake too long, and they will burn.)

3. What choice did the students have? (To watch the baking time of the cookies and turn off the oven or get busy with something else and forget about them.)

4. Was an information session held? (Yes. Page 394, line 4 from bottom starting with ". . . as they're taught," and ending with "the time," line 5.)

5. Why did it work? (Most people don't like to eat burnt cookies, and the students were allowed to learn from the results without any further verbal teaching or admonishing. Taking any student to task in front of their fellow students about a failure can interfere with their willingness to learn from the consequence, it seems.)

Situation 48, Page 395

1. What natural consequence was used to motivate a change in the students' behavior? (If you are asleep, you cannot hear when important instructions are being given. Page 395, line 17 to end of paragraph.)

2. Did the consequence flow naturally out of what was happening? (Yes. The conditions of the situation made it easy to fall asleep. Page 395, line 4 to "sleeping children.")

3. Was an information session held? (Not per se. The consequences revealed themselves as events transpired. Since no danger was involved, an information session was not a vital factor.)

4. What choice did the students have? (To allow themselves to fall asleep or see that they made themselves remain awake and alert.)

5. Why did it work? (The embarrassment and the discomfort of the inconvenience that resulted. Page 394, line 17 to end of paragraph.)

6. Did anything else influence the situation? (Yes, the teacher provided no payoff by demanding that students stay awake; therefore, the teacher avoided risking the development of a power struggle or the lure of negative attention.)

Situation 49, Pages 395-396

1. What natural consequence was used to motivate change in the students' behavior? (If you do not make an effort to learn the material, you will experience the discomfort of embarrassment and failure when being tested. Page 396, line 1 to "frustrated.")

2. Did the consequence flow naturally out of what was happening? (Yes. Mastery of new subject information and subsequent satisfactory school performance can only happen as a result of effort on students' parts. Learning does not just happen.)

3. What choice did the students have? (Choose to pay attention and then use and practice their understanding of what they were learning in their classwork and homework assignments, or choose not to. Page 395, line 9 from bottom to end of paragraph.)

4. Why did it work? (The students learned from their own experiences, the result of their choices. Page 396, line 1 to "assignments.")

5. Did anything else influence the situation? (No payoff of a possible power struggle or negative attention was present. Page 396, line 8 to end of paragraph.)

6. What part did an adult play? (The teacher set up the structure of the situation and did not supply any payoff.)

Situation 50, Pages 396-397

1. What natural consequences motivated a change in the students' behavior? (Page 396, line 5 from bottom to end of paragraph.)

2. Did the consequence flow naturally out of what was happening? (Yes. Time keeps passing inexorably, and if you let it slip by without completing your work, no way exists to turn your work in on time. The agreement was that no extensions of deadlines would be allowed. Page 396, line 13 from bottom to end of sentence.)

3. What choice did the students have? (They could choose to not procrastinate and get their work done and handed in or not to do so. Page 396, line 5 from bottom to end of paragraph.)

4. Why did it work? (The students were given the opportunity to speak to the problem and its solution. Page 396, line 13 to "consequence." Also, everyone was treated the same, which avoided resentment and revenge behavior. Page 396, line 13 from bottom to "deadlines.")

5. Did anything else influence the situation? (The rules covering the typewriting class regarding classwork and completion of assignments, time for doing classwork, and the deadline for completing assignments were clear and known to all. There was no reminding or other forms of pressure applied. Page 396, line 13 from bottom to end of paragraph.)

6. What part did an adult play? (The teacher called for an arranged time for a class discussion and then faithfully followed the solution that was chosen by consensus. Page 396, line 13 from bottom including "We held a class discussion . . ." to end of sentence.)

Situation 51, Page 397

1. What natural consequence was used to motivate the students to make a change in their behavior? (No sharing of water would occur with people who neglected to bring their water. Page 397, line 13 to end of sentence.)

2. Did the consequence flow naturally out of what was happening? (Yes, if we don't have water to drink when our bodies need it, we can become painfully thirsty.)

3. What choice did the students have? (They could remember to bring their water or forget it and become thirsty. Page 397, line 13 to end of paragraph.)

4. Why did it work? (Because they had all agreed on how to handle the problem and learned together that the whole group would not be able to complete their hike under such circumstances. The guilty ones felt the peer pressure of having let the whole group down. Page 397, line 17 to end of paragraph.)

5. Did anything else influence the situation? (Holding a meeting to search for a way to solve the problem. Being allowed and encouraged to consult about a problem and give their input on something that affects them helps students to take responsibility for the problem and its solution. This harkens back to the "no taxation without representation," one of the earliest dictums of this country's beginnings. Page 397, line 13 to "next hike.")

6. What part did an adult play? (The teacher allowed and took part in a joint meeting about the problem. Page 397, line 13 "We held a meeting.")

Situation 52, Pages 397-398

Using the questions below, do Situation 52

1. What natural consequence was used to motivate a change in the student's behavior?

2. Did the consequence flow naturally out of what was happening?

3. What choice did the student have?

4. Did anything else influence the situation?

5. Why did it work?

6. What part did an adult play?

SECTION T-42
STUDY QUESTIONS FOR
CHAPTER 62
INTERMEDIATE AND HIGH SCHOOL
LOGICAL CONSEQUENCES

Situation 53, Pages 398-399

1. What logical consequence motivated the students to change their behavior? (Page 399, line 10 to end of sentence.)

2. How was the consequence logically connected to the misbehavior? (If you can't take a shower safely, then don't take one. Page 399, top.)

3. What choice did the students have? (They could take a shower, observing safe practices, or not take a shower at all and go to study hall instead. Page 399, top, line 10 to end of paragraph.)

4. Did anything else influence the situation? (All the students talked it over and decided on the consequence if the unsafe practices in the shower did not stop. This brought peer pressure to bear on the situation. Page 399, line 9.)

5. Why did it work? (The teacher pulled back and allowed the students to work it out. Also, the teacher expressed no value judgment on which choice was made by individual students.)

6. What part did an adult play? (The teacher encouraged the students to talk over the problem and take responsibility for the problem.)

Situation 54, Pages 399-400

1. What logical consequence motivated the student to change his/her behavior? (This consequence is logically connected to the tardiness only in that it has to do with the ceramic lab. It borders on being seen as punitive by the students. Page 399, line 11 from bottom to end of sentence.)

2. How was the consequence logically connected to the tardiness? (It was connected to the activities in the ceramics lab.)

3. What choice did the students have? (They could be on time or spend five minutes on lab cleanup tasks. Page 399, line 11 from bottom.)

4. Why did it work? (The students talked it over and decided together what the consequence would be. This made the tardy student feel he/she had let his/her fellow classmates down. Page 399, line 13 from bottom to end of paragraph.)

5. What part did an adult play? (The teacher encouraged the class discussion of the problem and cooperated with the students' choice of consequence. The teacher also did not express in words or body language any value judgment of the choice the students had made.)

Situation 55, Page 400

1. What logical consequence motivated a change in the behavior of the students? (If the student is late, he/she misses taking the test because the classroom door is locked to insure no interruptions while the other students are taking the speed test. Page 400, line 9 to end of paragraph.)

2. How was the consequence logically connected to the misbehavior? (Being late results in being locked out and missing the test. Page 400, line 9 to end of paragraph.)

3. What choice did the students have? (To be on time or miss the test. Page 400, line 14 to end of paragraph.)

4. Did anything else influence the situation? (The teacher refrained from expressing any disapproval of the students' choice to be late. He/she allowed students their right to be wrong, and hopefully, learn from the results.)

5. Why did it work? (The consequence was logically connected and an atmosphere conducive to learning from experience prevailed.)

6. What part did an adult play? (The teacher chose the logical consequence and gave the students plenty of warning as to how class tests would be conducted and then followed through.)

Situation 56, Pages 400-401

1. What logical consequence motivated a change in the students' behavior? (Page 401, line 1 to end of paragraph.)

2. How was it logically connected to the disturbing behavior, "Complaints and Conflicts?" (Register early or choice of subject will be limited or non-existent.)

3. What choice did the student have? (Register late or register early.)

4. Did anything else influence the situation? (The guidelines and parameters are so clearly set up and so logically connected to the task of late, the student would find it hard to fight it and not comply.)

5. Why did it work? (No reminding or nagging occurred, just logical information given, and the student was left to comply.)

6. What part did an adult play? (The teacher thought up the logical procedure and made it clearly known to all. Then he/she sat back and let whatever happened, happen.)

Situation 57, Page 401

1. What logical consequence motivated a change in the student's behavior? (Page 401, line 14 to "without lunch for the day.")

2. How was it logically connected to the misbehavior? (If you have not remembered your lunch money, you cannot buy lunch. Page 401, line 15 to end of sentence.)

3. What choice did the student have? (Remember to bring and take care of his lunch money or not bother to do it and go without lunch. Page 401, line 13 to "the day.")

4. Did anything else influence the situation? (The mother *and* the son talked with the teacher and decided *together* what the logical consequence would be. The son also was helped to know what was important about remembering one's lunch money. Page 401, line 10 to "lose it.")

5. Why did it work? (Logical consequences will usually work, especially if no expressions of disapproval by any adult are allowed to creep in while putting the consequence into effect. The student is allowed to make the wrong choice and learn from experience without being judged.)

6. What part did an adult play? (The teacher arranged for the mother and son to talk it over with her and look for a solution. Also, the mother cooperated and agreed to allow the son to take part in the consultation.)

Situation 58, Pages 401-402

1. What logical consequence motivated a change in the student's behavior? (Page 401, line 1 from bottom to end of sentence.)

2. How was it logically connected to this behavior? (The teacher was not willing to put his/her energies into a procedure that would not work, but the student was free to use his time and energies in that direction. Page 401, line 1 from bottom to "to work.")

3. What choice did the student have? (To use a procedure that would work or pursue a useless one.)

4. Did anything else influence the situation? (The teacher refrained from being drawn into an argument and moved away from the situation, providing no payoff to the student for his misbehavior. Page 402, line 2 to end of sentence. Also, the teacher provided encouragement by complimenting the student on his successful piece of pottery, resulting from his choice of a workable method.)

5. Why did it work? (Since the student was gaining nothing from his rebellion and was only ending up with a collapsing

piece of pottery, he, on his own, decided to change directions to the method shown to the class by the teacher. Page 402, line 3 to "success.")

6. What part did an adult play? (The teacher decided to withdraw from the power struggle and let the student get on with his rebellious behavior and experience the results. He/she did not belittle the student by commenting on his change of direction and now ending up with a nice piece of pottery—only complimenting the results. Page 402, line 6 to end of paragraph.)

Situation 59, Page 402

1. What logical consequence resulted in a change in the student's behavior? (Page 402, line 13 from bottom to "participate.")

2. How was the logical consequence related to the misbehavior? (If you do not bother to do your part and get your permission slips, etc., by the deadline, you cannot take part in the State Special Olympics that year. Page 402, line 19 to end of paragraph.)

3. What choice did the student have? (To make the effort to get his/her permission slips and physical examinations turned in by the deadline or procrastinate about it and miss the deadline.)

4. Did anything else influence the situation? (Each student knew he/she had been thoroughly informed about the terms for taking part in the State Special Olympics. No harsh scoldings were used when they chose not to be sure their forms were turned in on time, and each was given the hope of taking part next year. Page 402, line 12 from bottom to "next year.")

5. Why did it work? (Because all the necessary parts of using a logical consequence were included.)

6. What part did an adult play? (The teacher thoroughly informed each student of the rules for taking part in

the event and explained each form to each student. He/
she then followed through and gave no tardy student
any extra special service. Instead, he/she let the logical
consequence happen. He/she also refrained from scolding,
instead pointing out the fact that they would have a chance
to take part next year. Page 402, line 17 ff. to "next
year.")

Situation 60, Page 403

1. What logical consequence motivated a change in the
   student's behavior? (No student without a pencil could
   borrow a pencil form the teacher or another student,
   and all assignments had to be in on time. The person
   without a pencil could use a chalkboard space to do his/
   her assignment, if he/she wished. Page 403, line 10 to
   "uncomfortable.")

2. How was the logical consequence connected to the
   misbehavior? (If you had no pencil and could not borrow
   one, how could you do your assignment comfortably at
   your seat and get it in on time?)

3. What choice did the student have? (To arrive at class
   with a pencil, or use the chalkboard, or not be able to
   do the assignment.)

4. What else influenced the situation? (The class talked it
   over and decided on part of the logical consequence, allowing
   everyone to feel like a part of the solution rather than
   it being arbitrarily imposed from above. Page 403, line
   12 to "agreed.")

5. Why did it work? (Because the logical consequence provided
   no benefits, just the discomforts of not turning in his/
   her assignment or doing it at the chalkboard which was
   tiring.)

6. What part did an adult play? (The teacher followed through
   on the stated consequence, making no expections and
   no comments. He/she arranged a class discussion about
   the problem and allowed and supported the students'
   additional choice of consequences.)

Situation 61, Page 403

1. What logical consequence motivated the student's behavior? (If you do not do your work, you have earned an "F." Page 403, line 12 from bottom to "that week.")

2. How was the consequence logically connected to the misbehavior. (In school, your work is graded so you receive an "F" when you do not do it. Page 403, line 13 from bottom to "that week.")

3. What choice did the student have? (To complete his work or not complete it.)

4. Did anything else influence the situation? (The teacher discussed what was happening with the student. Since Ben was retarded mentally, the teacher stated what the consequence would be. Ben was informed and warned and did not disagree. Also, he was not reminded or nagged, nor subjected to disapproval. Instead, he was given the space to work it out himself. Page 403, line 12 from bottom, ff.)

5. Why did it work? (Because all the elements of a logical consequence were employed and Ben himself disapproved of an "F" on his report card. Page 403, line 9 from bottom to the end of the sentence.)

6. What part did an adult play? (The teacher assessed the situation and set up the logical consequence after first discussing it with Ben.)

Situation 62, Pages 403-404

1. What logical consequence motivated a change of behavior in the students? (Page 404, line 3 to end of paragraph.)

2. How was the consequence logically connected to the misbehavior? (If you do not handle your materials correctly for a class setting, then you are deprived of their use for a day. It is not O.K. to make other people put away your materials.)

3. What choice did the students have? (To put away their materials or leave them around the classroom.)

4. Did anything else influence the situation? (Since the students arrived at the logical consequence themselves, they felt committed to abide by it. Nothing further was said about the matter by the teacher, nor was any disapproval expressed by the teacher if a student continued misbehaving. Instead, the agreed upon logical consequence was put into effect. Page 404, line 2 to the end of sentence; line 10; and line 12 to end of paragraph.)

5. Why did it work? (Because the necessary elements of a logical consequence were observed.)

6. What part did an adult play? (The teacher also accepted and employed the consequence decided upon in the class discussion. The teacher did not talk any more about the unacceptable behavior; instead, he/she let the logical consequence wield its effect. Page 404, line 1 to end of sentence.)

Situation 63, Page 404

1. What logical consequence motivated a behavior change in the students? (Page 404, line 19 to end of paragraph.)

2. How was the consequence logically connected to the misbehavior? (When you do not do your assignments, it will be reflected in your grade.)

3. What choice did the students have? (Do their assignments or choose to have their grade lowered.)

4. Did anything else influence the situation? (Sometimes voting can create a further problem of polarization. Consensus is usually best. Also, the students, through discussion, came up with the consequence and agreed upon it. This helped commit all the students to the situation and some peer pressure was in play. Page 404, line 12 from bottom to end of paragraph; line 15 from bottom to end of sentence; and line 16 to "in agreement.")

5. Why did it work? (Talking over a problem and helping solve the problem seems to generate cooperation in people.)

6. What part did an adult play? (The teacher had put in operation regular class discussions which made the outcome possible. Page 404, line 16 to "assignments.")

Situation 64, Pages 404-405

1. What logical consequence motivated a behavior change in the students? (Page 405, line 18 to "another day longer.")

2. How was the consequence logically connected to the misbehavior? (If you elect to abuse expensive school sewing machines, you are deprived of using the machines for a period of time and thus get behind in your work. Page 405, line 19 to "their desk.")

3. What choice did the students have? (To abuse the sewing machines or run them safely and properly as they have been taught.)

4. Did anything else influence the situation? (The reasons for running the sewing machines safely and properly were explained to the students. Page 405, line 12 to end of paragraph and line 18 to end of sentence. Pertinent information was given to the students, and class members talked it over and searched for a solution to the deliberate abuse of the sewing machines. Page 405, line 18 to "the machine:". Also the students set up the rule governing the use of sewing machines through consultation, which made the students more willing to obey them. Peer pressure also came into play when a machine was abused.)

5. Why did it work? (Because of the factors described above. Consultation together and peer pressure can powerfully influence behavior.)

6. What part did an adult play? (The teacher thoroughly explained why sewing machines needed to be run safely and properly, encouraged class discussion about the matter, and followed through by putting into effect the agreed

upon rules without further talk. Also, the teacher refrained from expressing disapproval when a rule was broken. Page 405, line 12 to end of paragraph and line 15 from bottom to end of paragraph. It also helps to greatly increase the penalty with each offense.)

Situation 65, Pages 405-406

1. What logical consequence motivated a change in the students' behavior? (Page 406, line 9 to end of paragraph.)

2. How was the logical consequence logically related to the misbehavior? (If you are not there, how can you fulfill your duties?)

3. What choice did the students have? (To be where they needed to be to fulfill their duties or decide not to bother.)

4. Did anything else influence the situation? (A conference was held with the two students about their lack of attendance to fulfill their duties, and periodic conferences were held to help with their personal problems. Page 406, line 4 to end of paragraph.)

5. Why did it work? (This time it did not work. Perhaps some of the elements of a logical consequence were left out? If all parts of a logical consequence are not included, it often does not work. At any rate, it laid a groundwork for future cooperation of future aids in the counseling office. Expect to be fired if you do not fulfill your duties. Page 406, line 14 to end of sentence.)

6. What part did an adult play? (The counselor set up a conference with the students about the ensuing problem and offered additional conferences about their personal problems. In addition, a contract was drawn up with the students in agreement concerning the terms of the logical consequence if the misbehavior continued. Page 406, line 4 to "as aids." This ended the problem: They were dismissed. Consult pp. 368-369 in *Action Guide* to see what might have gone wrong with the consequence.)

Situation 66, Pages 406-407

1. What logical consequence motivated a behavior change in the students? (The class would use some of its lunch time to make up the class time lost while it was settling down. Page 406, line 2 from bottom to end of paragraph.)

2. How was the consequence logically connected to the misbehavior? (The consequence made up the class time lost.)

3. What choice did the class have? (They could take a while to settle down and be quiet or they could get quiet right away.)

4. Did anything else influence the situation? (A class discussion about the problem was instituted. The students themselves came up with the logical consequence so there was no resentment or rebellion when it was put into effect. Page 406, line 2 from bottom to "decided.")

5. Why did it work? (Because the consequence fitted the offense and students, by talking it over and arriving at a solution, felt committed to it, since it was their own answer to the problem.)

6. What part did an adult play? (The teacher set up the class discussion and faithfully held to the parameters of such a discussion. See pages 291-292, Chapter 43, "Guidelines for Classroom Discussions"; and page 293, Chapter 44, "Ground Rules for Classroom Discussions.")

Situation 67, page 407

1. What logical consequence motivated the useful and satisfactory behavior of this class? (Page 407, line 15 to "noon rehearsal.")

2. How was the consequence logically connected to the exemplary behavior? (If the class members wish to play in the concert, they must study, practice, and rehearse or their skill will not measure up to the standard necessary

for playing in a concert. Page 407, line 17, points 1 and 2.)

3. What choice did the students have? (Choose to fulfill the requirements for playing in a concert or choose not to make the effort.)

4. Did anything else influence the situation? (The class talked it over together and decided together what the rules would be for playing in the concert. Page 407, line 14 to "class.")

5. Why did it work? (Today's individuals cooperate with decisions of which they take part through a true democratic discussion about matters which will affect them.)

6. What part did an adult play? (The teacher allowed and arranged such a discussion. He/she also abided by and accepted the decisions of this class group.)

Situation 68, Pages 407-408

1. What logical consequence motivated a change in the students' behavior? (Page 408, line 1 to end of paragraph.)

2. How was this consequence logically connected to the misbehavior? (Any student who does not make the effort to not lose his/her lock, has no lock and no protection for his/her belongings. Page 408, line 3 to end of paragraph.)

3. What choice did the students have? (To take care of his/her lock and remember to lock his/her locker or not.)

4. Did anything else influence the situation? (This solution about locks and lockers resulted from a class meeting about the problem of lost locks or neglecting to put the locks to use.)

5. Why did it work? (The students had a part in the solution.)

6. What part did an adult play? (The teacher arranged the class meeting for this discussion and put into action the resulting decisions.)

Situation 69, Page 408

1. What logical consequence motivated acceptable behavior of students on the track team? (Page 408, line 13 to end of paragraph.)

2. How were the consequences logically connected to the behavior of students on the track team? (Any infractions related to a member of the track team.)

3. What choice did the students have? (To obey the track team rules or not to do so.)

4. Did anything else influence the situation? (The rules were set up by discussion at a class meeting. Page 408, line 9 to end of paragraph.)

5. Why did it work? (The students took part in setting up the rules, and the rules made sense and were fair.)

6. What part did an adult play? (The coach instituted the group discussion to decide the rules that would affect aspiring track team members.)

Situation 70, Pages 408-409

1. What logical consequence influenced the behavior of the students in the ceramics class? (If you do not bother to clean up the wheel you used, you are not eligible to use a wheel for a time. Page 408, line 5 from bottom to "dog house.")

2. How was the consequence logically connected to possible misbehavior in the ceramics class? (A clean wheel was needed for the next student's use; therefore, if you did not cooperate so that all the students could start their work with a clean wheel, you would not use a wheel for a while.)

3. What choice did the students have? (To clean the wheel they used or not.)

4. What else influenced the situation? (All the students clearly knew what the rule was from the beginning.)

5. Why did it work? (The rule made sense and was fair and applied to all the students.)

6. What part did an adult play? (The teacher devised the rules and made sure all the students knew what the rule was. Also, the teacher put the rule into effect without exception and no further talk.)

Situation 71, Page 409

1. What logical consequence motivated a change in the behavior of the student? (If you don't bother to bring in the needed materials, you can't work with clay. Page 409, line 7 to "the others.")

2. How was it logically connected to the misbehavior. (If you don't have the materials neeeded for working in clay, how can you work in clay?)

3. What choice did he/she have? (He/she could bother to gather and bring in the materials for working in the clay or choose not to bother. Page 409, line 7 to "in clay.")

4. Did anything else influence the situation? (Being allowed to take part in the forming of the rules gave these students a feeling of fairness and commitment. Page 409, line 6 to end of sentence.)

5. Why did it work? (Today's individuals cooperate well with decisions they helped to formulate.)

6. What part did an adult play? (The teacher set up the opportunity for class members to discuss the circumstances of working in clay and how to handle any difficulties. He/she also made sure the rules were followed. Page 409, line 3 to end of sentence.)

Situation 72, Pages 409-410

1. What logical consequence motivated the student to change his/her behavior? (Page 409, line 12 from bottom to end of paragraph.)

2. How was it logically connected to the misbehavior? (The class members decided on rules for their Hawaii Special Olympics practice sessions. The consequence was connected to breaking one of those rules and taking part in the Olympics.)

3. What choice did each student have? (To follow the rules or break them.)

4. Did anything influence the situation? (The students being invited to take part in setting up the rules for practice time, and then when there was an infraction, the consequence was immediately put into effect. Page 409, line 6 from bottom to page 410, top, line 4, "Special Olympics.")

5. Why did it work? (The consequence was logical, agreed to, and put immediately into effect.)

6. What part did an adult play? (The teacher set up the opportunity for all to discuss and decide together what the practice rules and the consequences would be, and then followed through. Page 409, line 12 from bottom, ff.)

Situation 73, Page 410

1. What logical consequences motivated the student to change his/her behavior? (Page 410, line 17 to end of paragraph.)

2. How was the consequence logically connected to the misbehavior? (Their misbehavior resulted in their not being able to cook and thus receive a zero for their grade. If no needed preparation, then no cooking and no grade.)

3. What choice did the student have? (To choose to complete the necessary and agreed upon preparation or not to do it.)

4. Did anything else influence the situation? (A previous agreement had been made to the procedure. Page 410, line 10 to end of sentence.)

5. Why did it work? (The students saw the agreement as reasonable, needed, and fair. Also, they had been allowed to help set it up.)

6. What part did an adult play? (The teacher gave the students the opportunity to help construct the agreed-to method of operation. Also, the teacher presumably did not censor with body language the negative choice of a student, but let him/her get on with the learning experience.)

Situation 74, Page 410

1. What logical consequence motivated a change in the student's misbehavior? (Page 410, line 7 from bottom to end of sentence.)

2. How was the consequence logically connected to the misbehavior? (The misbehavior was being late to class and then expecting special, extra help during class time. The consequence of having to seek the extra help at her own inconvenience when she was late, related it to the misbehavior in that to do the work, the student needed the information. Refer to Section P-31, *Characteristics of a Logical Consequence*, in Part I, *Action Guide for Parents*.

3. What choice did the student have? (To be on time for class or not be.)

4. Did anything else influence the situation? (Observing the pattern of lateness, the teacher probably reflected about what would be a logical consequence in this case and how and when to communicate it to the student. In this example, it is not clear whether the student was informed in front of the other students or at a one-on-one time

with the teacher. One could say, "Please see me directly after class about this.")

5. Why did it work? (The consequence was fair, logical and inconvenient to the student. Informing the student of the change of procedure in private would eliminate any defensive behavior on his/her part.)

6. What part did an adult play? (The teacher devised the logical consequence and put it into immediate effect in a friendly, teaching manner.)

Situation 75, Pages 410-411

1. What logical consequences were thought of by the P.E. class members to motivate a change in the students' misbehavior. (Page 411, line 15 to end of paragraph.)

2. How were the consequences logically connected to the misbehaviors? (In this example, it is not stated what the consequences were—only that they had to do with how the P.E. class teacher did the referring. However, the teacher seemed satisfied with their effectiveness. The team captains were given the job of handling the "swearing," which was employing peer pressure with the consequence connected to playing in the game.)

3. What choice did the misbehaving students have? (To cooperate with the rules in the matter of "swearing" or not play the game. The teacher's choice of using the proposed refereeing suggestions eliminated the other misbehavior.)

4. Did anything else influence the situation? (The P.E. teacher's act of inviting the consultation of the class members for ways of eliminating the offending behavior; plus his/her very effective way of opening the discussion by seeking help with the students' part in the situation. The students felt recognized as individuals with some sense and not completely at fault.)

5. Why did it work? (All individuals today seem to respond warmly and positively to being invited to use their minds to try to solve problems that effect them. Young people and children can amaze us in this area.)

6. What part did an adult play? (The teacher arranged the setting that made possible the elimination of the misbehaviors. Page 411, line 4 to end of sentence.)

Situation 76, Pages 411-412

Using the questions below, do the last Situation in this series yourself.

1. What logical consequence motivated the student to make a behavior change in each case given?

2. How was the consequence logically connected to the misbehavior?

3. What choice did he/she have?

4. Did anything else influence the situation?

5. Why did it work?

6. What part did an adult play?

SECTION T-43
TEACHERS AND
FOUR MISTAKEN GOALS
OF CHILDREN

GOAL 1: (AGM) ATTENTION GETTING MECHANISM

The Child's Probable Goal and His/Her "Faulty Logic"

Child seeks proof of his acceptance and approval.
He puts others in his service, seeks help.
"I feel I have a place only when people pay attention to me."

Teacher's Involuntary Reaction

To be kept busy by child.
To help, remind, scold, coax, and give child extra service.
Is delighted by constructive AGM child.
Is annoyed.
"He/she occupies too much of my time."
"I wish he/she would leave me alone."

Teacher's Corrective Procedures

Give attention when a child is not making a bid for it.
Ignore the misbehaving child.
Be firm.
Realize that punishing, reminding, coaxing, scolding, and giving service are all forms of attention.

Teacher's Interpretation of Child's Goal to Him/Her

"Could it be that you want me to notice you?"
"Could it be that you want me to do special things for you?"
". . . keep me busy with you?"

NOTE: Always ask questions in a friendly, nonjudgmental way and not at times of conflict.

| GOAL 2: | POWER |

The Child's Probable Goal and His/Her "Faulty Logic"

Wants to be boss.
Does what he/she wants to do.
"I only count if you do what I want."
"If you don't let me do what I want, you don't love me."

Teacher's Involuntary Reaction

Feels leadership of the class is threatened.
Feels defeated.
Is angry.
"Who is running this class? He/she or I?"
"I won't let him/her get away with this."

Teacher's Corrective Procedures

Withdraw from the conflict.
Cease all talk.
Recognize and admit that the child has power.
Appeal for child's help, enlist his/her cooperation, give him/her responsibility.

Teacher's Interpretation of Child's Goal to Him/Her

"Could it be that you want to show me that you can do what you want and no one can stop you?"
"Could it be that you want to be the boss?"
". . . get me to do what you want?"

NOTE: Always ask questions in a friendly, nonjudgmental way and **not** at times of conflict.

| GOAL 3: | REVENGE |

The Child's Probable Goal and His/Her "Faulty Logic"

Tries to hurt as he/she feels hurt by others.

"My only hope is to get even with them."
"I can hurt!"

Teacher's Involuntary Reaction

Dislikes the child.
Feels deeply hurt.
Is outraged by child.
Wants to get even.
"How can he/she be so mean?"

Teacher's Corrective Procedures

Avoid punishment and retaliation.
Win the child. Try to convince him/her that he/she is liked.
Do not become hurt.
Enlist a "buddy" for him/her.
Use group encouragement.

Teacher's Interpretation of Child's Goal to Him/Her

"Could it be that you want to hurt me and/or the children?"
"Could it be that you want to get even?"

NOTE: Always ask questions in a friendly, nonjudgmental way and **not** at times of conflict.

GOAL 4: DISPLAY OF INADEQUACY

The Child's Probable Goal and His/Her "Faulty Logic"

Is in despair.
Tries to be left alone.
Feels hopeless.
"I don't want anyone to know how stupid I am."
"I can't bear it."

Teacher's Involuntary Reaction

Feels helpless.
Doesn't know what to do.

"I can't do anything with him/her."
"I give up."

Teacher's Corrective Procedures

Refuse to be discouraged yourself.
Don't give up.
Show faith in the child.
Encourage—Encourage.
Give recognition and appreciation of the smallest
constructive act.
Arrange encouraging experiences.

Teacher's Interpretation of Child's Goal to Him/Her

"Could it be that you want to be left alone?"
". . . you feel stupid and don't want people to know?"
". . . you can't help it?"

NOTE: Always ask questions in a friendly, nonjudgmental
way and **not** at times of conflict.

SECTION T-44
TIMES WHEN A
TEACHER SAYS "NO"

(These areas are not negotiable)

1. Life endangerment, or severe injury.

2. Seriously damaging to their health.

3. Breaking the law.

4. Seriously interfering with the comfort of the whole class.

5. Idiosyncratic value of the teacher such as chewing gum, abusive language, etc.

SECTION T-45
WHEN IT IS NOT
A LOGICAL CONSEQUENCE

If you are

1. using it to get your way, to win;

2. using it with anger in any of its mild or severe forms;

3. using consequences to impose demands rather than as a teaching/learning tool;

4. calling it a logical consequence when it has no connection at all to the misbehavior; and/or

5. using it without first discussing it with the student or students and winning their agreement to its appropriateness.

    Hold the discussion either in a one-on-one discussion or during a class discussion.

SECTION T-46
HOW TO MUCK UP
YOUR LOGICAL CONSEQUENCE

1. Putting the consequence into effect in an angry spirit—your actual feeling showing itself in body language and tone of voice.

2. Continuing to talk while the teaching/learning experience is happening—reminding, pointing out, admonishing.

3. Failing to trust the child's capacity to learn in this way.

4. Failing to trust in the capacity of a consequence to teach.

5. Neglecting to see the consequence as a sufficient penalty for the misbehavior.

6. Failing to believe that the child can learn even from the wrong choice.

   Giving him/her the right to be wrong and learn from it.

7. Forgetting to not stand in judgment of the child's choice of behavior during a teaching/learning process.

   The child is acquiring reasons of his/her own for choosing the preferred, appropriate behavior.

8. Neglecting to show a friendly, encouraging attitude as soon as the consequence is finished.

   This is when he/she begins to realize that the behavior is what you do not like, not him/her.

NOTES
Related to Week 6

SECTION T-47
TEACHER'S INDIVIDUAL STUDY
PLAN NO. 7

Chapter 67, Pages 437-448

1. What happened when you did your school practice activity for Week 7 where you used a consequence to correct a student's misbehavior? Use your notes page and describe how it went from the misbehavior to the student's reaction to the consequence. How did you feel doing it? How would you evaluate the result? What can you do in addition to using a consequence? (Encouragement in all its forms, class discussions, Encouragement Council, entrusting the student with a school responsibility, etc.) An excellent listing of possible school responsibilities by grade level can be found in *Teacher Study Group Leader's Manual* (1975) by authors Asselin, Nelson, and Platt, and can be ordered from the Alfred Adler Institute of Chicago, 110 Dearborn Street, Chicago, IL 60603. The Institute also carries a number of other books listed in the bibliography of your textbook.

2. Finish Sections T-39 through T-42, *Study Questions for Chapter 62, Teachers' Examples of Consequences.*

3. Having done your reading, do Section T-49, *Study Questions for Preliminary Note and Chapter 67.*

4. The C4R School—C4R stands for Corsini 4 R's for **R**espectful, **R**esponsible, **R**esourceful, and **R**esponsive— the four Adlerian long range goals for children who will grow up to be lovable, capable, cooperative adults. Many people are enthuiastic about this program, and a number of such schools are in existence now. The school has a limitation with some types of individual children, seemingly, not enough structure exists for them to function comfortably; however, for most children, even though doing badly in traditional school, they seem to thrive in all ways in this kind of setting. If, for some reason, after a few years, they have to go back into a traditional school,

they seem to do all right in that setting too. They have found their bearings, so to speak. If you would like to learn more about his school system, you can contact Dr. Corsini as listed in the bibliography of your textbook under his name.

5. Look over Section T-50, *One-Hundred-Six Adlerian Concepts* by Dr. Raymond Corsini. It will enhance and pull together all you have been studying.

6. This brings us to the end of our study of the Adlerian principles and methods as applied to teaching in the school setting. It is hoped that some light has been shed on what is going on with students today, suggesting ways to ease them along to another place with their teachers so that students can gain the benefit that is there for them. **PLEASE, NEVER GIVE UP—THE WORLD IS IN NEED OF YOU.**

SECTION T-48
TEACHERS' GROUP MEETING
NO. 7 FORMAT

Chapter 67, Pages 437-448

1. Tell each other about your experience this past week with your school practice activity for Week 7 where you use consequences for misbehavior in the classroom. Which student did you work on? What mistaken goal and what consequence did you use? How did you feel about doing it and what were the results? Evaluate everything that happened and the whole concept of consequences as a deterrent in school by teachers. Talk it over and use your notes page to record any insights and conclusions. Also, consider how you are going to follow it up. What kinds of encouragement are you going to use, for example?

2. One form of encouragement we have not discussed is the assignment of some school responsibility to help enhance the status of a discouraged student. There is an outstanding listing of possible school responsibilities by grade level in the *Teacher Study Group Leader's Manual* (1975) by Asselin, Nelson, and Platt, and can be ordered from the Alfred Adler Institute of Chicago, 110 Dearborn Street, Chicago, IL 60603. The Institute also carries a number of other books listed in the bibliography of your textbook.

3. Then do Sections T-39 through T-42, *Study Questions for Chapter 62, Teachers' Examples of Consequences*, relating them to your own recent experiences, when possible. If you cannot complete all the examples and still leave some time for Chapter 67, do as many as you can.

4. Go to Section T-49, *Study Questions for Preliminary Note and Chapter 67 on the C4R School.* This school system was uniquely created by Dr. Raymond Corsini based on his own adaptation of Adlerian principles and theories of the school experience of children of all ages, with the problems and concerns of teachers also in mind. It is well worth your time to be aware of what it is like. C4R

stands for Corsini's 4 R's for **R**espectful, **R**esponsible, **R**esourceful, and **R**esponsive. These are the four Adlerian long range goals for children who will grow up to be lovable, capable, cooperative adults. Discuss together this system's merits and any drawbacks you think it may have. Many people are very enthusiastic about the C4R Schools and there are now a number of such schools in existence. If you would like to know more about his school system, you can contact Dr. Corsini, as listed in the bibliography of your textbook under his name.

5. Do not miss Section T-50, *One-Hundred-Six Adlerian Concepts*, by Dr. Raymond Corsini. It is very helpful in drawing together everything you have been studying.

6. This brings us to the end of our time together as a group, studying the Adlerian viewpoint as applied to children in our schools today. Your teaching profession is so vital and important to today's developing youngsters and our society as a whole. The hope is that this Group Study has added to your awareness of what is going on between students and teachers at this time and has augmented your fund of teaching aids to help your teaching time become everything you want it to be. These young ones need so much what you have to teach them, that no effort made on all our parts can be too much.

7. One further suggestion: if you are enthused about incorporating these ideas and methods into your approach to teaching, you could plan to meet once a month for a while to compare notes and critique what is happening. Also, you could brainstorm how to handle any difficult students that some of you are trying to reach. Thinking together of what might be done to turn such a student to a positive, constructive direction towards school and learning could be helpful and yield results. Results are always encouraging and help lead us on our way.

Wishing all of you **"HAPPY TEACHING!"**

SECTION T-49
STUDY QUESTIONS FOR
PRELIMINARY NOTE AND
CHAPTER 67

Preliminary Note, Page 436

1. What kind of process does the word "discipline" describe for Adlerians? (Page 436, line 1 to "disciple.") So the word "discipline" means what? (Page 436, line 2, middle, to "you do.")

2. Then, according to this view, what does it mean to discipline a child in school? (Page 436, line 4 to "teachers.")

3. What do Adlerians see as useless and harmful means of discipline? (Page 436, line 7 to "harmful.") List some of the harms this kind of punishment can do to children. (Page 436, line 11 to "others.")

4. What kind of good behavior are Adlerian disciplinary rules intended to achieve? (Page 436, line 5 from bottom to "good behavior.") By what means are these goals achieved? (Page 436, line 3 to end of paragraph.)

Chapter 67, Pages 437-448

History of Adlerian Schooling Methods

1. Even in the early Adlerian school in Austria, what do you perceive as their goal with their students? (Page 437, line 3 from bottom to end of paragraph.)

2. What position did these early Adlerian educators take about handling children? (Page 438, line 8 to end of paragraph.)

The Corsini 4R School System

1. In contrast to these early Adlerians, with what has Dr. Corsini been primarily concerned? (Page 438, line 14

to end of sentence.) His nomothetic position has what as its particular concern? (Page 438, line 15 to end of paragraph.)

2. What was his unusual conclusion? (Page 438, line 16 from bottom to "problems.") What did he envision and try to devise? (Page 438, line 13 from bottom to end of paragraph.)

3. How did Dr. Corsini see the traditional school system? (Page 438, line 7 from bottom to "study.") Therefore, what did he elect to do? (Page 438, line 4 from bottom to end of paragraph.)

4. Who does Dr. Corsini see as mainly responsible for a child's education? (Page 439, line 4 to "education.") Who could best advise the child about his/her education? (Page 439, line 5 to "members.")

5. What does Dr. Corsini want children to have a chance to learn, besides academic subjects? (Page 439, line 7 to "play," and page 440, No. 14.)

6. Therefore, what were schools to be like? (Page 439, line 9 to "around.") According to Dr. Corsini, children have a basic wisdom about what? (Page 439, line 10 to "learn.")

7. What is part of the teacher's role? (Page 439, line 12 to "learn.") What does Dr. Corsini see as children's right in regard to learning? (Page 439, line 14, ff.)

8. To what school of therapy does this school system bear a resemblance? (Page 439, line 16 to end of paragraph.) Where would the similarity to a shopping mall rest? (Page 439, line 14 from bottom to end of sentence.)

Some Aspects of the C4R System of Schooling

1. Do you especially like any of the points describing a C4R School? (Page 439, No. 1, to page 441, No. 30.) Do you agree with any of them? (ibid.) Are any of them unclear? (ibid.) Individuals make notes on the notes page,

seeking answers as you study. Group members discuss together and note conclusions, watching for answers as they study.

How a C4R School Works

1. Why is every parent required to take a parenting course? (Page 442, line 2 to "school.") What kinds of tests will the children be given? (Page 442, line 3 to "abilities.")

2. How would you describe a student's usual day in a C4R School? (Page 442, line 9 to "classes.")

3. What other innovative choice does each child have? (Page 442, line 8 to "own choice.")

4. What is taught in this school? (Page 442, line 15 to end of paragraph.)

The Specific Disciplinary Program

1. What about rules in the Specific Disciplinary Program of a C4R School? (Page 442, line 13 from bottom to end of paragraph.) What is School Rule 3? (Page 443, No. 3, line 4.)

2. What is an idiosyncratic classroom rule? (Page 442, line 9 from bottom to "so forth.")

3. Therefore, what control over the teaching situation in his/her classroom will the teacher have in this system? (Page 442, line 6 from bottom to end of paragraph, and page 440, No. 13.)

4. What are the three school rules? (See top of page 443.) Four consequences exist for breaking one of the three school rules. What are the four consequences? (Page 445, line 14 from bottom to page 446 end of third paragraph.)

5. Why is no child ever imprisoned in a school room in a C4R School? (Page 443, line 8 to end of paragraph.)

6. Teachers are most hampered in their teaching by the "trouble maker" students in their class. What can be done about these students in a C4R Class? (Page 443, point No. 3, and page 443, line 15 to end of paragraph.)

7. What is the "go signal?" (Page 444, line 11 to end of paragraph.) When does a teacher use it? (Page 444, line 6 to "bothering her.") Is anything further done? (Page 444, line 18 to end of paragraph.)

8. When a child is given a "go" signal by a teacher, how does it affect him/her? (Page 444, line 18 from bottom, ff. to page 445, line 6 to "a seat.")

9. If a child does not want to go to any classroom, study hall, or library, or is "pointed out," what can he/she do? (Page 445, line 20 ff.)

10. What right of the teachers and right of the children does the C4R System preserve? (Page 445, line 7 to end of paragraph.)

11. What about Dr. Corsini's statement, "THERE IS ABSOLUTELY NO REASON EVER TO MISBEHAVE IN THE CLASSROOM, THE LIBRARY OR THE STUDY HALL"? (Page 443, line 10 to end of paragraph.) Does this statement hold up? Individuals reflect and answer on notes page. Group members discuss and share conclusions.

Consequences of Violations

1. Look at Page 443, line 1, ff., for the three school rules. What happens if any child breaks one of the school rules? (Page 445, line 14 from bottom to end of paragraph.)

2. Should a child break one of those three school rules three separate times, what would happen? (Page 446, line 1 to "them.") How about six violations in one year? (Page 446, line 4 ff. to "the School.") Any further violations

can lead to what? (Page 446, line 12, ff. to end of third paragraph to "the principal.")

3. What does a child who cannot be won over to cooperating within the limits of this school finally have happen to him/her? (Page 446, line 15, ff. to "another school.")

Results

1. How did C4R Schools compare with traditional schools in the six areas listed? (Pages 447 to 448, points 1 through 6.)

2. What other gratifying aspects are noted? (Page 448, last paragraph.)

SECTION T-50
ONE-HUNDRED-SIX
ADLERIAN CONCEPTS

Compiled by Raymond J. Corsini, Ph.D.

PHILOSOPHY

The iron law of social relations is equality.

Cooperation is better than competition.

We can not motivate others—we can only open windows so people can see out and open doors so people can move out.

All humans have three tasks in life: family, society, occupation.

Every human problem is an opportunity.

Today is the first day of the rest of your life.

If there is no order, there is no freedom.

In a democratic society, institutions such as the family should also be democratic.

One can harm a child in two ways: rejecting him [or her] and spoiling him [or her]. The second is worse.

A major problem in life is to gain courage.

HUMAN NATURE

Children have four general major goals: attention, power, revenge, assumed disability.

All behavior is goal directed.

We learn *how* to do it from the past; *when* to do it from the present; and *what* to do from the future.

If you have children, you have problems.

A bad child is a discouraged child.

We all need the courage to be imperfect.

A child needs encouragement; he [or she] does not need praise.

First we think—then act—then feel.

All human behavior is a movement from a felt-minus to a perceived-plus.

Man's [or a human's] most basic aim is to find where he [or she] belongs.

One's attitude and approach to life is known as life style.

A child needs encouragement the way a plant needs water.

Every child is different and if one disregards this, one violates his [or her] dignity.

The aggressive child and the apathetic child are both discouraged.

In our efforts to find our place in society, we develop a life style—an attitude and an approach to life.

Three four-year-olds: one is three, one is four, and one is five.

The human being is a purposeful, indivisible, responsible entity.

Humans are quantitatively like animals, but qualitatively different.

Animals are irresponsible. Humans are responsible.

People are more alike than they are different.

Human behavior is determined always by the individual. The environment never determines the behavior.

All human problems are social problems.

HUMAN RELATIONSHIPS

All people have equal rights to dignity, respect and fair treatment.

Respect implies freedom of choice.

Democracy depends on equality.

Democracy implies respect and order.

Rewards and punishments depend on the concept of inferiority and superiority; and consequently, they violate the spirit of equality.

Over protecting a child robs him [or her] of courage, initiative, and resourcefulness.

RULES FOR PARENTING

Only royalty should be treated like royalty.

Only give orders if you are ready, able and willing to enforce them.

Orders are never necessary except in emergencies.

Never praise a child for doing what he [or she] should have done— such as doing well in school.

Never try to find out "why?" from a child.

A child's money is his [or her's] to spend, save or burn.

Ignore bad habits.

When you don't know what to do, do nothing.

Never do for a child routinely what he [or she] can do for himself [herself].

If you solve one of your family's problems efficiently, you may thereby learn how to solve all the others in the family.

A dominant parent produces sly, shy, withdrawn, resentful, rebellious and hostile children.

Treat the child who is dependent on you the way you hope he [or she] will treat you if you are ever dependent on him [or her].

Allowance, like food and clothing, should be a non-negotiable right.

If a child refuses to cooperate with you, you can refuse to cooperate with him [or her].

Children become what the parents are.

TALK

Talk should be for communication, not punishment.

Never give a child an order—but if you do, only do it if you can and will obtain immediate compliance.

Never repeat an order—never.

All discussion about a child should be in his [or her] presence.

Talk to a child only when you and he [or she] are calm.

Mothers who talk too much develop "mother deaf" children.

Learn to talk with and not to children.

TRAINING

Do not train a child in public.

Criticism only emphasizes weaknesses.

Praise only praiseworthy efforts, such as a child risking his [or her] life to save his [or her] parents.

A child learns responsibility only by being given responsibility, which implies a chance to fail.

Every family should have a family council.

A *temper tantrum?* Escape! Immediately!

All learning is intentional, that is motivated.

The child knows best how much freedom he [or she] can accept.

Reward and punishment are means used by the superior to control the inferior.

Natural and logical consequences show respect.

Punishment can become a reward and so is doubly wrong.

We can only control ourselves and by so doing, we control others.

Parents in training children should deal with them consistently.

Learn to act and not talk in training the child.

Separate the doer from the deed. The doer is good, the deed may be bad. Children must be trained by their parents.

Train on strengths not weaknesses.

In training, aim for improvement, not perfection.

AGGRESSION

Aggression is best handled by withdrawal. Take your sails out of another's wind.

Punishment is arbitrary and motivated by anger, leads only to temporary correction and long term resentment and feelings of guilt and inferiority.

Children have a right to fight—but no right to bother others.

Egressing anger facilitates more expression of anger.

When angry, keep quiet; even better, disappear.

NORMALITIES

The touchstone of normality is social interest. Selfish people are sick.

It is normal to feel inferior. This feeling motivates a person to achieve more. This is due to a difference between one's self perception and level of aspiration. But too much of a good thing becomes bad.

It is normal to be ambitious. Bums, alcoholics, and the insane are ambitious. It is just that their ambitions are different.

EMOTIONS

Anger does not have to be expressed. It is not a gas that has to be let out. We do not just become angry. We are angry only when we want to be.

The emotions are at the service of the intellect. They serve the intellect's purpose.

Love is the consequence and not the cause of good behavior.

Anger begets anger; violence begets violence.

Never pity a pitiful or piteous child.

Do not communicate when angry.

Do not react emotionally to a child's provocations.

Love is unselfish. Anything else is not love.

SCHOOL

School should be the child's responsibility.

Establishing a curriculum and putting a child into a grade is degrading to the child's uniqueness and dignity.

The three R's of education should be: Respect, Responsibility, and Resourcefulness.

We should neither teach children what they already know nor what they cannot learn.

The child knows best *when* he [or she] can have something and *how* he [or she] should learn it. Adults know best *what* a child should learn.

Internal motivation is good; external is bad.

Report cards should go to students and not to parents.

Forced homework is useless and harmful.

A class council is essential in a democratic society.

Children learn best from their peers.

Grades are value judgments and are destructive to children—whether high, average, or low.

Parent-teacher conferences are disrespectful of children. The child must always be present. We should have parent-teacher-child conferences.

NOTES
Related to Week 7

ABOUT THE AUTHOR

Margaret Cater is the mother of four grown children and five grandchildren. When her own fourth child sank her "parental boat," she herself was forced to search for help and understanding of what was happening. These Adlerian ideas and methods gave her such gratifying and happy results, she became an indefatigable Adlerian family counselor and parent study group leader. Eventually, many pages of this Action Guide materialized from her efforts to help other parents understand and put to use successfully these quite novel ways of influencing children and guiding them to maturity.

Our present advanced, technological and high-information culture has given us a child to parent or teach in a classroom setting, who is entirely different and often sadly deficient in self-esteem and confidence, as well as angry. Our children, themselves, can be bewildered as well as bewildering. So, someone has to know the way to go. Mrs. Cater's awareness of this put a fire under her and set her back and forth across the Island of Oahu, Hawaii, and also to the Outer Islands. Wherever parents wanted a Study Group, she would go.

Her formal training entails a B.A. degree in Philosophy, a B.A. degree in Sociology, and an additional 30 hours in Sociology plus 30 hours in Psychology. She is a certified Adlerian Family Counselor, with training also in Marriage Counseling. She has led parent-study groups for the D.O.E. of Hawaii, for the Family Education Centers of Hawaii, for nursery schools, on military bases, and for church groups.

She prepared the Leader's Guide and Parent Manual to "The Practical Parent" at the request of Doctors Corsini and Painter. These were used widely throughout the United States.